2IH

Pr. 50

THROUGH THE BIBLE IN 365 DAYS

Daily Bible Reading Notes

Rev Dr Stewart Jones, Donemana Presbyterian Church, Northern Ireland.

ISBN 978-1-4452-2936-2
90000
9 781445 229362

Stewart simply wants you to get into a regular habit of reading the Bible – and even better – to actually get your way through all of it. Use your favourite translation. Get yourself 4 bookmarks for your Bible. You can of course, adapt this scheme, and stretch it over several years. Just keep at it and get there, eventually!

ALWAYS read asking for God's Holy Spirit to light up the pages for you – for His Spirit to open up His Word, assist you in recalling what you have already learnt, and helping you to apply what you read, so that, it is never just a mental exercise, but a deepening of your daily walk with your Lord and Saviour, Jesus Christ. Having said that, don't expect to understand everything! Getting a general overview, an idea of where things are in the Bible, is a success in itself.

Acknowledgements: The actual reading scheme is available from several sources, including a free download on the internet:

http://www.oneyearbibleonline.com/readingplan/oneyearbiblereadingplan.pdf

Bibles already divided up according to this reading plan are very useful, with only one bookmark needed.

Stewart first came across The One Year Bible published by Kingsway Publications Ltd, who produced the Living Bible Translation rearranged in such a fashion. They claim the actual reading of the Bible is about 10 minutes a day, but 15 minutes is more likely! The publishers have produced a range of other One Year Bibles since then. Stewart has adapted this scheme further, by only taking you through the psalms once, so if you are using your ordinary Bible you can look forward to the four book markers going down to just three in early July! When pushed for time, always, always make sure it is *God's Word* that you read.

References to various Christian writers or "Commentaries". These are usually to The Bible Speaks Today Series, or the Tyndale Old or New Testament commentaries, all of which are suitable for lay people and are published by IVP

January 1st

READ Genesis 1 v1-2v25

The beauty and goodness of creation. Verses 10, 12, 18, 21, 25, 31 "And God saw it was good. In Hebrew, "good morning" is actually said the other way round "morning good" – *boker tov.*

We are given a clear indication of where human life is first formed – the rivers bordering the area, and even some of the minerals found there.

Men and women have a unique relationship with their Creator. And despite all the things that follow down through the generations to come, we have one man, one woman, in a permanent relationship.

MATTHEW 1v1-2v12

Far from being boring reading, this family tree has some interesting names. Childless Tamar was poorly treated by her deceased husband's family and she dressed up as a prostitute to lure her father in law into getting her pregnant; Rahab the prostitute from Jericho found faith and married Salmon. Ruth the Moabitess, also found faith and married Boaz. And that's only the women who are mentioned. There are many interesting stories to go with the men's names too!

King Herod was insecure because he was not of the Davidic line – i.e. he had no Biblical right to the throne.

PSALM 1v1-6

This psalm tends to slam on the brakes for anyone who is walking into God's presence without having given the slightest thought as to the privilege it is to enter.

PROVERBS 1v1-6

The proverbs can be frustrating in the way that they jump from topic to topic, or make statements that make us want to come back and argue, because we know of exceptions, such as godly people who do suffer etc. Solomon did want us to use that grey matter in our heads, and to find a wisdom that is God given.

January 2nd

GENESIS 3v1-4v26

Suddenly the one thing that God told them not to touch becomes the centre of the garden, instead of being something forgotten altogether. There is also exaggeration, to make God sound even more mean – God never said they would die if they *touched* it. Satan then goes for the direct denial of what God has said, and once the rule is broken, the blame game, of blaming someone else begins.

Further sorrows come. Cain kills Abel. Sin has its grip in the world.

MATTHEW 2v13-3v6

Bethlehem was already a place of grief in the Bible – Rachel died here, giving birth to Benjamin, Joseph's brother. Being just down the road from Jerusalem, it had also been a place of sorrow whenever disasters fell on Jerusalem. Now it became a place where the baby boys were butchered by Herod in his determination to stop someone from the Davidic line appearing.

After the return to Nazareth, the story jumps approximately 3 decades, to when John the Baptist begins to prepare the people for what Jesus came to do. John was not dressed in a fur coat, but in a very rough material woven from camels' hair. His lifestyle and message were simple as he called for repentance, and for people to get ready.

PSALM 2v1-12

There are strong links between this psalm and a number of New Testament passages. The reference to the LORD's anointed being seen as a direct reference to the Saviour.

PROVERBS 1v7-9

A key verse in Proverbs: "The fear of the LORD is the beginning of wisdom."

January 3rd

GENESIS 5v1-7v24

The book of Genesis continues to throw up many questions. All cultures across the world which have their own creation stories also have very long lives. There are two ways of interpreting 6 v3 – either that God decided to cap these life times at 120 years maximum, or that there is a 120 year countdown to God's judgment in sending the flood. (Noah lives to 950 years, and others after him continue to live lives going into the hundreds.)

Who are these 'sons of God' mentioned in chapter 6? The passage is very cryptic. Some see two very separate branches of human development, others see fallen spiritual beings craving bodily experience. I'm afraid you are going to have to leave it there. Trying to take it any further only leads to endless speculation. The reference to 'giants' in verse 4 of the King James comes from Latin and Greek translations. Other translations based on the original Hebrew wisely call them the Nephilim. There are hints of something which goes beyond the scope of the Bible: ***The Scriptures principally teach what man is to believe concerning God, and what duty God requires of man.*** (Shorter Catechism) We may have to wait until we are in heaven itself to have these other questions answered! Meanwhile we have the Scriptures to make sure we get there!

One thing we do learn is that sin is now so full blown in the world that God considers wiping it clean. Noah's boat, far from being the happy childish little ship of our children's story books, is an immense object with the proportions of a coffin.

MATTHEW 3v7-4v11

These are strong words from John the Baptist!

John is shocked that Jesus wanted to be baptised, but Jesus sees the importance of identifying with the people He has come to save.

The temptations are a serious attempt to derail Calvary; changing stones into bread would be to avoid any of the discomforts of human life. His earthly life had to be that of a real man who could suffer. Someone who took the easy option of changing stones into bread was not likely to face up to the pain and suffering of Calvary. We know from elsewhere in the Scriptures that Jesus and the disciples knew what it was like to feel hunger – desperate disciples ate the heads of grain on the Sabbath (Luke 6v1.)

Jumping off a high point, for angels to come to His rescue, would have turned His ministry into a Paul Daniels' show. People would have been attracted for all the wrong reasons. Indeed, miracles such as the feeding of large crowds were inclined to draw the wrong attention. People would have made Jesus their King if he could guarantee more free lunches, in a part of the world where it was normal to go hungry in the lead up to harvest.

As for the last temptation...Satan offers worldwide rule without the Cross – if only Jesus will worship him.

PSALM 3 v1-8

As the title tells you (provided the translation you have shows the titles) this psalm goes back to that dreadful part of David's life in which he has to flee Jerusalem before the army led by his son Absalom. The background is dreadful. It begins in the competing families of David's household, and the failure of David to discipline his own children. There is the rape of one of his daughters by a half brother Amnon, who is subsequently killed by Tamar's full brother Absalom. (After David had done nothing about it for 2 years.) Absalom is first banned, and then is allowed back, but is not allowed to see the King, and then he is sent for...but by then the damage is done and Absalom plots to overthrow David. You can, if you wish, read the horrific story which is spread over several chapters of 2nd Samuel (13-19)

Although there are godly men who go into temporary exile with David, it is a time of terrible isolation for David, and there are many with their grievances who wish to rally to Absalom.

PROVERBS 1v10-19

Right up to date with how we have seen young people enticed into terrorism or more normal criminality here and further afield.

January 4th

GENESIS 8v1-10v32

The story of Noah's drunkenness is the bit they didn't tell you as a child!

MATTHEW 4v12-25

For a time Jesus does seem to have a roof over his head – Capernaum becomes a home from home and Jesus' work is based there for a while – leading to speculation that it was his own house that had a hole ripped in the roof by the friends of the paralytic on the mat.

Piecing together the calling of the disciples from the various Gospels does make interesting reading. As a child I had an impression (from Sunday School) of Jesus calling virtual strangers, but in fact they are people who have at least been around and are familiar with what Jesus is saying and doing. So for some of them, there is more than one incident that leads to a calling, which makes sense.

We are told of the extent of Jesus fame on both sides of the Sea of Galilee and the Jordan River, and far north into Syria.

PSALM 4v1-8

The circumstances of psalm 3 may still be dominating here. David is dealing with fickleness (v2), with hotheads (v4), and with defeatists (v6) – all well meaning supporters! True peace is found in God, rather than relying on the emotional state of those around us (v8).

PROVERBS 1v20-23

Wisdom crying out in the streets – not easy to ignore, but for many, turning away from God is a very deliberate act.

January 5th

GENESIS 11v1-13v4

The tower of Babel / Babylon. We may laugh at the technological advancements of their day (as later generations will laugh at ours) as they used bitumen for mortar and thought they could reach the skies. It was the arrogance of sinful men and women that led God to scatter and divide them by language. Throughout the Bible, from Genesis to Revelation, Babylon comes to symbolise godless society. As Derek Kidner says in his commentary on Genesis (Tyndale Old Testament series, IVP) it was their *sin* that reached heaven.

We are also introduced to Abram (his name is later changed to Abraham.) This is now approximately 2,000 BC. Sara his wife is also his half sister (such marriages are later banned in the scriptures.) There is a partial emigration, from present day Iraq to present day Turkey. After the death of Abram's father Terah, Abram at the young age of 75 heads down to Canaan, to present day Israel.

Abram's faith and trust in God, undertaking such a journey, is very commendable, but following a time of famine which makes a journey to Egypt a necessity, courage falters, and fear takes its grip, and he tries to hide the fact that Sara is actually his wife, for fear that he will be murdered by someone who wants her. Of course, pretending that she is just your sister, does lead other men to assume that Sara is available, and it was common in those days to seal alliances with a marriage. Could Abram not see that coming? But that is precisely how we are all so different. My fears may be laughable to you, and vice versa. Whatever they are, they are real enough to us and should be brought to the Lord for His help.

MATTHEW 5v1-26

How is Matthew's sermon on the mount, and Luke's sermon is on a plain? Actually the traditional site is a large flat area (especially to those coming in a present day tour bus), which is also quite a steep climb up from the Galilean shore. Few middle aged tourists wander far enough to realise that this nice flat area is an exhausting climb for anyone coming up.

As for content, each line is priceless. We are called to be the world's seasoning, or the world's light.

PSALM 5v1-12

Derek Kidner, basing his view on verses 6 & 9 in particular, describes "the menace of their propaganda" as one of the things David is feeling here; the presence of his enemies is never far away. David can rejoice, however, for His protection is in God.

PROVERBS 1v24-28

Having rejected Christian values and teaching, it will be a bitter regret when it is too late.

January 6th

GENESIS 13v5-15v21

When it came to Lot and Abram having to go their separate ways, "grasping Lot" grabs what was then a very fertile area. However, going to live down on the plains, got him dragged into a war. Abram has 318 men in his household, and manages to recover the captured people and their possessions.

We are introduced to Melchizedek, the priestly king of Jerusalem, who is clearly a worshipper of the one true God, and recognised as such by Abram, who pays a tithe of the loot to Melchizedek.

Abram is wise enough to refuse to take any reward from Sodom; he does not need to feel under any obligation to this evil city.

Twice in our passage we have God's promise to Abram – this land will be his, and he will have descendants that can't be numbered. The sacrificing of the animals and what Abram did with them, may seem bizarre to us 4,000 years on, but it was what happened when kings of that day drew up covenants. This is a covenant between God and Abram.

In a horrific nightmare, God makes Abram aware of the 400 years of slavery that lay ahead for his descendants.

MATTHEW 5 v27-48

Tough talking. We need to get to the root of sin in our lives. Jesus also speaks out on appalling attitudes to marriage and meaning what you say (oaths etc) and on the obsession with getting even with others (the Laws set under Moses were to stop retribution going too far; instead many always wanted the maximum revenge they could get.) This is a totally different way of living that Jesus is teaching, and it runs in contradiction of how many want to live.

PSALM 6v1-10

Psalms 6, 32, 38, 51, 102, 130, 143 are the seven penitential psalms. We need to recognise our sin and come to the LORD for forgiveness.

PROBERBS 1v29-33

Sometimes people only fully understand what it is they have chosen – in terms of lifestyle and personal values - when the consequences come home to roost.

January 7th

GENESIS 16v1-18v19

Impatience with God...the custom was not something which Sara and Abram invented, it was known in those times, but what bother it causes to this present day as the Arabs, rightly or wrongly, see themselves as the descendants of the servant girl's child! (There is no doubt that Ishmael went on to be the father of many tribes; whether we need to buy into the idea that ALL the Arabs are descended from him is another matter.)

We can only be appalled at Sara wanting to have a child through her husband getting the servant girl pregnant, and then Sara reacting so bitterly when it happens.

Ishmael is a teenager before Isaac is born.

Circumcision: hence forth a mark of God's covenant with the Jewish people.

The LORD's appearance at Mamre; the cynicism which has become a feature of Sara's life, stemming from hardened bitterness.

MATTHEW 6v1-24

Wrong understandings on prayer, fasting, and our possessions.

PSALM 7 v1-17

In this cry for justice, some see references to the situation over Absalom, and the way in which David discovered just how many enemies he had when the going became tough. We don't know who Cush was, but his tribe was the tribe of Benjamin, and many of its folk , being related to Saul, still had their bitterness and grievance about David replacing Saul and his line on the throne – and it showed, as soon as David was seen as being vulnerable.

PROVERBS 2v1-5

Ah, if only this was everyone's approach!

January 8th

Genesis 18v20-19v38

Abram, knowing that his nephew Lot is down there, pleads for God to hold back his judgement if there are 50, 45, 40, 30, 20 or even 10 godly people. Abram is learning something of God's grace and mercy. The judgment does come, and in the very revealing story of the mob outside the house, we understand why God decided to blot out this evil culture.

The story of Lot and his daughters shows how far they have sunk. One becomes the ancestor of Moab, the other the ancestor of the Ammonites.

The once fertile Dead Sea area is part of the great Rift Valley that runs down through Israel and on into Africa (eg Kenya). For those whose geography or geology is rusty, we are basically dealing with two huge rips in the ground, with the strip in-between plummeting far below sea level. The land had been very fertile, and the bitumen pools had been an important discovery from early days. However, the destruction of Sodom and Gomorrah, as the hot burning bitumen shot out of the ground and poured down from the skies, as it were, would have been the most horrific event that these people would ever have seen. Archaeology bears evidence that the dry and dead region once had a flourishing agriculture and villages and towns.

Matthew 6v25-7v14

Jesus continues to overturn deeply engrained wrong attitudes and values

Psalm 8 v1-9

There is a wonderful sense of praise in this psalm.

Proverbs 2v6-15

Just how do you want to live? Under God's guidance? In His wisdom?

January 9th

GENESIS 20-1-22v24

Good grief! Not again! Why does Abraham not learn?

And as for all that bitterness and cynicism that Abraham and Sarah have had in the past, and the entire stupidity over Hagar and Ishmael, God's promise is kept, and Isaac is born. It is dreadful that Hagar and her son have to be sent away – but even broken hearted Abraham (whatever he thought of Sarah's attitudes) realised what the future might hold for Isaac if the older Ishmael ever got the upper hand.

The story of God testing Abraham's faith was particularly testing now that the much treasured Isaac was all he had – but also it speaks volumes to us about when God's own Son Jesus died in our place – there was no substitute for Him, for He was dying for us.

MATTHEW 7v15-29

False piety and playing "religious"; just what are the fruits, and what are the foundations?

PSALM 9v1-12

Psalms 9 and 10 would seem to be companion pieces. We live in a fallen world, and at times see evil appearing to triumph, but God will rule and judge, and people will find their refuge in Him

PROVERBS 2v16-22

The attraction of reckless and wrecking relationships. There are different ways of translating the first line of verse 16 – the Hebrew "foreign woman" is translated as loose woman (e.g. RSV) or as a prostitute (Living Bible) – the people of Israel often had a fascination with the sexually obsessed pagan cultures around them. It is right up to date though - in these days when the press are full of stories of vice rings and the importation of women from other parts of the world, often into sexual slavery in 21st century UK and Europe, we know a lot about the attraction of superficial and fleeting encounters with the exotic, instead of real and meaningful permanent relationships.

January 10th

GENESIS 23v1-24v51

Abraham insists on buying the burial ground. The cave of Mach-pelah is still there, though Herod the Great built a magnificent building over it, with its huge tombs, inside which crumbling coffin like containers have been placed inside other containers, in their turn inside other containers over the millennia. Various members of Abraham's family are buried there, though claims that Adam and Eve are too is one you can privately scoff at once you are safely up the road! Whether it is wise to go there given the current Middle East situation is another matter. Stewart visited there in his early twenties, and took Patricia there in their journeys around the Holy Land in a Ford Fiesta, but until recently, tour buses avoided going anywhere near the area. The place is a place of Muslim / Jewish confrontation, with Jewish settlers trying to remain in the area, and was the scene of a Jewish gunman going berserk some years ago.

The search for a wife for Isaac. OK, this is not how we would do things today, but note the depth of prayer of even Abraham's servant. There is a clear sense of God's leading in the whole thing. If as much prayer went into seeking a partner for life today...

MATTHEW 8v1-17

The leper pleading for help, and Jesus' deliberate act of reaching out and touching someone who has probably not experienced the willing touch of another human being for a considerable time.

The godly Roman centurion, who accepts that the command of Jesus is all that is required – shames many others who have had the scriptures from childhood.

The story of Peter's mother in law reminds us that the disciples had homes and families too!

PSALM 9v13-20

Confidence in God rises.

PROVERBS 3v1-6

There are godly principles we have been taught; are you putting them into practice? "Write them on the tablet of your heart." (v3b)

January 11th

GENESIS 24v52-26v16

The hindering was not on Rebekah's part, but on her family's! Little wonder that 2,000 years later Jesus also spoke out when a would-be disciple was planning to stay at home until after his father's lifetime. Families can sadly, be the block to following God, instead of the place where God is found. (See the reading today from Matthew 8)

Abraham's home life left some things to be desired. He fathers more children, only to pack them off to leave Isaac alone as the one through whom the covenant with God was to pass down.

Rebekah and Isaac proved to have their favourites and must bear responsibility for the home they created; he may have been the eldest of the twins, but laid back Esau didn't give two figs about birthright and the whole covenant with God. The story doesn't say much for Jacob either, but in a couple of day's time we will read of how he meets an even bigger schemer in uncle Laban!

Meanwhile Isaac repeats a piece of stupidity committed on two occasions by his Dad. Fearful that others might kill him to take his wife, Isaac pretends that Rebekah is his sister. Funny some of the things we do, when we lose our nerve and stop trusting God!

MATTHEW 8v18-34

Would-be disciples are forced to think through the costs of following Jesus. See the earlier comment on the guy who would have sat at home until his father's life was over – there is no indication that his health was failing!

The experience of Jesus calming the storm was all the more shocking because the fresh water "Sea" of Galilee was the domain of his fishermen friends. This was their world, their place of trade. Suddenly it is the Carpenter who has power and dominion over that world in a way that reveals who He really is. Unnerving stuff for fishermen, who a few moments earlier were deeply frightened.

Jesus's power over demons brings home to everyone that what God is doing is on a scale beyond even what happened out on the lake. The local response is fear; many don't want what Jesus might do in their lives.

PSALM 10v1-15

An honest pouring out to God of what is on the Psalmist's heart. Are we ready for such honesty, such openness, such free expression to God of how the Psalmist felt? While guarding against self-righteousness on our part, we need to see this Psalm as a real cry to God when wicked men appear to be prospering all around us. If we are shocked by the language of parts of this Psalm – "Break the arms of these wicked men." (Living Bible, v15) – then pray to God that we are never in a situation where we really know, understand and identify with what the Psalmist felt – these evil doers believe no one can see what they are doing.

PROVERBS 3v7-8

Having brains, and knowing it, leads to one awful arrogance on the part of the "self made" man or woman. (v7 "Be not wise in your own eyes.")

January 12th

GENESIS 26v17-27v46

Strife between neighbours is nothing new, but Isaac strives to keep the peace, and provides for others. He was wise enough to know he needed good relations. Humanly speaking he was vulnerable amongst them. Once more Esau shows contempt for his spiritual heritage with two unsuitable marriages. The story of Jacob dressing up as Esau, and spicing up the meal to taste like game, has a lot to say about the parents and the home they created. And yet God is sovereign in all that is going on, for in God's grace the covenant is going to pass down through the very flawed Jacob.

MATTHEW 9v1-17

Jesus had been brought up in Nazareth, but he was based for some time in Capernaum, so much so that verse 1 describes it as home, leaving us speculating that is was Jesus's own home that was damaged (see another Gospel account) by those who lowered the lad down. Forgiving the lad's sins shocked the observers; what silenced them for the time being was when the lad went home healed. They were soon criticising again, with Jesus having called Matthew the tax collector and joining in a meal at Matthew's house. Jesus gave that answer about doctors being for sick people. Later on the disciples of John made contact. They were faithfully still doing the things that John had taught them, still preparing for the coming of the greater one...Jesus has to make the point that the "bridegroom" was with them. Jesus used a couple of illustrations to make the point that he was not merely patching up an old system, but bringing in a new age.

PSALM 10 v16-18

Once more a reminder that God is in control; and he has heard the cries of the poor and oppressed.

PROVERBS 3 v9-10

A reminder to set aside according to our means, part of what God has given to us, so that we can give to His work. Note this should be our first action when our pay comes in.

January 13th

GENESIS 28v1-29v35

In yesterday's reading, we read of Esau's determination to kill Jacob. He was very angry, and there was a real need to get Jacob off to somewhere safe. This was another sad development in home so divided by favouritism, and with the "games" that parents play, ultimately pitting their children against each other. To be fair to Esau, however, from what we read later, he does not seem to have been a "score" keeper. His anger was limited to the time it all happened. It is Jacob who remains troubled, never fully trusting his brother when they meet up again in later life, probably because Jacob knew how he would have thought about it if things were the other way about! Jacob's own heart will keep him troubled for years, then, because he will go on imagining that others think like him. Something to pray about, if you find yourself with a mind and heart like Jacob.

As for today's reading, there is that lovely picture of the heavenly staircase, and of God in His grace repeating to Jacob the promises given to Abraham and Isaac. There is that meeting between Jacob and Rachel, and the way in which seven years could pass so quickly as Jacob worked away, looking forward to the day when they would be married. Ah, but the schemer had met a real schemer in Uncle Laban, who palms off the poor unwanted Leah, leading to another generation of bitterness in a divided home.

MATTHEW 9v18-38

The faith of the synagogue ruler who is convinced that Jesus can raise his daughter is sorely tested with the incident of the haemorrhaging woman on the way. What a need there is to remember that others have their needs, grief and sorrows in the midst of our own. There is a lesson in the perseverance of the two blind men, but we can feel such deep sadness over the Pharisees who hate Jesus so much that they attribute Jesus' power to cast out the demon as an indication of how Jesus must be in league with the Devil himself. What blind logics we sometimes find in pious circles.

PSALM 11 v1-7

Fleeing is not always the thing to do. Sometimes Christians need to remember that God is still ruling, and the godly will see His face.

PROVERBS 3v11-12

Knowing that we are loved and disciplined at the same time has not always been an easy thing for us to get our heads around, especially if our own family life – or the life we have given our own kids – is far from balanced. God is balanced, even if we are not!

January 14th

GENESIS 30v1-31v16

Groan! More of this family competition, this time between a barren wife and her own rival, her sister, to the point of even giving their servant girls to Jacob so that more kids could be notched up that way. You would have thought this family would have learnt a lesson from the problems between Hagar and Sarah, back in Abraham's time. What is the application for today? Think of the hurt in our own society with broken homes, competing half families, rivalry between current and ex partners. Relationships are easy to break but the consequences are more than a lifetime. Eggs can't be unscrambled, as they say, but can you at least minimise and help to even partially heal some of those difficult family situations? (And with God's help, don't add to the mess our society is already in!)

Laban is quite a character himself, isn't he?

Some of that stuff about animal breeding may be puzzling. Just because Jacob used folklore ideas about rods being responsible for the colouring of sheep, does not mean that the Bible endorses the thinking behind it. The truth is that animals were more likely to be speckled and spotted, than pure coloured. In many ways, Jacob and Laban deserved each other, but Laban over the years proved to be a man who could not live any other way, without scheming. With Laban, it was almost compulsive. Did he have a straight forward, honest relationship with anybody? The whole incident led to Laban's own sons becoming very embittered, and it is interesting to note that when Jacob suggested to his wives that it was time to move on, neither was sorry to see the back of Dad. After the way he had treated them, they had nothing to miss! (see 31 verses 14-16 in particular.) Makes us ask some questions, once more, about the contribution we make to the happiness of our family circles.

MATTHEW 10 v1-26

No armchair discipleship here! Previous generations in our Churches had the luxury (or spiritual trap) that there was often "someone else" to do things. Many "passive" Christians thought they only had to pay, and go to Church, and that was their duty done. Can we really call that Christianity? Real Christianity is much more engaged, both in the world, and in a daily relationship with Christ as we really seek His will.

As he sent his disciples out, Jesus deliberately removed some of the comforts that they would have relied on, like all the extras they might have brought with them. He really improved their prayer life as they learnt to rely on God much more, from day to day!

PSALM 12v1-8

More reassurance for Christians living in a world in which dishonesty *seems* to pay.

PROVERBS 3v13-15

If only we would use that knowledge that we have of what is right or wrong, instead of looking over our shoulders all the time to see what society thinks!

January 15th

Genesis 31v17-32v12

More on those dreadful family relationships. Turns out that Jacob was right in expecting a violent response from Laban should he pull out of their various arrangements. There is an obvious application re the kind of parents with whom you can never talk anything through. And the fact that Laban never learnt to let go – still thought in terms of owning and controlling his own children even after they were married. Lots of application there! Disappointing is the response of Rachel who is so embittered that she has to take something which is of no use to her, but still needing to inflict some pain as she hits out at a father she has no love for.

As commented some days ago, Jacob now approaches Esau with very real fear, and makes every possible attempt to buy off Esau's anger. The truth is, as we shall find out tomorrow, that for all his many faults, Esau didn't think like Jacob. It is Jacob's own suspicious and twisted mind which will never allow him to relax while Esau is still around. Another piece of the irony is that Esau passes on nothing of his spiritual heritage. His people end up as heathen as all of those around them. It is through Jacob the twister that the knowledge of the one true God is going to be passed down. A lot to think about there!

Matthew 10v27-11v6

More challenges for the fearful Christian, constantly looking for approval from all the wrong people.

Have some sympathy for John the Baptist; prison life was beginning to have its toll. Sometimes we never stop to think of how vulnerable even people like him could be to depression and exhaustion. We sometimes expect too much of other believers. Jesus gives a practical answer that should help and encourage John.

Psalm 13 v1-6

We are too used to the television soaps in which problems only last 2 or five episodes. In real life we have to hang on in there much longer, learning to trust in God, and rely on his strength.

Proverbs 3 v16-18

Taken on their own, these couple of lines can come across a bit simplistic. The best way is to take them together with the rest of God's Word. Things do not always go well for those who truly love the Lord, but could you imagine what it would be like to have no faith, no belief, nothing to help you move forward? This is Godly wisdom.

January 16th

Genesis 32v13-34v31

Jacob's waves of presents for Esau, then the fact that he puts his wives and children across the Jordan for safety overnight, says a lot about Jacob and his fear of Esau. Do we not cringe, when the next day he places his own children in priority of who is loved more? Fearful of what Esau might do, Jacob arranges his family in a column. He places the concubines and their children first, and then Leah and her children, and then finally Rachel and her child. Imagine being at the head of that column (Dad doesn't care if I get killed off first!) At least Jacob goes out ahead, repeatedly bowing as his brother approaches with his 400 men. Esau has no desire for revenge, but Jacob and Esau will never be fully reconciled simply because of Jacob's own fearful heart.

The wrestling match the night before: As the deeply disturbed Jacob is alone on his side of the Jordan, he wrestles with God. Jacob is left with a physical scar, a limp. With his hip out of joint, and in excruciating pain, Jacob is forced to "cling to his opponent for support." (Joyce Baldwin The Message of Genesis, Bible Speaks Today series, IVP 1986, p137) Jacob comes away with a new name – Israel (God strives.) Hopefully the schemer has also learnt that it is God who is in control.

Dinah: How do we interpret this story? Is this a description of rape or seduction? In a male dominated society, the incident might be judged as rape because all the proper channels of courtship and marriage have been ignored by the King's son. It was a society in which it was up to the girl's father to literally give her away to the person of his (the family's) choice. Commentators do take different positions here, but all are agreed that Shechem has behaved abominably. On first reading it does seem as though we have a remorseful rapist who wants to marry his victim. At best we have an arrogant prince who assumes that Jacob would be glad to have him as a son in law and he literally forces the issue. It is possible to interpret it as Shechem using his power and position to entrap and seduce a woman who was powerless to say "no" to a King's son. In recent years there has been considerable discussion of these issues in society and the workplace. We are told nothing from Dinah's perspective, and this is most revealing in light of how the story develops from this point. Dinah's family were less concerned for Dinah, and more concerned about how they were wronged.

There are a lot of wrong motives in the subsequent story. The locals can see the wealth and success that Jacob's family would bring to their town, if they can be encouraged to settle permanently. The local townsfolk agree most readily to circumcision. Dinah's brothers, on the other hand, take what was a symbol of their covenant with God (circumcision) and encourage the locals to accept this so that, on the third day when the townsmen are very sore, all of Jacob's sons are able to ride in and massacre the town, taking the children, women, herds and wealth of every kind. The rape/seduction of Dinah does not justify the butchering of every man and the seizure of every woman and child. As for poor Dinah, her marriage was short lived as she is "rescued" from her now dead husband's house. Did anybody actually care about Dinah? Her brothers' answer to Jacob, that Shechem had treated their sister like a prostitute suggests more concern over family pride. Did they stop to think of what now became of their sister? Her last mention is in Genesis 46 v15 in a list of Jacob's descendants.

Matthew 11v7-30

Jesus speaks about John the Baptist and confirms that John was sent by God to get the people ready. Jesus describes the people as being a bit like the children, playing weddings one moment, and funerals the next, in the way they failed to respond to the message.

Chorazin and Bethsaida are local places which have witnessed miracles. How great the responsibility was upon them! Jesus mentions Tyre and Sidon (further up north, on the coast) as places that will have less to answer for on the day of judgment. He would have really shocked his listeners with his comments about Sodom (down on the shores of the Dead Sea, destroyed in the times of Abraham) as having less to answer for, because they did not have the opportunities that these local people have had under the ministries of both John and Jesus. Ouch!

Psalm 14v1-7

The fool who imagines there is no God. Both judgement and rescue are on the way.

Proverbs 3v19-20

The Creator's wisdom and power are brought home to us again.

January 17th

Genesis 35v1-36v43

Jacob himself realised, at the end of yesterday's reading, that he would have to move away from the area of Shechem, and now God told him to move to Bethel. His very much extended household now included many who did not share his relationship with God (presumably the women and children seized in Shechem were still with them, amongst others) and even Rachel had taken household "gods" belonging to her father. All of these idols and any connected paraphernalia(the ear-rings may have been charms) had to be left behind, although it is significant and worrying that they were buried, not destroyed, as this left open the possibility that they might be retrieved.

God reminds Jacob that he has a new name Israel. He had been called Jacob, meaning 'may he be at the heels' – a name which could be taken in several ways, including some good, but open to be taken in a bad way too, as one scholar has put it – 'grabber' - because of the way he had grabbed his brother's foot at birth. But Jacob had unfortunately been true to his name in adult life. God had a new life for Jacob to live.

Rachel's grave remains to this day, a heavily protected Israeli building on the edge of Palestinian Bethlehem.

As for Reuben's appalling behaviour, it also brings into focus the problems of a polygamous household, the competing wives and families, the servant girls without rights who become concubines as the two actual wives, Leah and Rachel, competed to see who could have the greater number of children in their "camps." Not much real love in the situation, and no respect for his father from Reuben either.

We are given significant information about Esau's descendants who will appear again and again in the Old Testament as the Edomites. The significance of Esau's marriages is that he became absorbed into the pagan culture of the region; archaeology reveals the idols of the Edomites.

Matthew 12v1-21

The constantly worrying thing about the Pharisees is that they saw themselves as the ones who truly respected the Scriptures – in their zeal they objected to very hungry disciples snapping off heads of grain in their hunger on the Sabbath (poor people were allowed to take grain like that) and to a man being healed on the Sabbath – working again. Jesus death is subsequently plotted.

Psalm 15 v1-5

The Psalm should be seen as a challenge to the worshipper to examine his or her heart as they approach the place of worship. This is one of David's psalms, written in earlier life – how his own words must have embarrassed him when things were far from blameless in later life, and David had every reason to be crimson faced. Forgiveness, mercy and grace are found in Jesus Christ who restores the one who truly repents.

Proverbs 3v21-26

"Preserve sound judgement and discernment "– or as the Living Bible put it, "Have two goals: wisdom- that is, knowing and doing right- and common sense."

I write these notes the morning after an evening in which someone has been pushing me to "rig" something when there is no reason or need to "rig" anything – doing things the honest way is going to produce the same results, but with a clear conscience as to how they were obtained! These verses from Proverbs are what we might call sanctified common sense; but they say things that still need to be repeated.

January 18th

Genesis 37v1-38v30

The story is familiar to us all, but my Sunday school teacher never made me think about the foolishness of Jacob (having favourites, and showing it) or Joseph (not always wise in what he shared.) Jacob and Joseph were Bible heroes and therefore could not be criticised!

The Bible story is there in all of its fullness so that we do learn from the crass stupidity and thoughtlessness of those, who in God's grace, were nevertheless used by Him. The sharing of Joseph's dreams brought much anger and bitterness into His home, coming so soon after the special coat. That does not excuse what the brothers did to him, but over these past number of days you have seen something of how Jacob devalued his other wives and his children by them. Only Joseph and Benjamin, Rachel's children seemed to matter. It was a household seething with hatred.

Meanwhile, one story that was not appropriate reading in Sunday school! The story of Judah and his sons, refers to the Biblical custom of the brother or the male next of kin of a dead man marrying the childless widow to raise children in the dead man's name. The story of Ruth is one of those episodes, and a happy one. However, in today's reading we are given a glimpse of how dark things could be on the fringes of Jacob's household.

Following the sale of Joseph, Judah moved out, not surprisingly, as he had to listen to Jacob crying over Joseph every day, and of course Judah had a very guilty conscience over the whole thing and his part in it. He got involved with a Canaanite girl and raised a family. We are not told what Er did, but he was particularly evil. Onan was then told to marry the widow Tamar, but took steps to avoid getting her pregnant. In other words, he used the accepted custom for his own gratification but denied the widow a child. He also died, and again we are told most clearly it was through God's judgement. At that point Judah sent Tamar back to her childhood home. The next part of the story may shock you – first of all there is Judah's use of a "prostitute," suggesting it was not the first time, since Tamar was clearly relying on that as part of her plan. It is also the desperate act of a young widow denied a family. No, none of it is edifying reading, but Tamar is right there in the family tree in Matthew 1 v3. That is may be the bit that shocks you most!

Matthew 12-45

In desperation the Pharisees attribute Jesus' power to the Devil. Blasphemy against the Holy Spirit is mentioned in this context, and is a debated point amongst Christians. In the context of this passage, we see those who are so determined to call the work of God Satanic in their utter opposition to it.

Jesus speaks of knowing a tree by its fruit – and the "fruit" of these Pharisees' lives was very revealing. The request for a miracle, coming after all the other miracles, deserves contempt. This is to be a showman type miracle, rather like what the Devil suggested in the wilderness – a temptation Jesus refused to succumb to. Some tough hitting words follow.

Psalm 16 v1-11

A fitting passage after some of the things in today's other readings.

Proverbs 3v27-32

Good basic morality, and wise words about not copying the world around us. There is something seriously wrong with us, and our understanding of God, if we think we have to use evil. Think back to our readings about addictive “fixers” and “riggers” like Laban. Not much belief in God if you have to live like that!

January 19th

Genesis 39 v1-41v16

Short term, mid term, long term? How you view life, and the lessons you take from it. Joseph could have thrown his faith away after the incident with Potiphar’s wife (or the lack of an incident, which is why he ended up in jail.) Or Joseph could have lashed out at God when the cup bearer forgot to use his influence to get him out of jail. God’s long term plan was for Joseph to be next to Pharaoh, in order to save his own family...but could you trust God that long, in jail?

Matthew 12 v46-13v23

Yes, Jesus had half brothers and sisters. They are the children fathered by Joseph after the birth of Jesus. They were not always helpful, nor did they see things from the perspective of the coming cross.

Jesus spelt out the parable; the hardness was not in the story, more in the hearts of the listeners.

Psalm 17 v1-15

This could be a difficult prayer to pray “I have been honest and have done what is right...” (Living Bible) but sometimes Christians do beat themselves about, just a bit too much. The problem is that they blame themselves when innocent, and excuse themselves and deny wrong doing when they are in the wrong. This psalm does deal with those times when you are innocent.

Proverbs 3 v33-35

Contrasted destinies. Which track are you on?

January 20th

Genesis 41v17-42v17

Joseph puts the great plan into action.

Meanwhile Dad back in Canaan sends 10 sons down to Egypt...

Matthew 13 v24-46

Ah, the first illustration is just what the Church on earth is today!

However, Jesus wants us to never lose our awe at what the Kingdom of God really is about.

Psalm 18v1-15

So many different ways of expressing how God is our Fortress, our Rock...

Proverbs 4 v1-6

Parents have their faults; part of growing up is undoubtedly discovering how not to do things (having watched your parents!) But there is also sound wisdom, and a godly heritage that are too quickly forgotten. Get wisdom, get insight...

January 21st

Genesis 42 v18-43v34

What dreadful temptations must have gone through Joseph's mind as he sought to test his brothers after all of these years! He was deeply moved, but could not show it, when they expressed sorrow amongst themselves in Hebrew for what they had done to Joseph all those years ago.

Much later, when Jacob wants to send them down to Egypt a second time, they stress just how serious this Egyptian prince was that they must produce their youngest brother, Benjamin. They also bring twice the amount of silver that Joseph had put into their sacks.

On arriving, they are united with imprisoned Simeon, but are then taken to the palace for a feast. How this Egyptian prince can remember such detail, including the order of their ages, is such a mystery to them!

Matthew 13v47-14v13

The reference to his brothers and sisters – remember that Joseph and Mary had a normal family life after the special birth of Jesus.

Herod continues to have a troubled conscience following the murder of John.

Psalm 18 v16-34

There is a strong sense of deliverance, but also recognition of the life that ought to spring from loving the Lord. Some may struggle with comments such as "He trains my hands for battle" but David knew just how things might have ended on many an occasion if the Lord had not been with him.

Proverbs 4v7-10

This is above all, a wisdom from God Himself.

January 22nd

Genesis 44v1-45v28

Now the story moves fast! Benjamin is arrested on the way back, and all the brothers arrive back before Joseph. As Judah pleads for Benjamin's life, Joseph can keep up the pretence no longer!

Matthew 14v14-36

The feeding of the 5,000 plus does not seem to prepare the disciples for the spectacle of Jesus walking on the water. To be fair to Peter, he did at least get out of the boat and walked on the water briefly before he lost his nerve. That was more than the rest of them!

Psalm 18 v35-50

There is a strong sense of being where he is, by God's leading and by God's direct intervention.

Proverbs 4 v11-13

God will guide – are we willing to take the guidance?

January 23rd

Genesis 46v1-47v31

Jacob and his family move to the safety of Egypt, as the famine becomes steadily worse. Jacob does not forget, however, that their ultimate destiny is not Egypt, but always the promised land.

Matthew 15 v1-28

Some dreadful petty criticism of the disciples leads Jesus to ask why the Pharisees have abandoned more essential things such as parts of the Ten Commandments – they had found a way round giving proper support to aging parents. The disciples still struggle with the difference between externals and what is really taking place in the heart. Jesus draws out the faith of the Canaanite lady.

Psalm 19 v1-14

David can see God's power and presence behind the created universe. And just as there are the laws of physics, so there are God's laws that are there for our own good and peace.

Proverbs 4 v14-19

Slippery paths exist and they must be avoided.

January 24th

Genesis 48v1-49v33

Jacob deliberately places his right hand on Joseph's younger son.

Also, Joseph's sons will inherit as though they were Jacob's – the loss of Joseph and Benjamin's mother Rachel still hurts Jacob hard in later life – she had died giving birth to Benjamin. Her grandsons will then inherit their place in the promised land as though they were her sons.

Jacob's "blessings" to his other sons are very revealing as to what they say about them. There is also the prophetic recognition of the Kingly line that will come from Judah.

Matthew 15v29-16v12

The feeding of the four thousand.

Jonah as a picture of the resurrection, which will be the sign that the Pharisees seek.

As Jesus tried to warn the disciples to be very wary of the Pharisees and Sadducees ("beware of the yeast of....") they interpreted it as a dig aimed at them because they had forgotten to buy bread!!!

Psalm 20 v1-9

A key verse – "Some nations boast of armies and of weaponry, but our boast is in the Lord our God."

Proverbs 4 v20-27

Again, what godly wisdom has to offer.

January 25th

Genesis 50v1-Exodus 2v10

Jacob is buried back in the promised land (modern Hebron)

Joseph's brothers have still not figured out their brother – they even invent a tale about what Jacob said before he died. There was no need for that. Joseph was sincere, but his godly faith was not understood by the rest.

Time passes, and a new administration, with no sense of owing anything to Joseph and his memory, comes to power in Egypt. Even during the times of Joseph the Egyptians had revulsion for the sheep keeping Hebrews, but now fear of how immigrants appear to be swamping the countryside leads to a policy of genocide. Ironically, Moses is adopted by Pharoah's daughter, and his own mother employed to look after him.

Matthew 16v13-17v9

Caesarea Philippi is in the far north, in a pagan area. The worship of Pan was popular here, and the local stream coming out of the mouth of a cave led locals to believe it flowed out of the mouth of hell. Here of all places, Peter acknowledges Jesus as the Christ.

Given the nearby location of Mount Hermon, some protestant scholars see Hermon as the location for the transfiguration.

Psalm 21 v1-13

David as King has been very aware of God's help and blessing. Are we as thankful?

Proverbs 5 v1-6

In our own society, otherwise strong and powerful figures have come to ruin in the whole area of their sexuality.

January 26th

Exodus 2 v11-3v22

Moses has lived a life of luxury in the palace, and copes poorly with the stark reality of what is happening outside. Whatever his age, he is very much the palace adolescent and soon to be the palace runaway. Impulsive and with no clear plan, to say nothing of the actual murder of the Egyptian, Moses explodes in anger. He could have stopped the beating without having to lift a finger or harming the Egyptian in any way. If he is to lead his people to freedom, it will not be done this way, and the killing of the Egyptian ultimately leaves the Israelites suffering for many more years as Moses has to flee until the present Pharaoh is dead.

He had a lot to learn about human nature. Having saved the life of a Hebrew, Moses expected the Hebrew to keep quiet. Instead Moses meets mockery and contempt the next time he intervenes, and before long the Israelites have either gossiped freely or were forced to admit who killed the Egyptian when he was finally found.

Moses has to spend time struggling in a much more lowly role, to learn a lot of life's hard lessons. If these years seemed wasted, they were certainly not. Moses needed to know all about leading sheep through the desert fringes if he was to lead a whole nation through the wilderness. There were places along the route that he needed to know like the back of his hand. The sheep would soon teach him a few things! The scale would be vastly different, but he would have to take a people who had lived along river banks for 430 years and teach them all about wilderness survival.

The burning bush which did not actually burn was an intriguing way for God to appear to Moses.

Matthew 17 v10-27

John the Baptist had denied that he was literally the prophet Elijah back from the dead. Jesus confirms that John the Baptist had nevertheless fulfilled the prophecy.

There are lessons about having faith – faith enough to see things through in the power that God gives.

Behind the miracle of the fish with the four drachma coin in its mouth we see how Jesus will not cause offence where it is unnecessary. Matthew had perhaps another reason for recording the story some decades later. When the Romans eventually pulled down the Jewish temple, they reassigned the Jewish temple tax to the upkeep of one of their own pagan temples in Rome. It became a very embittered issue. It was an even more embittered issue to the ex Jews who were now Christians. They needed to know that Christ Himself had once paid the temple tax, albeit in the days when the real Jewish temple still stood, even though it was a place of much opposition to Him.

Psalm 22v1-18

A shocking but honest account of how David worked through a pretty devastating experience of feeling deserted by God – and also, in verse 1, the words of Jesus on the Cross as he took the wrath of God in dying for Your sins and mine.

Proverbs 5 v7-14

More advice on the consequences of an adulterous relationship.

January 27th

Exodus 4 v1-5v21

First of all we raise our eyebrows to the number of miracles God enables Moses to do, so that the people might see that he does represent the Lord. Then we are dumbfounded with Moses' excuse about a speech impediment, and we are almost scandalised when God has to send Moses' brother Aaron to do the talking for him. Not exactly glowing enthusiasm for what God wants in his life, but are we any better?

God is pretty frank with Moses about how Pharaoh will hold out until the final plague.

The incident at night is puzzling, though Moses and Zipporah clearly recognised God's hand in it. Clearly Moses and his wife had a disagreement over circumcision, which was a sign of belonging to God's covenant. It took a pretty extreme situation, whatever that was exactly, before Zipporah agreed.

Matthew 18 v1-22

Jesus continued to challenge the wrong perceptions of his disciples (v1-6.) The language of verses 7-9 seems extreme, but Jesus is challenging his would be disciples to adopt some radical dropping of things that hinder their walk with God. And he wants us to understand that there are real issues for each of us.

The parable of the sheep does of course bring home that God is concerned for each one of us.

Verses 15 -17 are important, and are written into the Code of our Presbyterian Church. These are principles that are fundamental in handling serious disagreement amongst Christians.

Verses 18 & 19 are not a blanket agreement to just anything, but reflect the Jewish understanding of the Divine presence resting upon those earnestly studying God's law. (RVG Tasker, Matthew, Tyndale NT Commentaries, 1961, p177.) From a Christian perspective, we see God's commitment to those who, having come together in His Name, are seeking what is right for the work of His Kingdom.

Verses 21 & 22. Peter's limitation on forgiving 7 times might have seemed reasonable. Christ does not want us to keep counting to 77, but it is also a direct reference back to Genesis 4 v23-24 – Lamech killed a young man for wounding him – in Lamech's own words, he had his revenge 77 times over. What Christ wants, is the very opposite of what Lamech did in going over the top.

Psalm 22v19-31

This is a turning point in the Psalm. After the frankness of a man who feels that God has deserted him, David is working it through in prayer – and God is coming to his rescue.

Proverbs 5 v15-21

Frank and pretty colourful language on the subject of being satisfied with your spouse. Interesting poetic ways of expressing it.

January 28th

Exodus 5 v22-7v24

A classic manoeuvre, on the part of Pharaoh: drive the people against Moses by making their conditions so bad that they will blame Moses for ever having intervened! Of course, you and I know that the people have been suffering from before Moses was even born, and later on, in the wilderness, we will read of them pining for the wonderful conditions they left behind in Egypt, with the apparently wonderful range of vegetables they had back there!!!

It is of course easy to see that kind of reaction in others, but how do you catch yourself on if you are in the shoes of the people who are turning against Moses? Or more importantly, if you are the person with the very selective memory, lashing out against God? A lot to think about there – when were you last guilty of a selective memory, and perhaps turning against or blaming some godly soul who only wanted the best for you, and who was doing everything possible to help?

The showdown with Pharaoh's "magicians." Moses and Aaron are sent by God with a genuine miracle to perform in Pharaoh's presence. The miracle is seemingly reproduced by Pharaoh's "magicians." Whether the "magicians" did this by slight of hand – trained performers like present day "magicians" used by Pharaoh to manipulate the simple common people – or more worryingly – that this was a real manifestation of occultic power – has divided scholars. Some missionaries have warned that in the west we have not seen occultic or demonic power as it exists in parts of the world.

One point is simply that instead of responding to a demonstration of God's power, Pharaoh dismisses it all. Likewise, Pharaoh's "magicians" are also able to turn water blood red. So my men can match yours (however they managed to do it.) Pharaoh is a long way yet from listening to God.

Matthew 18v23-19v12

Many Church going people today still cannot get their heads around God's grace, and what it might mean (as a recipient of that grace) for how I might live it out in my response to others. Which actually puts the next issue – the trap question on divorce – into a different light. Jesus has just been explaining the depths of God's grace, and God's subsequent anger when those who have been forgiven so much by Him show no signs of extending that grace to others. Now that is just about the last thing you find in our divorce courts – grace.

Psalm 23 v1-6

A beautiful psalm, but perhaps we need to see it for many other occasions and not just death! When was the last time you lay out in long dry grass on a warm summer's day? Maybe you need to learn to lie down in green pastures, and trust God to give you that tremendous peace.

Proverbs 5 v22-23

It is sometimes said, rather cynically, that the fraudster is caught out when he can't remember which lie he told to whom, and when. A life of constant dishonesty always exacts its price upon those who live by it. And sometimes it exacts its price when someone who lives by lies can't take at face value the word of an honest man or woman who would have helped him or her without seeking anything in return. It is very sad to be the honest man facing such situations in which people imagine you to be just like them.

January 29th

Exodus 7 v25-9v35

Maybe it's just my sense of humour but can you see the funny side of Pharaoh's men reproducing the snakes, blood, frogs – and then failing to produce the gnats? Having camped beside Loch Lomond on a warm summer I would have thought that Pharaoh should have been relieved when his "magicians" failed to add to the numbers of gnats! Interestingly, when Pharaoh's men failed to duplicate the miracle (by fraud or however) they took seriously that Moses was not just better at slight of hand, but that these were real miracles, real power, with a real God behind them. It took a very brave magician to go up to Pharaoh (a "god" himself in the land of Egypt) to tell him that these things were done by the finger of God. Pharaoh will not learn – well, not the right lesson anyhow. From now on he does not ask his magicians to replicate the miracles; they have let him down, a bucketful. But does Pharaoh want to listen to God? At least some of the ordinary people saved their cattle from the hailstones by bringing them in from the fields, and God's grace is there in the way the crops of wheat and emmer (spelt) were unaffected by the timing of it all.

What are we to make of Pharaoh's admission of having "sinned" and his requests that Moses should pray for him? This is manipulation of Moses' faith and of God's grace. Not a word of sincerity in it all. Playing "sorry" is only another card up Pharaoh's sleeve in his world of alternating diplomacy and tyrannical power. As soon as the plague is over, Pharaoh sees himself as having won in a very cruel and dangerous game, exploiting the simple faith of Moses when nothing else would succeed. Of course, at a personal level, the only cost to Pharaoh so far has been his personal pride at having to go through such mock sorrow. None of his people, their crops or their livestock have actually mattered to Pharaoh. God will, as a last resort, touch what – or rather who – actually does matter to Pharaoh.

Matthew 19 v13-30

The disciples in their panic try to cut down on the many pressures that Jesus was facing. Jesus had to overrule them. What kinds of irrational decisions do you make under pressure? Are the children in the home pushed aside? A husband or wife pushed aside? What was the logic in the disciple's decision that somehow or other the children did not matter? How badly do you handle pressure, and what – or who suffers as a result?

There is of course the lesson that children do matter to Jesus.

And then there is the story of the rich young man. Funny enough, Jesus does not question this account of a sinless life towards others – but he does put his finger on all the omissions of the things that could have been done to alleviate the suffering around him. The young man's wealth was a huge stumbling block.

Trust Peter to come up with the rather inappropriate question as to what they were going to get out of following Jesus!!! Perhaps at this point a warning about being careful about some of the "prosperity gospel" stuff that is sometimes around in Christian circles – Jesus spoke of how they would receive a hundred fold, but he did not necessarily mean in the bank account – there are many other ways of finding deep satisfaction in following the Lord.

Psalm 24 v1-10

Another one of those Psalms that in later life must have made David's ears go red with lines like "He who as clean hands and a pure heart…" Sadly there were times when David behaved abominably in later life. He did, however, learn of God's grace and forgiveness in those times.

The Psalm is best seen in how it came to be used by later generations; a spiritual self check-up by the reader as he or she approached God's House in Jerusalem. The various sung versions of this psalm help with its impact on us today.

Proverbs 6 v1-5

Important words of warning as to who you get into business with, or who you may be "covering" who may very well land you right in it! There are times when Christian people realise, rather belatedly, that they are literally in business with someone whose values and ethics are a complete contradiction of their own. Here in Proverbs the believer is told to get himself out of such setups as soon as he can. It does not mean that we cannot ever be in business with someone who does not share our faith, or that we cannot put up a surety for someone who does not know the Saviour, but we need to be very wary of all circumstances in which we leave ourselves open.

Our honesty and openness can be abused. We do not want to become so hard that we refuse to help, but walking lives that are marked by God's grace and love does not mean that we are to walk blindly, but with real discernment and with our eyes fully opened in this evil world. Pray for discernment.

January 30th

Exodus 10 v1 – 12v13

God in His grace and mercy challenges people again and again – but not forever. When is the last time? The frightening thing is that God has been giving Pharaoh opportunity after opportunity – but now it is God who hardens Pharaoh's heart and that of his officials, as God's hand begins to close in judgement.

The Passover is of course the meal that Jesus and His disciples celebrated together at the Last Supper. Unleavened bread is all part of the get-ready –to-go preparations as God's people leave Egypt after 430 years. The blood of the lamb on the door posts is of course a reminder for Christians that it is through the blood of THE Lamb that we escape God's great judgement.

Redemption is a central theme in all of God's dealings with His people – and a preparation for what God would do on Calvary

Matthew 20 v1-28

This is a story to which adults and children of a certain age react in very different ways. Adults are offended when those who join the work force towards the close of the day are paid the same as those who were there from early morning. The owner of the vineyard would appear to be more concerned than all go home with the money they need. After all, these people were available for work, facing hunger and increasing hopelessness until this employer came along and took them on. The salary is pretty good, but those who have worked all day resent the employer's ideas. Funny enough, younger children tend to agree with the employer's idea of fairness.

It is of course an illustration of grace. Do we resent others who have been forgiven more? Are we constantly watching others, slighted by every good thing from above that comes their way?

Jesus speaks of His coming death. He is frank and clear. The disciples of course don't want to hear this talk, and the incident that follows, which is so cringe worthy, only illustrates how they are on a different wavelength. Mummy Zebedee has great dreams for her two boys. She imagines them on thrones on either side of Jesus; which is rather ironic, since it will be a cross, and thieves on either side – which is why Jesus asks the question, “Can you drink the cup I am going to drink?” The rest of the disciples are of course furious that James and John’s mother “got in” before them. There is also the problem that the disciples need to learn what Jesus has been teaching and illustrating in His own life – servanthood.

Have you fully grasped what Jesus wants in your life? Or are you still following your agenda?

Psalm 25 v1-11

This is a beautiful psalm. Some background: this is an acrostic psalm, which means it has a verse beginning with a letter of each Hebrew letter (except one, and there is an extra verse at the end in this case.) All of this is lost on us in the English, but a lot of hard work has gone into this piece of poetry with all its themes of God’s protection, guidance, pardon, the psalmist’s confidence in God, His goodness, justice and loving care (Rogerson & McKay Psalms 1-50 The Cambridge Bible Commentary, 1977 page113)

Proverbs 6 v6-11 Sanctified common sense, though it comes as a bit of a rocket with no warning after the other issues in the first 5 verses. Dissatisfaction in life brings many temptations, including the temptation to opt out and take to the bed or the settee.

January 31st

Exodus 12 v14 – 13 v17a

Communion is such an important celebration to us, so we should have some understanding of the importance of Passover, from which our Communion developed when Jesus gave new meaning to the wine and unleavened bread. Passover remained the most important celebration in Old Testament times, and to Jewish people today it is still so central.

Here we have the description of the first Passover meal, eaten as outside the Egyptian firstborn are being slain by God. It is the last of the plagues, and sadly it has had to come to this. On the last day of the 430th year of their time in Egypt, the people of Israel begin to head “home.”

Matthew 20 v29-21v22

The Gospel story is heading towards its climax – the cross. Little did these blind men realise this was the last time Jesus would pass their way. Note, they understand who Jesus is – the crowd are trying to stop them from shouting that out! Later, the crowd in Jerusalem (probably largely made up of people who have come up from

Galilee) repeat these things as Jesus enters the city. There are touching details such as the donkey and its colt, and what the disciples are to say. These things were also prophesied by Zechariah (9v9).

Jesus' entry into Jerusalem would have reminded people of how the temple was "taken back" after being defiled in the period between the two Testaments (164 BC) when the people sang "Hosanna" and waved palm branches. As Jesus relived that part of His people's history we should not be surprised that He moved on to the temple, where the part that should have been available to gentiles for worship was taken up by stalls and animals. Like Judas Maccabaeus in 164 BC, Jesus strove in to cleanse the temple, but in this case it is from Jewish defilement.

Jesus' treatment of the fig tree is best explained as being to do with the fact that the fig tree is one of the symbols of Israel in the Old Testament – this is God's judgement on the nation, which would happen in the terrible slaughter of 66-77 AD.

Psalm 25v12-22

There are statements of how the psalmist expects things to be for believers,("he will spend his days in prosperity") and there are his real problems he is facing now. There is a lot to work through here. Following Christ is not a guarantee of a blissful, uneventful life. At the same time, there are promises to claim in the midst of struggle.

Proverbs 6 v12-15 More comment on what the writer of Proverbs can see in everyday life; lessons for those coming behind, things to recognise in a very evil world.

February 1st

Exodus 13v17b-15v19

The first lesson to learn is that God does recognise the limits of His people. They were in no fit state to take the most direct route, through present day Gaza, which would have meant taking on the highly experienced Philistines. Still not a route to take today! God leads them by a pillar of cloud during the day, and a pillar of fire at night. But is God leading them into a cul-de-sac, with the sea in front, and Pharaoh's army behind? The division of the sea was so unexpected, and an early lesson that God had not brought them out into the wilderness to let it all end here. Something to remember in life's apparent "cul-de-sacs." Quite a hymn of celebration!

Matthew 21v23-46

Jesus gives the Jewish leaders a question which they are afraid to answer. They can't afford to say anything derogatory about John the Baptist, but if they complement John then they need to explain why they didn't do as he said.

Jesus lets fire with several parables – which son really obeys – the one who says "yes," but does not do it, or the one who says "no," realises he is wrong, and goes out to obey? Then Jesus speaks of how prostitutes and others repented when they heard John, but these people (those who seemed to be saying "yes" to God in appearing so religious) had never repented. Ouch!

Then the story of the heir murdered by those leasing the vineyard – they were a bit slow on realising that Jesus was speaking of them – the people who were supposedly looking after God's vineyard – Israel.

Psalm 26v1-12

A lot here to make us think. No doubt David believed what he was claiming here ("for I have led a blameless life.") Is that always the case when believers are facing problems? Having said that, there is comfort here for the believer who is genuinely innocent and who is crying out for God to vindicate him.

Proverbs 6v16-19

Pretty direct here!

February 2nd

Exodus 15v20-17v7

430 years in Egypt meant that the present generation knew very little of the everyday lives of Abraham, Isaac, Jacob etc. Just as well that Moses had spent those years wandering around in this area with his father-in-law's sheep. The first problem is always water in a region like this. How quickly they forget what God has just done back at the Red Sea. The name "Marah" will appear again as the name that an embittered Naomi takes in the Book of Ruth.

Food is the next problem. First we ever heard of the wonderful and plentiful things they had back in Egypt! How fickle memory is! What then did God save them from back in Egypt, if things really were that good?

God gave them quail (quite tasty, but you need a couple on the plate – I've tried it) and manna. They don't trust God from day to day, and have to learn the lesson when the manna goes off that they tried keeping overnight. They also have to learn to gather twice as much on the sixth day, cook what they are keeping, and accept that there will be no manna on the ground on the seventh day. This daily trusting of God in the most basic of things proves to be quite a struggle, and until we learn to get past that point, our spiritual lives are not going to move forward. Basic, daily, even mundane things are often the real testing ground.

Before we leave the story, we should note that the issue of the Sabbath, and Sabbath rest, is a big one for God in the Old Testament. It is a big issue, for a whole pile of reasons – rest for us, time to worship Him. We need to work out some of the principles in our complex 21st century lives, with shift work and sometimes obligatory work when we want to be at worship. We don't want to make the Sabbath a misery (and somehow miss the point) but there are basics – rhythm and order in our lives, even respect and honour for the Creator, who also rested. We shall see, again and again, that Sabbath rest is important even for those leading a pretty rough existence in the wilderness.

The water issue comes up again. This time it is the complete absence of water, rather than just a bitter supply. Once again God is portrayed as bringing them out to kill them in the wilderness. The place will be remembered in both the Old and New Testaments for the rebellion and backbiting – a landmark we wish was not there. It is a lesson though, in how quickly and how deeply bitterness and rebellion mount up.

Matthew 22v1-32

The guests who don't come – too busy for God. In fact, the messengers are sometimes badly treated. Others are gathered in.

There is however, one person who comes into the feast, but refuses to wear the special robe made for him. All have been admitted on the same footing, but this man is arrogant enough to believe that what he has is good enough. The King (God Himself) will have none of that. He provides the means, all come on the same basis, into God's heaven.

Trick questions follow. The one about taxes to an unpopular invader; then one about whose wife she will be in heaven (bear in mind that the Sadducees didn't even believe in the resurrection, so they were mocking more than Jesus here.)

Psalm 27v1-7

There is a real awareness of God's saving grace here. Here is a believer who wants to take the time for what we often forget to do.

Proverbs 6v20-26

Belated words, recognising the benefit of growing up in a godly home? If you had that, you are probably only starting to appreciate the rich spiritual heritage you have, to say nothing of the stability of the home you had as a child.

February 3rd

Exodus 17v8-19v15

A real lesson in prayer here.

The Amalekites will appear again and again.

Wise advice from Moses' father-in-law. Moses had to learn to delegate. Many Christians don't know how to delegate and the result (exhaustion, anger, stress, or just not coping with the work or situation) is hardly glorifying to God.

At Mount Sinai God will give the commandments. God appearing to the people is to be one of the other most significant events of their history. There are important lessons about the holiness of the God they are approaching. While we approach through what Jesus has done for us (and what a privilege it is to say "Abba", Father) we can be flippant, careless and sometimes indifferent. We need to feel the fear that was felt around the mountain back in those Old Testament times, to give us a grasp of what our privileges are in Christ today.

Matthew 22v33-23v12

Trick questions again. Jesus sums up the laws in two sections.

Jesus then gives them something to think about. If the Messiah is descended from David, how come David calls Him Lord?

Jesus warns about religious show (of which there was plenty.)

Psalm 27v8-14

Hold on, in there! God is coming. "Be strong and take heart and wait for the Lord."

Proverbs 6 v27-35

Adultery – given as an example of reckless sin with a multitude of consequences, some of them severe and destructive and leading to chains of reaction from others.

February 4th

Exodus 19v16-21v21

The sheer breadth of all the commandments given here is breathtaking.

Matthew 23v13-39

I once said in church that many, if they only knew it, are happier with the Pharisees.

Here we have a lot of religious hypocrisies exposed. Long prayers from those who are evicting widows (business is business?) Converts, still learning, still vulnerable, made worse as they are waylaid into the wrong things by pious sounding individuals. False, sinful definitions of which oaths can be broken (White lies versus black lies – what happened to truth?) Tithing popular, but justice, mercy and faith missing?

Some very hard words about the past, and how the wrongs continue into the present. People go on to revere those whom they didn't listen to, when it mattered. All of this would indeed catch up with this society.

Psalm 28 v1-9

A recognition of where our safety lies. And a reminder that God will punish those who continue to rebel against him.

Proverbs 7 v1-5

Godly wisdom, sanctified common sense, is not to be ignored. God has shown what He wants in our lives. Do we want to listen?

February 5th

Exodus 21v22-23v13

Practical laws had to be laid down – if you think any of these are harsh, they are best seen as setting maximums. There are basic decencies expected, where the law exceeds anything we have today, such as coming to the rescue even when it is your enemy struggling to get an animal back on its feet, or it is your enemy's animal that has strayed. There are particular concerns for the poor and the immigrant.

Matthew 24 v1-28

Herod was currently funding a rebuilding of the temple, with some very impressive stonework. It came as a shock when Jesus prophesied what would happen approximately 40 years later. Far from being a comfortable future, real struggles lay ahead for those seeking to follow Jesus. Things would happen on worldwide scales. They were to be aware that many would make false claims about Jesus' return.

Psalm 29 v1-11

For some a thunder and lightning storm is particularly frightening. Not for David – he enjoys the power and the strength of it all – and behind it all, recognises that God has tremendous power and strength too. If we are impressed with creation, how much more so ought we to be impressed with the Creator.

Proverbs 7 v6-23: more comment on society where marriage is not respected and upheld

---

February 6th

Exodus 23v14-25v40

If you are lost in these descriptive passages, bear in mind that these people were called to live a life marked by the presence of their Lord and God.

In the details of the Ark and all the other things that Moses was told to have made, have we slipped, in our day and age, into an attitude that anything will do God? Here only the best will do in the worship of God.

Matthew 24v29-51

Warnings of the end times continued. Rather than living in fear of this, let's get on with living for Jesus, so that, whenever it comes, we are not ashamed to be suddenly in His presence.

Psalm 30 v1-12

A flood of emotions here! David has at last emerged from earlier trials into happier days. He does confess, however (verses 6-10) of a period of over-confidence and its dire results.

Proverbs 7 v24-27

The warnings of death in a promiscuous society are right up to date.

February 7th

Exodus 26v1-27v21

Sheer dedication to God will produce all of this! The best will be given in service.

Matthew 25 v1-30

Attitudes – carelessness, lack of preparation, even an unwillingness to invest and use what God has given us to his glory. Obvious lesson re "talents."

Psalm 31v1-8

David is working through, with God, difficult times of stress.

Proverbs 8 v1-10

Note how God's wisdom is directly relevant to all these places from everyday life.

February 8th

Exodus 28 v1-43

A lot of ministers are uncomfortable with robes – some even with clerical dress itself, largely because congregations often "love it" for all the wrong reasons – there is a need for many lay people to realise that the last thing we need are added barriers to real life ministry. Some folks do want Church to be, for them, a relic of a bygone age. The world outside has no time at all for formal dressing up, formal titles, or anything that suggests pomposity. Sadly, what some Church going people just love, only confirms in the eyes of many people outside the Church that it is irrelevant to their present day lives. Even those denominations which don't have clerical dress or robes soon find other ways of making worship and contact with pastors unnecessarily formal and somewhat distant.

There is also a need to realise that we are living in the times since the first coming of our Lord. He never instructed his early disciples to engage in this kind of dressing up. These descriptions of very formal, holy vestments belong to the Old Testament, to that time before the coming of our Lord, when the High Priest entered the Holy of Holies once a year in fear and trembling. Everything about the Temple worship, its structures, its dress, reminded people that they served a holy God whom ordinary people could not approach. At Mount Sinai they stood behind protective barriers, as sinners, who would die if they crossed the line.

In sharp contrast, the Gospel brings the message that the gulf between God and man has at last been bridged; through faith and trust in the finished work of Christ upon the cross we can dare to call God "Abba" - which was absolutely scandalous to many people who heard Jesus say that. The fact that Jesus has died for our sins means we do not need the reminders that properly belong to Old Testament times, of what it was like before Jesus died in our place. We are not outside the curtain anymore. We are not back in the Old Testament temple with its Holy of Holies, its elaborate sacrificial system, its court for the priests, its court for Jewish men, its court for women, and finally its outer court for gentiles (us!)

If you are puzzled by the last few verses of today's reading, the simple explanation was the need for practical modesty as the priests were going up steps etc.

Matthew 25v31-26v13

The first part of our reading brings home what the letter of James will later give strong emphasis to; the need for a practical outworking of our faith. If we can't even offer someone a drink of water, show some compassion for a stranger in difficulty, or have some concern for someone in very difficult circumstances, then it does raise the question whether the Gospel has really penetrated our lives.

Jesus is very frank to the disciples as He tries to prepare them for His death.

The Perfume: This was a very extravagant gesture; even the disciples were highly critical of someone who wanted to express love for the Saviour. Are we too judgmental of how others want to show their love of Jesus? Does it reflect on a mean streak towards God in us?

Jesus spoke of how the woman was anointing his body for burial. Had she grasped the truths which the disciples did not want to hear?

Far from being crass or uncaring about the poor, Jesus was only too well aware that "the poor" were often used as an excuse for doing nothing that might seem extravagant, by people who didn't at the same time do much for the poor either!

Psalm 31v9-18

David is in considerable inner turmoil and has very real enemies to contend with. Walking with the Lord is not going to be a life of continuous highs with no worries. Taking it to the Lord and trusting Him – really putting into practice all those things we know in our heads, but sometimes need to actually put into practice as steps of faith – is something which we need to learn again and again.

Proverbs 8 v11-13

Wisdom in the Bible is always something far more than just brain power, or educational achievements, or even streetwise wisdom. Real wisdom begins in a living relationship with God.

February 9th

Exodus 29v1-30v10

The ordination of Aaron and those who are to follow is itself a reminder of the need for atonement, the need for sacrificial blood, the need for consecration. Even when we get lost in these details, we realise this is a God who takes sin seriously, and who takes seriously how those who serve Him ought to live. If we find the details and the extent of it all overpowering, it is a reminder that we are not to make light in anyway of the need for Calvary.

Matthew 26v14-46

Countless theories have been put forward to explain why Judas did what he did. What were the first seeds of sinful attitudes that opened up his heart and life to the darkest of deeds? The description of the Last Supper records that Judas knew that Jesus knew, before he left to carry out the deed.

Peter's boast about his own loyalty to Jesus would haunt him before very long.

They all found it hard to cope with how Jesus was talking and acting at this time of annual holiday. As we have seen, Jesus had talked plainly to them before now. He needed their fellowship and prayer support in that time in the Garden of Gethsemane.

Psalm 31v19-24

Here we read more of David's working through with God the deep despair and exhaustion of which we read yesterday and the day before. This may indeed have been a long process. There is recognition of hastily spoken words (v22) of accusation towards God.

Proverbs 8 v14-26

Again emphasis on how real wisdom is God-given.

February 10th

Exodus 30 v11-31v18

We continue to be reminded of major themes; the need to be ransomed; the fact that rich and poor are alike before God, the whole seriousness with which we should understand God's holiness and otherness. Recipes for incense and anointing oil, no matter how attractive they might smell, were never to be used by the people for themselves.

Special attention is given to the concept of the Sabbath; rest and worship are important. True, many of us have to live lives with very complicated work patterns and requirements outside of our personal control, but we need the rest and we need to put regular, quality time into our relationship with God.

The irony though is that our modern British society has now become so secular that it is more secular than many other parts of Europe! I'm currently writing these notes on holiday on a Spanish island, where even the tour operators don't run bus trips or boat trips, if only to give hard pressed holiday trade workers their rightful rest! That brings home just how far wrong things are at home.

We read at the end of our passage about the 2 tablets of stone which God gave Moses with the Ten Commandments on them; sadly tomorrow we will find out what the people were up to while Moses was taking all of this time with God.

Matthew 26 v47-68

Judas arrives; the sheer audacity of that betrayal kisses! Could he not do it by simply pointing?

The disciples flee after some initial violence.

Jesus is then taken across the valley. You can follow the route – the steps up to Caiaphas's house are still there. Peter has the courage to follow at a distance and is presumably the witness who gives us the details of what is said, and what happens at the trial of Jesus. It is to his credit that Peter will also give the details of how (in tomorrow's reading) he denied his Lord. (Well, who else was to tell that story?)

Psalm 32 v1-11

A shorter psalm, bringing home the unnecessary inner turmoil of unrepented sin. Bring things to the Lord, and know that peace restored! As David says, don't be a mule!

Proverbs 8 v27-32

Real wisdom springs straight from the side of God Himself.

February 11th

Exodus 32v1-33v23

Sometimes when ministers come back and hear what went on during their holidays…Moses was not on holiday, he was on top of Mount Sinai with God for forty days and nights, only to discover that while he was away, the impatient people below had written him off as never coming back, and even worse, had "another" god "made" in his absence.

We identify several problems immediately. Time and time again in Old Testament history, we read of times when the people appear to be loyal to the one true God, but before long we discover it was the strong personality of a particular leader that kept them there. To put it bluntly, Moses had only to disappear up a mountain for just over a month for the people to start idol worship.

Secondly, how did these people so quickly, and so easily, go back to idol worship? A few chapters ago, were you not impressed with the apparent solemn commitment made to the covenant with God? It does leave us concerned today about the apparent "health" of many of our rural congregations. We seem to have more involvement in rural areas, but that is not the same as having real commitments. What many of our people want, or would settle for, is often something very different from a personal faith and trust in Christ. Under a thin veneer of Christianity there can be a lot of "folk religion" and ministers are under pressure to deliver what the people want. That is precisely what Aaron did.

Thirdly, the idea of one God but no idol was one they kept struggling with. They wanted something they could picture and see, and being agricultural folk, seem in their history to have had a weakness for golden calves and similar idols, possibly tied in with ideas of fertility cults that were common enough in the area.

Fourthly, they could not get their heads round the idea of what "holy" meant, they could not understand the concept of God being holy or that he might want His followers to live lives very different from the paganism around them. Throughout these years, and for centuries after they enter the Promised Land, they do seem to have felt cheated when they saw all the idolatrous, adulterous lives of their pagan neighbours.

Fifthly, they had some tremendous experiences of God – the crossing of the Red Sea, the experience of Sinai itself – and a few days ago we actually read of 70 of the elders, together with Moses Aaron, Nadab and Abihu actually seeing God, and the sapphire pavement under His feet, and having a meal in God's presence – but these experiences don't seem to have borne much fruit in terms of serious understanding and commitment. Lives, hearts and minds are not changed. There is no link between what they have come through, and how it should have "clicked" in their hearts and minds. There is no radical conversion to the one true God.

When Aaron made them their new calf idol, they promptly called it "Jehovah," made burnt offerings, and had one wild immoral party. At this point God sent Moses down the mountain. The first set of commandments carved in stone by God Himself were smashed as Moses threw them to the ground before destroying the calf and then instigating a judgment which led to three thousand deaths, followed by plague.

Matthew 26v69-27v14

The Galilean accent gave Peter away. To his credit, he did follow Jesus that far, but it was so poorly thought out, that he did the very thing he had been so determined to avoid doing. Mind you, the only one who could have told the others what happened was Peter himself – at some later point he clearly shared his own failing, so that others might learn.

Judas changed his mind when he saw that Jesus was condemned to death. If Judas was surprised at that, or suddenly remorseful, just what had he expected would happen?

The hypocrisy of the religious leaders who could not take "dirty" money back, but instead bought a field to bury strangers.

We see something of Pilate's unease over the charges against Jesus.

Psalm 33 v1-11

A happy psalmist! There are moments of absolute peace and contentment too!

Proverbs 8v33-36

Find that God given wisdom!

February 12th

Exodus 34v1-35v9

The Commandments are once more written in stone, and Moses is given precise descriptions of how the covenant is to be kept with God. This time when Moses came down the mountain the people were terrified by the glow on his face caused by being in God's presence – so much so that Moses had to veil himself

Matthew 27v15-34

Pilate could see through the accusations being made against Jesus, and his wife was very unsettled as well. Pilate was very sure he had a way out, and was taken aback when the crowd and the religious leaders settled for Barabbas.

To be fair to Pilate – and few ever pick up on this – he did demand to know what Jesus had done to deserve death. Once his own Jewish people made clear that they wanted Jesus dead, Pilate had his revenge, of sorts, upon them by making clear that when this man was crucified it was for being the King of the Jews – hence the particular mockery and cruelty that was inflicted upon Jesus. He did nothing to alleviate the suffering of Jesus – in fact it was increased because of the charge, but he was angry about it all, nevertheless. And his soldiers, despite inflicting the torture, were just as accurate in reading what was going on – we see their reaction tomorrow.

Psalm 33v12-22

Knowing exactly who to trust (the Lord.) War horses represented the high tech war weapons of the day – they are no substitute for having a right relationship with the Lord.

Proverbs 9 v1-6

There are those who have so hardened themselves against listening to God that there is a particular perverseness about it all.

February 13th

Exodus 35v10-36v38

A happier period out in the wilderness. There seems to have been a genuine spiritual stirring, so much so that a point was reached when the people had to be told they could not give anymore! We see that only the best will do for God, and the highest skills and training are used. There is no sense of "making do." The shabby or second rate will not be used. God's people did not "play poverty" and were more than able to meet the need. This portable House of Worship would be a fitting forerunner to the Temple.

Matthew 27 v35-66

The Chief Priests and others mock, but at the end of it all they are as unnerved by His death as they were by His life. The tearing of the huge and heavy curtain in the temple, and the resurrection of a number of godly men and women, was more than ample proof as to who Jesus was.

Psalm 34v1-10

God's help is known, but many have to be told to ask!

The background is of a period before David became king, when he allied himself rather foolishly with Abimelech (also known as Achish – the Philistine King of Gath) and David had to pretend to be insane in order to get away. It was a time when David realised he had got himself into a right deep hole. (Story is found in 1st Samuel 21 v10-15)

Proverbs 9v7-8

An unteachable spirit is not unknown today!

February 14th

Exodus 37v1-38v31

Yes, we get lost in the details, but here is more of that love that does not hold back on giving the best for God's work.

Matthew 28 v1-20

These men left to guard the tomb are not fools. We assume by the fact that they report to the temple authorities rather than the Roman authorities, that they are actual temple guards – understanding much, much more about Jewish teaching and expectations. All the more appropriate that they witness the resurrection! Bribery was the only answer the temple authorities had!

Psalm 34v11-22

Having had a rather close one, by relying on his own (not so) smart thinking, David has learnt to trust in God, not his own wisdom!

Proverbs 9 v9-10

A fitting comment after the background explanation over the past couple of days to our psalm portion!

February 15th

Exodus 39 v1-40v38

We come to our final reading today from the Book of Exodus. Beautiful robes are made for the priests, the Tabernacle is finished, the priesthood is anointed, and finally the cloud and pillar of fire which signified God's leading and His presence rest upon the tabernacle – when the cloud lifts the people are to follow in their journeys through the wilderness.

Mark 1v1-28

You will notice a fair bit of similarity between Matthew, Mark and Luke. John's Gospel is clearly coming at the Gospel story from some different, though complimentary angles, but it is pretty obvious that Matthew, Mark and Luke have a central source, either Mark's Gospel itself, or some earlier draft of it. Evangelical Christians don't have a problem with that idea itself, though you can read whole books that theorise on this until you bore yourself silly. These three Gospels are known as the "Synoptic Gospels."

Anyway, Mark does NOT begin with the Christmas story – something which you may not have thought of before! John Mark, to give him his full name, begins with John the Baptist. Mark was around for some of the events himself (see Acts 12v12.) Some think that the young man of Mark 14v51 might have been John Mark. It is also possible it was his home that was used for the last supper. A major "inside" source for Mark would have been Peter himself.

Anyway, Mark tells us of John the Baptist as the forerunner –it is not until you read through Acts that you realise just how far John the Baptist's influence had spread round the coast of the Mediterranean Sea – he was better known than we appreciate! We are also told of Jesus' time in the wilderness, though Mark doesn't give us the details of the temptations. We read of the arrest of John the Baptist, and the call of Peter and Andrew, James and John. We read right away of a confrontation with demonic powers in the service at the Capernaum synagogue.

Psalm 35 v1-16

If you are taken aback by the tone of this psalm, then pray that you never understand what it is like to be in circumstances that make you pray like this! David has a real sense of his own kindness and love being repaid with evil.

Proverbs 9 v11-12

Make up your mind what you are going to live by!

February 16th

Leviticus 1 v1-3v17

We start Leviticus! One of the things you will discover is that there are many different types and forms of sacrifice. A burnt offering of meat was offered as a substitute for sinful people. Offerings could be according to the means of the person offering it, but it was important that the animal was without defect. It was not acceptable to get rid of a damaged or deformed animal by passing it off as a burnt offering. People were to understand that God takes sin seriously. As chapter 1 verse 4 puts it, "The person bringing it is to lay his hand upon its head, and it then becomes his substitute: the death of the animal will be accepted by God instead of the death of the man who brings it, as the penalty for his sins." (Living Bible.)

A grain offering was obviously an offering that could be brought by very poor people, though grain could never be offered up to atone. Scholars suggest this is more likely a situation in which the intention is respect or honour, rather than atonement. In these circumstances, a portion would be burnt, but the rest was given to the priests for food.

Other types of sacrifice included thanksgiving or fellowship, in which the blood was thrown against the sides of the altar, the fat was burnt, but the actual meat was used for a special meal by the person presenting it, and his family or friends. We will read more details about these sacrifices on another day, including portions that were kept for the priests, as a way of making provision for them.

Mark 1 v29-2v12

It will come as a surprise to many to discover that Simon Peter had a mother-in-law, and therefore a wife! We have the healing of Peter's mother in law, a leper that Jesus actually touched, and the paralysed man carried on his bed by his friends, as well as all those who had packed for healing in the immediate aftermath of Peter's mother-in-law.

Packed into these busy and demanding days though, is the time for private prayer – absolutely essential to Jesus!

Note that the house which had its roof opened up by the friends of the paralytic was probably "home" to Jesus in Capernaum.

Psalm 35v17-28

David has a strong sense of others gloating at his misfortune, of real evil intent on the part of many looking on. The need for vindication is not just for David's sake though; there is a need for right to be seen and to be upheld in a wicked world that does not take the Lord into their considerations.

Proverbs 9v13-18

"Folly" is personified and compared to a prostitute! Loud and brash, and with many false promises, former clients are now in the grave.

February 17th

Leviticus 4v1-5v19

A distinction is made between someone deliberately setting out to disobey the commandments, and someone who finds himself in the sorrowful position of having broken God's laws without setting out in an attitude of defiance. Sin is still sin though, and must be atoned for.

The start of chapter 5 also deals with the serious sin of omission when it comes to withholding evidence in a law case. Sins of omission regarding God and the things of God are also mentioned within the details of the passage.

Mark 2v13-3v6

The call of Levi (Matthew) leads to absolute horror when the Pharisees realise that Matthew invites Jesus to a special dinner with his tax collector friends. What a witness though, on Matthew's part, as he sets off on a new life!

The Sabbath comes up twice in our passage – the disciples were so hungry they were actually eating ears of wheat from fields they were passing – something which poor people were allowed to do, but the Pharisees accused them of "harvesting" on the Sabbath. They were also extremely angry when Jesus healed a man with a deformed hand on the Sabbath. The idea of the Pharisees getting together with the Herodians was just mind blowing, but such was the united hatred for Jesus. Back in college in the late 1970s I can remember the Late Professor Teddy Russell saying that the Pharisees and Herodians getting together must have seemed as unlikely then as Sinn Fein and the DUP...well, we have seen some strange things.

It is not so long since in our readings from Exodus that we saw the importance of the Sabbath in the Old Testament. By these times, however, Sabbath keeping had become a matter of extreme pettiness and religious point scoring. Why do you do things as you do? Out of real honour for the Lord, or in a spirit of petty self-righteousness? Jesus could recognise that healing, helping, caring were not a contradiction of the intention of God's laws.

Psalm 36 v1-12

Sin lurking in evil hearts is contrasted to a God who cares for people and animals alike. What are we going to model our hearts on? Some deny there is a God at all, and plan and live that way.

Proverbs 10 v1-2

The joys and sorrows of parenthood when the children become young adults are briefly mentioned here, as is the fact that anything that is ill-gotten will be seen, eventually, to be of no value.

February 18th

Leviticus 6v1 – 7v27

Basic honesty is demanded in matters such as property entrusted to your care, finding lost property etc, being truthful, not being guilty of extortion in your dealings with others etc.

Regarding sacrifices, the priests and others are constantly reminded that they handle holy things. There are strong penalties for being flippant or defiant in these matters.

Mark 3 v7-20

We are told of the vast crowds and their demands upon Jesus. Mark also emphasises the very real and heightened spiritual battle going on during the earthly ministry of Jesus. We also read of how the teachers of the Law tried to make out that Jesus was driving out demons because Satan had given Him the power to do so! They were so determined to discredit Jesus, and yet could not deny the reality of what they saw happening.

Although there are complicated theological arguments over what is meant by blasphemy against the Holy Spirit, and the fact that it says here that such a sin will not be forgiven, most folk get the general idea that attributing the work of Jesus to the Devil is most certainly an extreme thing done by people wholeheartedly opposed to the Gospel and who are very self confirmed on a hell bent path.

In the midst of this very real spiritual battle, with frequent confrontations with demons, Jesus actually calls the twelve inner disciples.

And in the midst of all of this, we have Jesus's own family – mother, half brothers and half sisters, who want to put to an end all of this ministry and take Him home and "straighten Him out"!

Psalm 37 v1-11

Envying the wicked and their apparent successes in life is a very common problem for many professing Christians. It leads to a bitter heart that imagines that we have somehow been "short-changed" in life because of our faith.

Proverbs 10 v3-4

These verses from Proverbs fit in well with our psalm portion. There is always that niggling doubt in our hearts that sin still pays. Proverbs gives a resounding no.

February 19th

Leviticus 7v28-9v6

The regulations continue regarding the sacrifices.

We continue to have provision made for the priests.

We continue to have the preparations and actual ordination of Aaron and his sons.

The emphasis on the blood continues. Blood must be shed for sin. This constant emphasis helps us to understand why Jesus had to go to the Cross.

Mark 3v31-4v25

By the day of Pentecost we will find that Jesus's family will, in the light of the resurrection, finally believe in Him and what He came to do. Until then though, they will have their own ideas as to what His ministry should be about.

Jesus, having had to have a boat on standby because of the vast crowds surrounding Him on the seashore, finally uses it as a pulpit. Mark gives us the parable of the sower and its application in great detail.

Psalm 37 v12-28

Our Psalm portion continues to deal with this deep seated suspicion that some have that the ungodly have all the fun.

Proverbs 10 v 5

It is practical common sense that can be adapted to many different ways of making a living.

February 20th

Leviticus 9 v7 – 10v20

Initially things seem to go well, but then two of Aaron's sons suddenly show a complete disregard for what they have been taught. The New Century Bible commentary puts it this way:

Their action with it was also usurping the role of the high priest, and therefore included presumption, or perhaps jealous impatience. Their behaviour was not just an accidental slip in a minor detail of ritual, but a cavalier disregard for the most serious meaning of the events they were part of.

(Carson, D. A.: New Bible Commentary : 21st Century Edition. 4th ed. Leicester, England; Downers Grove, Ill., USA : Inter-Varsity Press, 1994, S. Le 10:1)

God's judgment comes immediately – they are burnt to death.

It was a stern warning for a family who had already had a very cavalier attitude – bear in mind that a few days ago, while studying Exodus, we saw how readily Aaron had fashioned a golden calf idol.

Mark 4v26-5v20

There are some parables. As Mark tells us, this was a very typical way in which Jesus taught publicly.

The disciples are left in awe and shock when Jesus calms the storm.

Another very dramatic event is the drowning of the herd of pigs after the demons leave the man and enter the pigs. The response of the local people is that they beg Jesus to go away!

Psalm 37v29-40

We continue thinking through this terrible temptation to be jealous of evil people and their apparently glamorous lives.

Proverbs 10 v6-7

Proverbs confirms that God's judgment will be seen.

February 21st

Leviticus 11v1-12v8

This is complicated stuff to get into but it is at the heart of what being Jewish was and is now, so I can't escape giving some explanation. In the Old Testament, animals are divided according to whether they belong to the land, water or air. Within those 3 categories, we are then given guidelines as to what can be eaten. Regarding birds, those that are banned from the table are primarily birds of prey or birds that eat dead animals, and it is easy to understand that common sense hygiene would take them off the menu. Disease etc can be passed down the food chain. Regarding water, the Israelites were told they could eat what was clearly a proper fish (fins and scales). Regarding land animals, they had to be hoofed animals that chewed their food (ruminants or those that appeared to be ruminants). Animals outside those categories were not to be eaten. Few insects are a healthy thing to eat, but an exception was made to grasshoppers and locusts.

It is obvious though, that hygiene alone will not explain these rules (though it certainly would have been an issue regarding e.g. pork in a warm country in times of poor preservation) and many books have been written, by both Jews and Christians. At this point I think we need to leave all the complicated arguments behind and make a few simple points.

Firstly, everything about life in the Old Testament was distinctly different from the pagan tribes and nations around them. God's people as a nation were distinct. To this day, every meal in a practicing Jewish home is a reminder of being Jewish, of belonging to a particular nation. Unlike Christianity, Old Testament Judaism was very much about a national covenant with God.

Secondly, what about Christians today?

Christ Himself had something to say on these food laws – see Mark 7:14–23 **particularly verse 19.** And the story of Peter's vision in Acts 10 was that God had demolished all these distinctions between "clean" and "unclean" – though the chief point of the vision was that the barrier between Jew and gentile was now gone. Acts 11 and 15 deal with these matters, although it has to be pointed out that there were occasions when Paul caught Peter slipping back into Jewish attitudes towards gentile Christians and not eating with them. Food was no longer to be a barrier, and the barrier between Jew and Gentile was gone.

I probably need to say something too on this idea of a national covenant between the Old Testament nation of Israel and God.

Unfortunately some Christian uses of the idea of a "covenant" (particularly Presbyterian ones!!) lead to confusion. God does not work through "national covenants" no matter how much some of our people down through the centuries would have liked things to be that way. (Scottish Presbyterians were trying to work through how Church and State relate and so in their history tried to have covenants that spelt out the King's role and position.) All of this confuses the issue. Ulster Protestants, or Scottish Presbyterians, can't put themselves back in Old Testament days and argue for a national covenant with God in which they virtually put themselves in the place of Old Testament Israel. There is no doubt that there were some Presbyterians in the past who were probably happier in the Old Testament than in the New, and that itself should sound warning bells. God works through personal relationships with Christ as our Lord and Saviour. Christ's death on the Cross brings us into a totally different scenario.

Mark 5 v21-43

Many different demands – as Jairus is on a life or death mission to get Jesus to his house, a woman who had been socially ostracised for years because of her particular illness reaches out, touches His clothes, and is healed. There are many things we could say about this healing. Far from her making Jesus unclean through touching Him, she is healed instead. And despite having a pushing crowd all around Him, both Jesus and the woman know immediately that healing power has been at work. The healing is more than just something physical; this is a socially ostracised woman restored.

Meanwhile, what Jairus feared has happened. He has failed to get Jesus there in time. Jairus and other will learn that Jesus' power does not stop before death – he can bring the little girl back.

Psalm 38 v1-22

There are many other threats, but the problem of sin which until now has not been dealt with, leaves David vulnerable.

Proverbs 10 v8-9

An unteachable spirit v8.

The contrast between a man of integrity and one of crooked paths v9.

February 22nd

Leviticus 13v1-59

Such huge numbers, living in close proximity, meant that the people wondering through the wilderness together had to take seriously any sign of disease to avoid contagion. We might wonder what all of this has to with us today, but look at all the practical programmes Christians are running today to try and improve the lives of others, whether in the developing world, or closer to home.

What is being called "leprosy" here is a Hebrew term that includes clinical leprosy, but also some very unpleasant moulds and mildews that could destroy garments and building materials. As far as human disease was concerned, the Jewish priest was trying to distinguish between a type of ringworm, various skin disorders such as eczema, impetigo, acne, and clinical leprosy. There was a strong emphasis on isolating the disease to protect a community that had nothing of our present day medicines, but the priest also had a role in checking and declaring clean those who had recovered and who were clearly not a threat to the rest of the community.

Mark 6 v1-29

His home town was particularly hard to preach in.

The disciples were sent out 2 by 2 to get some initial experience, and were given instructions that were to ensure their focus on the work and their priorities in it.

Herod was a superstitious man because he had killed John the Baptist. Mark explains the background to John's death.

Psalm 39 v1-13

Both Psalm 38 and Psalm 39 appear to be against a background of illness. David is aware of how frail life can be. He has also been on his guard (keeping silent) against words that might later be regretted in coping with his current difficulties.

Proverbs 10 v10

We tend to think of "winking" in a moment of harmless jest, but this winking at sin, a totally different matter.

February 23rd

Leviticus 14v1-57

Given the life-long social isolation that clinical leprosy causes, it was a matter of immense relief when someone was declared free of disease – either never had it, or was actually healed. The priest and the ritual served to restore the person and to put to an end all social stigma. The sprinkling of the bird's blood enabled the healed man to rejoin the community. The bird's death was a reminder of what might have happened if the Lord had not healed.

The rest of the ritual requires very lengthy explanations beyond what we can give here.

As for plaster work etc, we continue to read of the need to end unhealthy moulds and mildews that would do nothing for the health of those living in the house.

Mark 6 v30-56

The feeding of the 5,000 came on top of a very demanding day – indeed, the disciples had barely reported on their experiences of having been out, 2 by 2, visiting villages and towns. Jesus sent the disciples on ahead – presumably to protect them from very demanding crowds, as we realise that these people were used to have to "make do" in the last month or two leading up to harvest, when supplies from the last harvest would have run out. A miracle such as this would have sent shock waves through the area. A man who could feed crowds and fill up rumbling stomachs!

However, the disciples got into difficulty out on the lake. This could happen to experienced fishermen, due to the hills and mountains around Galilee, which could lead to sudden storms without any obvious warning. Having said that, they found it hard to connect what happened on the land (the feeding of the people) with what Jesus could do on the water. The water was *their territory*, which is why miracles in *their domain* frightened them all the more!

Psalm 40 v1-10

That experience of being lifted by God out of a situation of utter despair!

Proverbs 10 v11-12

As I write this, a woman in England has been sentenced for faking the kidnap of her own daughter. While we are left wondering who else was involved in the case, police and others cannot understand how someone could turn on the tears, and put on such a believable act. What a contrast there can be between mouths – those that are truthful, and those that are so evil.

Verse 12 continues to contrast what words can do – stir up old quarrels, or bring love where there has been past injury.

February 24th

Leviticus 15 v1-16v28

The first part of our reading continues to give guidance to a community trying to prevent infection. Gonorrhoea was one of the things in particular which these guidelines were trying to isolate. Care was being taken when dealing with things out of the norm. There were also concerns for basic hygiene even where there is no disease. The second part of our reading deals with the day of atonement. This for Christians speaks volumes – Christ is our Lamb, He is also our High Priest, and on His death upon the cross, the curtain that separated sinful people from a Holy God was torn in two.

In the Old Testament ritual, one goat is sacrificed, the other carried the people's sins away. Much symbolism here that Christians would come to understand.

Mark 7 v1-23

Having been reading through Leviticus, we have heard a lot about ritual, and ritual cleaning.

Jesus' disciples come across as pretty relaxed on the ritual. In the ensuing argument, Jesus makes clear that the emphasis is wrongly on the outside, and not on the heart within.

Psalm 40 v11-17

We cannot deliver ourselves from these things; we have got to trust in the Lord.

Proverbs 10 v13-14

Wisdom and foolishness again contrasted.

February 25th

Leviticus 16 v29-18v30

We hear more about the Day of Atonement, and then some final rules about what is appropriate in worship. Then some more rules, including those that avoid marrying too closely, and rules outlawing some of the worst practices of the pagan tribes around them, including child sacrifice, homosexuality, and sexual relations with animals.

Mark 7 v24-8v9

These are significant stories, emphasising that while Jesus' ministry was directed primarily to the Jewish people, it was not exclusive to them. Faith is found, very persistently, in a distressed mother up in what is present day Lebanon. The "Ten towns" were significant non Jewish settlements, and the feeding of the four thousand is seen by some as a similar event to the 5,000, but this time in a gentile or non Jewish area.

Psalm 41 v1-13

The opportunity to help (v1-3) is contrasted with the opportunity to hurt (v4-10)

V13 is the doxology marking the end of the 1st book of psalms. In our Bibles we have one book of psalms, but in Hebrew there are five "books." Book 2 begins with our next psalm, no. 42

Proverbs 10v15-16

Comparisons are made between wealth and poverty – and then between the wages of righteousness, and those of wickedness. The first set of comparisons seems obvious, but they lead on to the second set, which is what the writer wants to teach.

February 26th

Leviticus 19v1-20v21

The key to this passage is found in this: "You must be holy because I, the Lord your God am holy."

The implications of holiness come into the whole of life, including looking after the poor by leaving corners of the field etc for the poor to glean the fields, basic honesty and justice, including how workers are treated, how you treat the disabled...

Some rules are to avoid mimicking the pagans, who would have trimmed hair and beards in certain ways as part of their practices. Some of the rules were to do with horticultural practices of the time, such as allowing fruit trees to develop for several years before harvesting, crops were to be rotated, not sown together...

Some of the rules prevented clothes being made which produced rashes in warmer climates (like mixing wool and linen.) Sexual relationships were to be in the proper context of marriage. Practices involving mediums and other occult practices were strongly forbidden. Mark 8 v10-38

Cynicism which demands miracles – had they not witnessed many already?

When the disciples forgot to do the shopping, they assumed that Jesus' comment about yeast was a dig at them! Instead he was warning them of what both Herod and the Pharisees – two very different groups – were doing to their society and to people's understanding of God.

We have an interesting miracle in which Jesus heals in stages.

Right up in the far north, in pagan Caesarea Philippi (where Pan was worshipped, and the locals were convinced that a stream emerging from a cave was the mouth of hell) Jesus discusses who the people think He is. Peter is convinced He is the Saviour, but once Jesus begins to talk plainly about the cross, Peter wants to hear none of it.

Psalm 42

As the dear pants for water… A lovely thought as we start into book 2 of the psalms.

Proverbs 10v17

Another strong contrast.

February 27th

Leviticus 20v22-22v20

The emphasis on holiness continues. Some of the rules on the priests not having defects themselves may seem harsh, but they parallel the rules on giving the best to God in sacrifice.

Mark 9 v1-29

The transfiguration…a tremendous experience which Peter would have liked to have lasted forever.

At the bottom of the mountain, though, a great deal of ministry is to be done, and the disciples are unprepared for a very difficult case, and learn the lesson that ministry must be based in prayer.

Psalm 43v1-5

There is a need to be vindicated, but there is also recognition that we need the Lord. As Derek Kidner put it in his commentary: "the dark moods alternate with increasingly affirmative prayer."
Proverbs 10v18

Words and the true state of the heart are contrasted.

February 28th

Leviticus 22v21-23v44

Again, giving the best to God, not bringing damaged and unwanted animals for sacrifice.

Various Old Testament festivals are set out.

Mark 9 v30 – 10v12

The disciples cannot / will not understand Jesus when He talks plainly about the cross.

They have been arguing over who will be the greatest!

There is also jealousy of someone who is not part of their circle, but who has been performing miracles in the name of Jesus.

There are a number of very significant sayings recorded here.

There is also a strong contrast between the Pharisees and Jesus on the subject of divorce. They had made it very easy for a man, and left women very vulnerable by their teaching.

Psalm 44v1-7

National defeat seems to be the issue here. They know what God has done in the past.

There is heart searching going on here. Why are the seemingly innocent suffering? As one Christian writer has put it, defeat is not unknown in the reigns of loyal, godly kings. Sometimes God's people are caught up in a much bigger picture. National disaster does not necessarily mean that God is punishing them.

Proverbs 10v19

I like the Living Bible version of this verse: "Don't talk so much. You keep putting your foot in your mouth. Be sensible and turn off the flow!"

March 1st

Leviticus 24v1-25v46

There are two ways of taking the symbolism of the lampstand – how Israel were supposed to be, as a light to the surrounding nations – and how the true light, Jesus, had yet to come.

We may gasp at the outcome of the blasphemy. Haven't we come a long way, the wrong way?

In Chapter 25 God's people were being encouraged to use the best agricultural practices of their day, but there is also a very important spiritual principle behind the concept of the Jubilee – every 50 years - the cancellation of all debts, the return of property to the original families etc – all an attempt to prevent any of the families losing forever what they had when they entered the promised land. There are also rules to stop a fellow Israelite from being exploited (see the verses on interest!) There is an emphasis on social justice and humanitarianism.

Mark 10v13-31

Children are not just "the Church of tomorrow" but very much part of the Church today.

These verses are very much abused by people who demand certain "rites" such as baptism but at the same time intend to bring the child up in a way that ridicules the profession of faith and the promises of giving a Christian home. It is the children who are being brought up in homes like that who are the ones being kept from Jesus, by the parents who have no intention of giving Christian values in the home. What is very scary, are the values and godless outlook being passed on to kids by parents and grandparents who claim a Church connection but whose entire outlook on life is a denial of what Christianity is all about. If people want to bring their children to Jesus, then they'll give them a home that encourages them to love Christ.

The story of the man who claimed to have kept the six commandments that deal with our attitudes towards other people (as distinct from the first 4 that deal with our attitudes towards God) shows us someone who claimed to have never done the negative (he claimed to have never broken those laws) but who hadn't done much that was positive either – when challenged to distribute his great wealth to the poor he walked away, for he was very rich. Living for Jesus, as we ought to do if we really love Him as our Lord and Saviour, is not just about the things Christians don't do, which is sadly how most people in Northern Ireland see it, but is really about doing and being, for Jesus.

Psalm 44v8-26

We continue looking at a psalm that is trying to make sense out of why defeat has been allowed to come at a time when the people have been faithful. People are being demoralised as a result, but they are working through how to handle setbacks that are not the result of sin or of unfaithfulness. The concept of suffering for being faithful, is much better understood in the New Testament.

Proverbs 10v20-21

The link between the heart and the tongue.

March 2nd

Leviticus 25 v47-27v13

The concept of the year of Jubilee continues; even the Israelite slave is to be freed, and a man seeking to buy himself out of slavery finds that the price is set according to whether the year of Jubilee is near or far. The whole concept of "Jubilee" is very radical, so that no family group loses out on what God promised them before they entered the Promised Land.

This is followed by reminders that they will know blessing in the land if they obey, and they will know defeat, plague and exile if they disobey. Thankfully, the passage also speaks of repentance and restoration to come.

Chapter 27 takes us into the whole area of vows and offerings. Dedicating yourself or family members, or even one of your animals to God's service was to be taken seriously; people could be bought back out of that service, but the price was meant to stop unrealistic and insincere dedication to service. If the whole concept sounds rather weird to you, well think of young Samuel given to God's service by his parents. That story perhaps more than any other helps us to get our heads round what this passage is talking about. Samuel's parents were absolutely sincere and set on what they did. A more foolish couple, making a promise that they then regretted, could have bought back their son, but at a price that would have taught them not to make rash and unfulfilled promises. An animal promised to God's work could also be redeemed. The lesson though is clear; don't stand in God's presence making promises you have no intention of keeping; promises made to God are better not uttered than to be made with little thought and then broken. More on this tomorrow.

Mark 10 v32-52

Jesus talks plainly about what is going to happen in Jerusalem, but of course the disciples continue to think that Jesus is being rather melodramatic and that the revolution they think He is going to launch will lead to glory...we can just hear our Lord groaning when, no sooner has He talked about the coming crucifixion, than up come James and John, asking that they get a throne on either side of Jesus when the forthcoming struggle is all over! And then the rest of the disciples are angry that James and John have seemingly jumped in ahead of them all!

How much did blind Bartimaeus understand? He has grasped that Jesus is indeed the “Son of David” and the healed man joins the crowd surging up to Jerusalem.

Psalm 45 v1-17

Described as a wedding song, and clearly for a royal wedding, Christians have found other meanings in it too. Verse 4 inspired the Palm Sunday hymn, “Ride on! Ride on in majesty.” (Derek Kidner’s Tyndale commentary.) There are reasons for seeing the kingly figure of the psalm as someone else than just a mere mortal – see verse 6: “Your throne O God...” As Kidner puts it: “it is an example of Old Testament language bursting its banks, to demand a more than human fulfilment...” (page 172.)

Proverbs 10v22

God’s blessing upon our work is essential if it is to have real value. The translator of the Living Bible took this verse rather differently: “The Lord’s blessing is our greatest wealth. All our work adds nothing to it!”

March 3rd

Leviticus 27v14 - Numbers 1v54

The lessons over dedicating something to God’s work and then wanting to pull back from the promise continue to be made. In my last congregation I remember one little old lady who got herself into quite a tizzy after accidentally dropping her house keys on to the offering plate – of course we gave them back at the end of the service and told her to not get upset – the whole thing was an accident! But at least she understood the concept that you do not lightly take back what you have seemingly given to God and it took a house visit to convince her that she could indeed keep her home! There are too many promises that are made in the hearing of others that go unfulfilled in God’s work.

The census at the start of Numbers brings home to us the huge numbers being led out of Egypt and across the wilderness, and the very practical arrangements that had to be put in place.

Mark 11 v1-25

The triumphal entry, even on the back of a colt, does fulfil the expectations that the people had from the Old Testament regarding the coming Messiah. If you are puzzled over Jesus's judgment on the fig tree, try to understand it as a figure for what he was just about to do / did actually do in the Temple. The whole of chapter 11 is more connected together than we often realise. There is a "leafy show" in all that is happening in the Temple – plenty of religious activity, but as barren as the tree.

Psalm 46 v1-11 A favourite of many, and when put to the tune "Dam Busters" we quickly grasp the concepts of God seeing us through tremendous events that have shaken whole generations.

Proverbs 10v23

What we find our pleasure in says a lot about us.

March 4th

Numbers 2v1-3v51

Don't despise organisation, administration etc – it all has a practical purpose in God's work. Interestingly is how the Levites were thought of as those dedicated to the Lord's work, given as a gift in place of the rest of the nation.

Mark 11v26-12v17

Yesterday's comments are strengthened further by the story of the vineyard and the wicked tenant farmers – everybody understood that Jesus was talking about the religious leaders. When faced with the trick question over the taxes to the hared Romans, Jesus left them in knots.

Psalm 47 v1-9

A lovely psalm of praise – yes, not all the psalms are about problems! Sometimes there is simply sheer joy in the Lord.

Proverbs 10 v24-25

The insecurity of the wicked is brought home to us.

March 5th

Numbers 4 v1-5v31

Detailed organisation, with large numbers of people available in service. What a contrast with the Church of today, in which a small group of people are often worked into the ground trying to juggle many tasks.

Serious disease has to be isolated in a huge camp of people living very closely.

Other parts of today's reading may leave us puzzled. There are elaborate rituals and oaths, with very clear warnings of judgment, when personal trust has been shattered, either over property or in relationships. Clearly a liar is inviting God's judgement upon him or herself.

Mark 12 v18-37

So much of the debate from the Sadducees and other groups was an attempt to score points over Jesus, rather than to actually clarify a serious point, or indeed to bring people into a better understanding of God and what He wants in our lives. When you get into religious argument, is there a constructive point to it at all?

Psalm 48 v1-14

Mount Zion, Jerusalem, thought of as the holy city, and the joy that could be taken in her very stones. This is only true as long as its inhabitants grasped more than some superstitious understanding of what it meant to be known as the holy city. For much of its history it fell far short of what it should have been as the place of God's abode. It is, however, a tremendous experience to approach Jerusalem from the distance and to see the city suddenly coming into view.

Proverbs 10 v26

The sluggard!

March 6th

Numbers 6v1-7v89

The vows of a Nazirite – this is a vow made for a specific time period, when someone has set aside themselves for special service. Samson was basically to be a Nazirite, set aside for God's service, but as you read again his story with adult eyes and hearing you will be appalled at what poor effort he made to actually live a life dedicated to God. Paul and other Jews amongst the first generation of Christians (there are references in the Book of Acts) did continue with these vows of dedication for specific periods. Having said that, Christians need to be wise in avoiding making promises of the impossible and to pace themselves in consistent life and service.

The second part of our reading tells of very generous gifts brought to God's work, but note the absence of any feeling or sign of competition.

Mark 12v38-13v13

Outward show, playing the part, living lives of secret inconsistency – here are some warnings for those who are "busy" at "God's work." There are indeed some terrible experiences ahead for those who are really serious in following Jesus. Endurance is a totally different matter when it is costly to follow Jesus.

Psalm 49 v1-20

An appropriate reading following up on some of the things we have just read in Leviticus.

Proverbs 10 v27-28

Right priorities and consequences.

March 7th

Numbers 8 v1-9v23

Dedication, dedication...We might get lost in some of the details here, but if only we had an understanding of what it ought to mean to live lives really dedicated to our Lord.

Passover is important as the story of God's great deliverance of the people from Egypt, and also as the festival that Jesus will give new meaning to, in the bread and the wine.

The cloud and the pillar of fire were a constant reminder of God's presence amongst His people.

Mark 13v14-37

Specific teaching on the end times, but also serious warnings on being taken in by those who claim to know the timing, as well as being ready for the return of Jesus. There will be those who will exploit the whole idea of Jesus's return for their own false purposes.

Psalm 50 v1-23

Serious misunderstandings about real discipleship. Not empty, hypocritical ritual, but a real living for God.

Proverbs 10v29-30

Similar thoughts.

March 8th

Numbers 10v1-11v23

The journey begins well, but our reading soon turns to the grumbling and complaining that is to characterise just too much of their time under God's guidance. The wonderful fish, cucumbers, melons, leeks, onions and garlic of Egypt; strange what they have forgotten about how the Egyptians planned genocide by killing them with crippling labour and drowning the baby boys!

We read of manna that fell with the dew.

We also read of God promising them so much meat they will be sick of it! (See tomorrow's reading!)

Mark 14v1-21

Once more we speculate what was the very last straw that triggers the betrayal by Judas. A strange but prophetic act by a woman who pours a very expensive flask of perfume over the head of Jesus?

Might not be our idea of showing such intense devotion, but do we find ourselves amongst those who mutter "waste" and who suddenly show concern for the poor? Ah, we don't like to be upstaged by the love of others! Here was someone unafraid of looking silly or weird in her love for the Lord.

And the man carrying the water was not afraid to be seen to be compassionate either (normally a woman's job!)

Psalm 51v1-19

What it really means to repent! This was a terrible act – taking another man's wife, trying to cover up who had fathered the baby, having the woman's husband murdered and then imagining that nothing is known. David's failures had plummeted to new depths at a time when everything else in life was so successful.

Proverbs 10v31-32

Strange then that people still go looking for perverse advice!

March 9th

Numbers 11v24-13v33

Quail – tasty little things, though rather small on the plate. The Lord's judgement also came upon these people who had muttered about all the lovely things they had left behind in Egypt.

More mutterings, this time from Moses's own brother and sister, over his Cushite wife.

A group of spies are sent into the Promised Land, but the majority of them lose their nerves, and bring back a negative report about how impossible it will be to take the Promised Land – decades more will be lost wondering in the wilderness.

Mark 14v22-52

The Last Supper. Jesus gives new meaning to the bread and wine. Peter tries to assure Jesus he will never desert or deny him.

We have the scene in the Garden of Gethsemane; many think that the young man who got away stark naked was John Mark, later to become the Gospel writer (Mark).

Psalm 52v1-9

David has experienced treachery.

Proverbs 11v1-3

Personal integrity is also the issue here.

March 10th

Numbers 14v1-15v16

This act of rebellion, in which the people openly discuss electing a new leader to bring them back to Egypt (what kind of a welcome did they think they would get there???) ends with God striking down the 10 who had brought the discouraging report. God's judgment comes upon the whole nation. A generation will perish in the wilderness, and never enter the Promised Land. That joy will be for the next generation, and also for the two faithful spies who had tried to encourage the people to enter the land, trusting the Lord.

A belated attempt to enter the Promised Land, after God's judgement upon their disbelief is announced, ends with a thorough "hiding" delivered by the Amalekites and the Canaanites. A whole generation had just "blown it" with God.

Mark 14v53-72

You can still trace these steps today, very literally in places, right up to the Church built over the High Priest's house. While Peter had the courage to follow Jesus that far, he had given no thought as to how he would pass himself there; what Jesus had said came true, as Peter swore and cursed and denied knowing Jesus.

Psalm 53v1-6

The fool who denies there is a God. What God sees as He looks down on humanity is a society living with that delusion; a society that believes there is no God to answer to.

Proverbs 11v4

As the Living Bible puts it: "Your riches won't help you on Judgement Day..."

March 11th

Numbers 15v17-16v40

Thanking God for the harvest was marked by the harvest loaf from the coarse flour of the first grain.

Distinctions are made between sins of ignorance and those that have been very deliberate.

Tassels are added to Jewish clothing to remind them that they are to live by God's Laws.

Another rebellion against Moses is led by a Levite and members of the tribe of Reuben. This is a very serious rebellion, involving 250 prominent community leaders. It is brought to an end by an earthquake and fire, and plague.

Mark 15 v1-47

Jesus is sent by the Sanhedrin to Pilate; they want him to pass the death sentence. Pilate is no fool, and realises the whole thing is a frame up. He is not going to be "put out" though, for the sake of Jesus, but in placing the signboard, Pilate is a very proud man who does not like being forced and blackmailed to do anything contrary to his own personal judgment. He has his revenge on the Jewish leaders for forcing his hand. Much of the severity in how Jesus is badly treated by the Roman soldiers is Pilate's peculiar way of making clear that if this man is going to die, it will be for the very excuse the Jewish authorities used to force Pilate's hand - Pilate will make clear to all that they handed over their own king, and the board above the head of Jesus will spell that out.

The scene at the Cross is deeply moving, even to the most hardened of Roman Officers. The accompanying earthquake rips the curtain in the Temple that divides ordinary people from the Holy of Holies. The Roman officer explains that "truly this was the Son of God" and at last – when all is seemingly lost from a human perspective Joseph of Arimathea has the courage to ask for the body of Jesus.

Psalm 54v1-7

David knows what it is like to be hunted and betrayed. The circumstances of Psalm 52 were upsetting enough, but on this occasion the rejection has come from members of his own tribe.

Proverbs 11v5-6: The courses that people have chosen in life bring their consequences.

March 12th

Numbers 16v41-18v32

Yesterday we read of the rebellion against not just Moses, but against God for having taken them out of "lovely Egypt" (The Living Bible.) The problems continue, with Moses and Aaron now accused of killing "the LORD's people." Once again the people bring down God's judgment upon them, and sadly Aaron's calling as High Priest has to be confirmed by a miracle. People crave for power, not just in politics, but within the Church and Christian work too.

Mark 16 v1-20

Can we even begin to imagine the immense sadness of these brave women who set out to do what they see as the right thing – embalming the body after a rather hurried burial on the Jewish Sabbath (Saturday) only to find an angel calmly waiting for them. What made it so difficult for His disciples to cope with the resurrection was the whole bloody (literally) awfulness of crucifixion. It was not just that someone had closed their eyes and gone to sleep – what crucifixion did to the body, and the terrible awfulness of the corpse afterwards, made it very difficult to cope with the idea of seeing that person again.

There was no doubting that the person had died. So when He was seen again, and the disciples and others got their heads round the shocking experience of resurrection, the impact was tremendous.

Psalm 55 v1-23

The Psalm deals with an overwhelming sense of being engulfed by enemies, and the particularly disturbing betrayal of a friend. Yet the psalmist, in working this through in prayer, is able to conclude, “Give your burdens to the Lord.”

Proverbs 11 v7

The ultimate con act has got to be conning yourself; the evil man who has given no thought to what comes next after this life.

March 13th

Numbers 19 v1-20v29

It is too easy to skip over the first part of this reading, not realising its deep symbolism. If you really want to get to grips with this, get Gordon Wenham’s Book Numbers – there are also some important links with the Gospel too – as in Hebrews 9 v13-14 where the blood of Christ is compared to the ashes of the heifer here. The passage ends with the death of Aaron and the handing on of the High Priesthood to Eleazar.

Luke 1 v1-25

This is volume one of a two volume account of Jesus and the early Church – Luke also wrote Acts. Here he gives us the details of John’s birth. You thought you knew the Christmas story, but Luke chapter 1 has so much that we often overlook! What a lovely godly couple we have here in Zechariah and Elizabeth. (A bit unfortunate that he informed an angel that these things are impossible!)

Psalm 56 v1-13

Pressures that lead to such terrible tossing to and fro all night. Whether it is leading an army, or the pressures of very different work, we need to learn to trust God and His promises.

Proverbs 11 v8

The proverb is a timely challenge to those thoughts that we have when we imagine that things are really the complete opposite! Be wary of those times when Satan poisons your mind to think the very opposite of what is true about God.

March 14th

Numbers 21v1-22v20

While the Israelites were down in Egypt, the full evils of Caananite society have come to fruition. This is often revealed by what the archaeologists discover of Caananite society. There is to be no welcome home for the Israelites. Not even the descendants of Essau (the Edomites) want their long lost relatives back. The story of Balaam is disturbing, in that this is a man who knows something of the one true God, and he has been hired to curse the Israelites, presumably in God's name.

Luke 1 v26-56

Unlike Zechariah, who expressed doubt at the word of an angel, Mary asks 'how.' There is some beautiful poetry in this passage. Here ordinary people are aware of how God is beginning to bring to pass things for which their people have been waiting for a very long time.

Psalm 57 v1-11

Learning to be calm and confident in God.

Proverbs 11v9-11

A lot packed in here. Skills to rebuild are a lot more desirable than words that bring destruction. Although people may flatter an evil man when he is in power, the honest truth is that a city sighs with relief when he is gone.

March 15th

Numbers 22 v21 – 23 v30

We are meant to see the funny side of the story, but Balaam will end up blessing, not cursing the people of God.

Luke 1 v57-80

Now that the angel's words are fulfilled, Zechariah can speak again. Both Zechariah and Elizabeth insist on the name already given by the angel. Inspired by the Holy Spirit, Zechariah speaks these lovely words.

Psalm 58 v1-11

God's judgement is coming upon those who may seem unassailable now. There is a God who judges justly here on earth.

Proverbs 11v12-13

A lot of sanctified common sense. Needless arguments with the guy or woman on the other side of the garden fence; the dangers of gossip, and the trustworthy person trying to put a dampener on damaging nonsense.

March 16th

Numbers 24v1-25 v18

Balaam has no choice other than to bless as God intended.

Sadly, the people of Israel bring their own destruction, as they join in with the wild sexuality of the local Moabites and the accompanying worship of Baal.

Luke 2v1-35

We know about the shepherds, but in this passage we also read of Simeon – it had been a long wait to see the Messiah!

Psalm 59 v1-17

We need to grasp that "God is changeless in his love for me." (Living Bible, verse 10)

Proverbs 11v14

The proverb states the obvious, but that is not what the people always deliver at the ballot box!

March 17th

Numbers 26v1-51

OK, so these are long lists – but they are also part of the preparation of going to battle to enter the Promised Land. Moses needs to know the manpower that is available. What man power is available for God's work today in your local Church?

Luke 2 v36-52

Another godly person there (Anna), to give assurance and a timely word from God. Simeon and Anna are real examples of how believers ought to be in old age – which can be a very selfish and inward looking time of life.

Psalm 60 v1-12

Self confidence has been broken; it needs to be back in the right place – in God.

Proverbs 11 v15

Wise counsel; believers have sometimes rushed into business partnerships without giving real thought as to the values and aspirations of those in whom, or with whom, they are investing so much.

March 18th

Numbers 26v52-28 v14

The story of the daughters of Zelophehad is one of great fairness, and the protection of families in which there was no male heir.

Moses will see, but not enter the land. Sin does have its consequences. Joshua will lead the people in.

There are final instructions on the sacrifices that are to continue.

Luke 3 v1-22

John's ministry begins as he prepares the way. Why did Jesus Himself come to John to be baptised? – Jesus identified with those for whom He would one day die.

Psalm 61v1-8

God as our towering Rock! Also an awesome promise of how we are going to live as those who know the Lord as our Rock!

Proverbs 11v16-17

A careful watch on the character we are contributing to in our own lives.

March 19th

Numbers 28v15-29v40

You may be thinking, haven't we heard some of this before? Actually what we have here are regulations for what the priests were to do for the nation as a whole, as distinct from what individual lay people might bring due to sin or whatever in their own lives. One commentator makes a very interesting point, that these requirements are actually a promise – a promise given to the people while they are still in the wilderness, that God will meet their needs, and in so doing, provide the very things these sacrifices will require. These sacrificial requirements point to the settled and prosperous life that God had promised them in the land that was to be theirs.

The Old Testament calendar, by the way, is very different from ours and starts at a very different time of year.

The main thing, though, to pick from all of this, as we read through these regulations for worship for the whole nation, is that sacrifice is at the heart of worship. We live in the aftermath of Calvary; these complex regulations should bring home to us what a difference it makes that Christ has been our one perfect sacrifice. We should note, amongst all the other festivals, the fact that the first 10 days of the seventh month are a penitential season that culminates in the day of atonement. Sin is to be taken seriously, as is our need to turn back to God.

Luke 3 v23-38

Where are they all now, in eternity? Interesting question about all of those names! Some shone brighter for God than others. Some interesting stories to be traced through the Old Testament, if you have a Bible with a good index and a good bit more time. Joseph's family tree is important as he accepted Jesus as His own, and raised Him.

Psalm 62 v1-12

Again the theme of God as my Rock. Human frailty is reflected in the Psalm, as are some warnings about the temptation to try and succeed the wrong way.

Proverbs 11v15

What good is wealth without health – we might say. An obvious warning about the short term gains of making our way in life the wrong way.

March 20th

Numbers 30 v1-31v54

The first part of our reading deals with promises that should not have been made in the first place – promises made which very much impinge on others and their rights too.

The Midianites had sought to lead the people astray and had done so largely by introducing them to rather promiscuous lives and erotic pagan worship. You begin to understand Moses' anger on hearing of the number of women his men had captured, suggesting that some of the men fought this war for very different motives!

Luke 4v1-30

The temptations seem strange to us, because we could not make bread from stones etc. Part of the point of the whole thing, is that Satan sought to derail Jesus from ever living a real life – with hunger etc – and Satan would have successfully derailed Jesus if could have got him to go for the spectacular, in drawing people to Himself, as an alternative to all the pain and suffering of the Cross. Without the Cross happening, the whole core of what God had planned would have been missing. Fluttering down unharmed, from the highest point, as an alternative to the Cross, would have drawn the crowds, and done nothing to atone for the sins of men and women.

The eloquence of the "local boy turned preacher" initially impressed the Nazareth congregation – but His words regarding their hardness of heart (especially when compared to some foreigners) stung hard. You get a very impressive view from the Nazareth hospital gates of the hill from which they would have tossed Jesus over.

Psalm 63v1-11

We are rarely thirsty enough to fully understand the deep longing for God expressed here, but I can remember the sheer relief of finding a stream out in the desert long after having exhausted a 2½ litre bottle.

Also an interesting idea of lying awake in thankfulness – not in terror.

Proverbs 11v16-17

God's timing may be very different from ours, but He will have the last word.

March 21st

Numbers 32v1-33v39

Some difficult things were wisely and skilfully handled here. First of all, the Promised Land was west of the Jordan river, but some of the people could see what wonderful sheep country existed where they were. This issue could have split the people, for all the Israelites were supposed to travel over together and fight together. Thankfully they did keep their promises and did cross over to help the others, though it must be said that long term it was a foolish decision to opt to stay on the east bank of the Jordan, in the present day country of Jordan.

The place names are not all easy to tie down, but one of the most fascinating parts of Israel has got to be the wilderness between Israel and Egypt – some spectacular desert features, including moon style craters caused by the Rift Valley that runs right down from the Dead Sea into Kenya in Africa. Gives you a deep understanding of dependence upon God – I nearly ran out of petrol driving round some of those place names!

Luke 4v31-5v11

Capernaum was to be a home from home for Jesus – a base for much of his Galilean ministry. Some impressive ruins – Simon Peter's house was very close to the Synagogue. As we saw from Mark's Gospel, Simon Peter had a mother in law – we tend to forget that at least some of the disciples had wives and family obligations.

The story of Jesus preaching from Simon's boat has its particular lessons, especially when Jesus "interferes" in Simon's sphere – right at the very heart of his work. When Jesus could demonstrate such power out in the boat, those kinds of miracles seemed to hit Peter harder than anything done back on the land. There was no part of life that Jesus could not touch – and that shocked hardened fishermen who thought they knew it all about boats and fish.

Psalm 64v1-10

Again, a real sense of the depths that evil men will go to, together with their cunning and their planning – which means it will be an even bigger shock for them when God acts.

Proverbs 11v18-19

Just about any celebrity magazine today will illustrate this one!

March 22nd

Numbers 33v40-35v34

The entire evil culture of Canaan had to be destroyed.

The Levites did not have a particular region set aside for them – they were to serve the Lord, but just as the sacrificial system helped to provide for them, so they needed to be given cities in which to live, and they clearly had sheep, cattle etc that needed pasture. However, some of those cities would serve as cities of refuge to which others who were accused of serious wrong doing – murder or manslaughter - might flee for safety until a trial was properly arranged before the dead person's family took the law into their own hands.

Rules had to be made to distinguish between a genuine accident and murder. Rules were made regarding the need for someone who has accidentally killed someone to stay away – in the City of Refuge, and to not even consider returning home until after the life time of the current High Priest. Sadly the laws had to recognise the limitations of the people when it came to grace and forgiveness.

Murder was to be taken seriously; murderers were to be executed, but the evidence had to be strong and would never rely on one witness. Unlike Islam, which came much later than both Judaism and Christianity, the murderer could not "buy his way out."

Luke 5v12-28

If you will...a leper recognised the power that Jesus had. Jesus still had to advise him to go through the normal channels to be declared well so that he could be properly integrated back into society.

The healing of the man carried by his 4 friends is of course a favourite for many. It also reveals the extent to which Jesus was already under investigation by the authorities down in Jerusalem.

Our reading also ends with the call of Matthew – a scandalous act in itself, given he was tax collector!

Psalm 65 v1-13

Worship, thanksgiving, requests – many different facets of prayer here. It does make you ask, is your prayer life balanced between all the various things that ought to be in it? Or is it one long shopping list?

Proverbs 11v20-21

As I said before, God will have the last say!

March 23rd

Numbers 36v1- Deuteronomy 1v46

The Year of Jubilee was an important concept as the people were about to enter the Promised Land. Over the years, families would have various degrees of success. Some would become wealthy, some would end up in poverty, but the Year of Jubilee was to be one huge reset button, when all land would go back to the family to whom it originally belonged. It had ideas of social justice and equality behind it. How much the Israelites ever put it into practice is another matter.

The daughters of Zelophehad had been granted land since there were no men left in their family, but that itself threw up the possibility that men from other tribes could through marriage end up inheriting land smack in the middle of this particular tribe. Although the matter was resolved, it does show how human minds run ahead when it comes to land!!!

The rest of this reading tells us how what should have been an 11 day hike became a 40 year struggle in the wilderness, all through sin.

Luke 5v29-6v11

What dubious company – Matthew and his friends!

Jesus comments that it is the sick who need a doctor, and it was to spiritually sick people that Jesus came!

The Pharisees also felt that Jesus' ministry was not austere enough to be religious! There are plenty of professing Christians today who think just like them! Jesus came to bring forgives, peace and joy. Some present day Christian fellowship and worship could do with some real joy in it.

The story of the disciples eating heads of grain on the Sabbath (poor people were allowed to do that kind of thing when they were hungry) shows that things were far from the continuous partying that the Pharisees tried to portray Jesus and his disciples as having all the time.

Ultimately Jesus was also tackling wrong perceptions about the Sabbath, especially when the Pharisees objected to Jesus healing someone on the Sabbath. Some of our Presbyterian forefathers in their own austere legalism would have been very happy with the Pharisees' line – but things have clearly swung too far the other way today.

Psalm 66 v1-20

What a tremendous sense of worship. When did you last remember to say thanks?

Proverbs 11 v22

We can all tell our proverbial stories about the tight fisted person who held on to something until it crumbled and gave neither himself nor anyone else any pleasure. Some take pleasure in holding on to something they don't want or have no use for, rather than let somebody else have it. Perhaps we need to have the wisdom to see that generosity to others can be an investment – both in them, and in the future. No man is an island, and it is a very lonely existence to even try. The day comes when we need to be part of a community.

March 24th

Deuteronomy 2v1-3v29

The recap on the desert experiences continues. It is interesting to note that, despite how the Old Testament (and God) are portrayed by many who are critical of all of this warfare, there were a number of serious attempts to avoid bloodshed and war.

Luke 6 v12-38. Sermon on the Mount (Matthew), or Sermon on the Plain (Luke)? Depends on your perspective – it is a steep climb up from Capernaum, to the very level bit where the coaches take you to, as the recognised spot for all of this. Many of the tourists who arrive by coach don't realise the steep climb the journey up from the water's edge actually is, especially if they have arrived from somewhere else and begin the descent down from this point by the main road, to the shore's edge.

Anyway, a tremendous amount of teaching is packed in here. Don't, however, try to divorce this from the Cross, from Calvary. Too many people would like to stop here, and ignore the rest. But the Sermon on the Mount/Plain is a manifesto for those who have come to experience the new life through Christ – it is not an alternative to salvation through what Jesus had to do on Calvary. We can only begin to live this new life because we know forgiveness, salvation and new life as a result of Calvary.

Psalm 67v1-7

Always interesting the number of occasions we are reminded in the Old Testament that God's salvation is for more than just the people of Israel. That vision was there, again and again, if not actually acted upon in the Old Testament. Less excuse for us – we have the great commission as part of our manifesto.

Proverbs 11 v27 Sanctified common sense – but still needs to be said.

March 25th

Deuteronomy 4 v1-49

As Moses' life is coming to an end, we learn that things were going to go drastically wrong in a couple of generations' time.

Some of us are old enough, not to actually remember the 2nd World War, but to remember the way in which those who lived through it never seemed to stop talking about it (the days when the guys with the medals – the war "veterans" at the cenotaph, were actually of working age.) Our comics, or "comicuts" were still full of war stories of the Japanese and Germans in the 1960s. There was still a link with a very significant past for the kids who thankfully were born after all of that, but for the generation coming after their generation – i.e. 2 generations further on, the War means very little.

So it was for the generations who came after Moses, Joshua etc. And God warned, here in our reading, that this was going to happen. The miracles etc would soon be forgotten, denied and ridiculed when there were no eye witnesses left to all the things which had happened out in the wilderness. The crossing of the Red Sea would become a story to snigger at, as would the stories of Sinai etc, etc. The time of the Book of Judges was a very difficult and confused period – a hard period of peaks and troughs, of turning to God with long periods of paganism and mixing the true faith together with whatever else they found or even invented.

Luke 6v39-7v10

The blind leading the blind...the guy with a whopper of a beam in his eye trying to help someone with a splinter...the tree that doesn't produce according to stock...all these are meant to be obvious illustrations of needing to recognise our own spiritual needs.

The story of the Roman soldier was of course a shocking illustration of how faith is found in the unexpected – leaving us asking the serious questions why we don't find that faith in those who should know it all given their background and strong teaching they received from childhood.

Psalm 68v1-18

There are enemies, but there is a strong conviction of what God is going to do, and there are references to those treasured memories of his past action – which we are to be reminded of.

Proverbs 11v28

A lesson for today's stock market and those who live as though there is nothing else.

March 26th

Deuteronomy 5 v1-6v25

A reminder for the people of Israel that the covenant is not just in the past, but with the present generation. A reminder of the most essential of the commandments. A reminder too, to pass it on the next generation.

Luke 7 v11-35

The story of the widow getting her son – and her life –back.

Also Jesus has to calm the worries of John the Baptist; bear in mind John was under great stress, in prison – he did literally lose his head.

Jesus speaks up for John when He addressed the crowd.

Psalm 68 v19-35

What a beautiful picture of the procession going up to the earthly temple...one day it will be the whole earth.

Proverbs 11 v29-31

A reminder of how we can leave ourselves with no backyard to live in! Relationships are important, as is anything that is character building.

March 27th

Deuteronomy 7 v1-8v20

Moses continues to set out the things the people of Israel are not to do when they enter the Promised Land – the trouble is that this list sounds more like a catalogue of what they did do, after both Moses and Joshua were out of the way.

The warning not to forget the Lord when you have plenty (8v11) is as relevant today as then.

Luke 7 v36-8v3

The terrible ironies of this story – the prostitute who has grasped the Gospel message, and the Pharisee who is mortified that Jesus would allow himself to be touched by someone like her.

By the way, Luke places this story which happens at the house of Simon the Pharisee in a very different time period (quite early on in Jesus' ministry) from that recorded in Mark and Matthew involving a woman and perfume and Jesus, at the house of Simon the Leper. (Though Simon the Pharisee might be an ex leper still called Simon the Leper.) Matthew in chapter 26 (Mark 14) tells us of a woman in Bethany pouring very expensive perfume on the head of Jesus, and Jesus telling those who were indignant that the woman had prepared him for burial. Apart from Luke, the other Gospels have the anointing very close to the crucifixion.

John (chapter 12) identifies Mary (sister of Martha and Lazarus) as the person who pours the perfume on His feet at a meal in Bethany "where Lazarus lived" and the story in John's Gospel has Martha serving at the table. John also tells us about how disgusted Judas Iscariot was at the waste, leaving us wondering was the incident pivotal in turning Judas against Jesus.

This story here in Luke is definitely of a prostitute who wipes Jesus' feet with tears and hair and pours perfume on them. I'm left wondering was there more than one incident at different stages in our Lord's ministry. Maybe I'm on my own on that one. However, key features seem to be disgust (in 3 of the accounts) at who did it, disgust at the "waste" – the irony of something "wasted" on our Lord, all of which portray a lack of understanding about the Gospel message, and frankly not much love for Jesus on the part of those who question a very generous gesture towards Him. Which of course begs the question, how much love have we for Jesus?

The subsequent story of the two men who were forgiven two very different (in size) debts makes a very clear point. Those who have been forgiven more tend to love more.

Psalm 69 v1-14

The psalm has a number of themes – the innocent suffering, yet David in v5 speaks of his own folly and his own sin/guilt. Tomorrow's reading though, takes us to the bit that speaks of how "they gave me vinegar for my thirst" putting the psalm into a very different context for the Christian, and perhaps understanding better some of the tensions where David seems to be speaking about himself, and then speaking prophetically in a way that is much more appropriate from Christ Himself.

Proverbs 12 v1 I especially like the Living Bible version of this verse: "To learn, you must want to be taught. To refuse reproof is stupid."

March 28th

Deuteronomy 9 v1-10v22

If you are finding Deuteronomy hard going, then here is a quote from a sermon I preached in the closing months of my time in Bangor, which brings home why Christians should sit up and pay attention:

Deuteronomy is of special interest to Christians today because the very first followers of Jesus saw a special significance in its message. It is referred to in 17 out of 27 New Testament books. There are over 80 references in the New Testament. I think we would be very unfair to the early Christians if we explained this away by saying they quoted Moses a lot because they wanted to impress their fellow Jews. The early Christians also faced an immense task, one that was just as frightening as the task faced by their

ancestors all those centuries early. Jesus had sent them to take on, not just the promised land, but the whole world with the Gospel. Looking through the Old Testament, Deuteronomy was one of four major books that they homed in on, as they searched for Old Testament teaching that they could relate to the task they now faced.

Luke 8 v4-21

Parables you should know. Also another reference to the half brothers that Jesus had – children whom Joseph had by Mary after Jesus was born.

Psalm 69 v15-36

Yes, the relevance to the cross is so obvious in today's reading – not just the vinegar, but the scoffing at the pain of the one you have pierced (v26).

Proverbs 12v2-3 Things that need to be stated, given that the world will often try to tell us the opposite.

March 29th

Deuteronomy 11v1-12v32. Moses continues to speak to a generation who should know better. They have witnessed much.

Luke 8 v22-40

The exhaustion of Jesus was very real, but so too was the peace with which he could sleep "at funny times." Things were obviously very bad when the fiercely independent fishermen realised the danger and knew they could not get out of it on their own.

Further power is shown when Jesus lands on the side of the lake next to present day Syria – when the herd of demon possessed pigs throw themselves into the Lake. There are 2 different reactions from crowds – those who fear Him, and want Him to leave, and those who are glad to see Him.

Psalm 70 Again a cry for help.

Proverbs 12 v4 A comment on what good and bad marriages do to the other person within them.

March 30th

Deuteronomy 13 v1-15v23

The need to test out some of those things that people claiming to be "spiritual" claim or teach. Best to know your Bible well enough that you recognise what is from God.

Regarding the list of what is clean and unclean for eating, there is a lot of practical common sense in it, in terms of, e.g., eating carnivorous animals exposes us to much more risk of disease. While we are not bound as Christians to the full Jewish laws on what to eat or not to eat, the people in the Old Testament were asked to live lives markedly different from the pagan nations around them; there is a principle in that to recognise. Interesting teaching on setting aside part of our income for God's work, and some serious social teaching on looking after the needs of others, including the very radical cancellation of debts at the end of the seventh year.

Luke 8 v41-9v6

A very trusting father in a desperate situation.

The second story reminds us that the disciples much also become practical doers and get out there, and do it!

Psalm 71 v1-24

Trusting God from childhood into old age. What a witness in itself! But an important prayer and a comfort to those who are facing new difficulties in later life.

Proverbs 12v5-7 The need to be steady in our faith when we are seriously tempted to adopt what others do.

March 31st

Deuteronomy 16v1-17v20

The people are reminded of festivals to be kept.

Included is that they ought to remember others.

The reminder to appoint judges etc, is a reminder that part of worship is living and conducting life in a way that really honours God.

Luke 9 v7-27

Guilt over John continues to plague Herod who had him killed. This obsession with wanting to see and hear Jesus will last until he eventually gets to see him – at Herod's request.

After the feeding of the 5,000 people make their responses. Some see Jesus as a prophet back from the dead etc. Peter recognises that Jesus is the Messiah. He still has a lot to learn as to what being the Messiah means.

Psalm 72v1-20

The final of David's psalms - there is prayer for Solomon who is to take his place as King; these prayers include that the new king will take care of the helpless and poor. He is to judge and rule with righteousness. What is your prayer for the next generation.

Proverbs 12 v8-9

A number of things are thrown together in the space of a few lines; wisdom versus a warped mind, living in the real world, and not in a make-believe one.

April 1st

Deuteronomy 18v1-20v20

Proper support for the Levites as they serve God.

Again a reminder of some of the most horrific customs that currently existed in the land (and archaeology bears this out, such as child sacrifice.) The people of Israel are not to take up these customs. (They did, later.)

A reminder again of justice requirements, including the cities of refuge so that those who have caused an accidental death get a fair trial.

Practical reminders about the honest and fair treatment of others.

Trusting God in times of war and rules as to how war is to be conducted.

Luke 9 v28-50

The transfiguration- quite a privilege for the handful who were there, but also real problems waiting for them as they come down from the mountain.

The disciples still will not take in this talk of betrayal and all the things that are ahead in Jerusalem.

In fact, they still haven't grasped what Jesus has been saying about service and servant hood, as they argue over who will be the greatest.

Psalm 73 v1-28

Dealing with the temptation to admire the apparent success of the wicked.

Proverbs 12v10

A strange way of judging a godly man? Not at all!

Caring for an animal, is contrasted with the wicked man who can't even do something "good" without an evil motive and an evil intent.

April 2nd

Deuteronomy 21v1-22v30

Practical rules dealing with a situation in which a grieving family or tribe might be inclined to literally lash out at the nearest settlement. The seriousness of the loss is recognised (the sacrifice of a heifer) which contrasts with the frustration and anger of modern day relatives who are often frustrated that "nothing has been done" and that there is no apparent closure.

We probably have much more trouble coming to terms with the rule about the treatment of captured women, but see this has an immense improvement upon what often happens in our "modern" age on the battlefield – the on the spot rape and sometimes subsequent killing of women. If someone sees a woman they want on the battlefield, she is to be taken home, allowed to shave her head etc and allowed to mourn her own family for a month. This is serious business, and waiting for the hair to grow back will make many a man think twice about seizing some beauty in war. There are also rules given about how she is to be treated if things do not work out.

The rule about the man having two wives, and how to treat the children of the unloved wife, is frankly right up to date. Children are not to be "punished" or favoured according to how the relationship between their parents did or did not work out.

The rule about a stubborn son may shock us on first reading it, but it takes the responsibility out of the parents' hands. Parents driven to consider the most extreme thing that parents could ever consider, are to hand the matter over to the city authorities. At the same time, the ultimate sanction remains in place. Something to think about in our dreadful society with some very violent and frankly sick behaviour being committed by very hardened "teenagers."

Rules about keeping an eye out for a neighbour's animals, or helping someone in difficulty getting an animal back on its feet – all rules about basic decency and good neighbourliness in a rural community.

The rule about women not wearing men's clothing, and vice versa, is not an attack on women wearing jeans or trouser suits – women tend to be very obviously women in such outfits!!! No, this is someone deliberately trying to look like the opposite sex – this is cross dressing, a totally different issue, and right up to date in our gender bending society.

Conservation even comes into some of the rules regarding taking eggs or young out of a nest (leave the mother) – bear mind this is not mindless killing or taking of wildlife for a collection, but people out seeking food.

Other rules include false accusations used in a divorce case, and an attempt to distinguish between rape and seduction. To really get to terms with what is meant in some of these verses get hold of a good Bible commentary, before you jump to conclusions and criticise the Bible.

Luke 9 v51-10v12

James and John, the "sons of thunder." How strange that their faith on other occasions is not strong enough to do the things that really matter, but apparently here it is strong enough to call down fire from heaven upon a Samaritan village!

Some comment on would be disciples – including once again the story of the man who wanted to stay at home until his father was dead – no indication that his father was ill or frail! Family responsibilities, when they are not that serious, are sometimes used dishonestly to avoid obeying God.

Jesus always insists on getting out and actually doing discipleship. No armchair Christianity here. Hospitality is to be accepted, but Jesus draws the line at comparing the hospitality in one home with another!

The solemn pronouncement against a community who do not want to hear the Gospel is not made lightly.

Psalm 74v1-23

Jerusalem has clearly been destroyed in this psalm – God had sent prophet after prophet for quite some time to warn the people, and the majority would not heed the prophets. Much responsibility had to be borne by the kings and authorities. Having said that, this psalm comes from the mouth of one of the godly who have had to suffer, along with the rest, the outcome of a nation's disobedience. God does allow His sanctuary to be torn down, when the practice outside (and according to Ezekiel, much of what was going on inside too) betrays His core values.

Proverbs 12 v11. Sanctified common sense again. We should know this, yet it has to be said again.

April 3rd

Deuteronomy 23v1-25v19

The opening words seem very tough, and perhaps you are thinking, where is grace here? For a start, this is an outlawing of practices they have seen elsewhere – the making of eunuchs in the palaces of Egypt and other surrounding kingdoms, or deliberate self mutilation. I'm writing these notes at a time when a woman who underwent some kind of sex change, but leaving her internal organs intact, is now a pregnant man (complete with a little beard), causing much bemusement in the press.

Having said that, we will see a softening of these words later on in one of the prophets, where there is recognition of godliness in people who did not inflict these things upon themselves. Verse 2 comes across as extremely hard in some translations; the context is that the people of Israel are to stay clear of the Canaanite practices which had temple prostitutes whose children were dedicated at birth to pagan gods. Moses is also underlining that marriage is the proper basis of society. Remember that they did go off the rails in the wilderness at one point – the pagan culture of Canaan was very explicit sexually. We may emphasise grace, but bear in mind that these people had to learn that this is a God who takes sin seriously. This nation was in a covenant with God, and they were to live in a way that pleased Him.

The Moabites did much to harm God's people, and the terrible thing about the story of Balaam, is that he was employed to curse the people in the name of the one true God, but then bear in mind the story of godly Ruth, the Moabitess who became a direct ancestor of David!

One of the things we discover is that God takes sins of omission seriously – standing by when someone needs our help is a sin. The Ammonites had no compassion for the people of Israel.

Incidentally, some of the later rules in this passage (v19ff) about letting the poor pick up the remains of the harvest, were key in the survival of Ruth and Naomi, and Ruth's eventual marriage to Boaz.

Many of the other rules in this passage are to do with personal hygiene, public health, helping the helpless, being dependable etc.

The rules on divorce. "There are no laws in the Old Testament which actually establish divorce." (Brown, R, **Message of Deuteronomy**, BST series, IVP page 227) That statement comes as a shock to many. Divorce was widespread in the Middle East, and so the rules in this passage are to be seen as an attempt to protect people and marriage, against a background in which divorce was so easy and for some very flippant reasons. The Canaanites had little regard for marriage.

Luke 10v13-37

Some knee height stones show the remains of Chorazin today. With privilege comes responsibility – if only places like Tyre and Sidon had seen these miracles.

The man who came to test Jesus with a question came away with more than he bargained for, in the story of the good Samaritan!

Psalm 75 v1-10. "Joy in God's great reversals" is how Derek Kidner describes Psalm 75 in his commentary. (Tyndale Old Testament Commentaries.)

Proverbs 12 v12-14 The foundations of people's lives soon show through.

April 4th

Deuteronomy 26v1-27v26

Our harvest celebrations are at the end of harvest, but here at the beginning of harvest the people of Israel were to rehearse the story of how God brought them out of Egypt and into the land of Israel. Rules are given for the care of the Levites, migrants and orphans and widows.

In chapter 27 the people of Israel – when they do make it to the Promised Land – are to be reminded of the standards that God requires of those who profess His Name.

Luke 10 v38-11v13

The story of Martha and Mary is well known to us. The Living Bible describes Martha as "the jittery type...worrying over the big dinner she was preparing."

We also have the short version of the Lord's prayer here (yes, there is a short, and a longer version! Many people mistakenly think one is Roman Catholic and the other Protestant, but they are both in the Gospels.)

Jesus teaches persistence in prayer, and the fact that if we with all of our flaws know how to give good gifts, how much more so does our heavenly Father. The Holy Spirit is mentioned here – the one who continues to work away in the Christian's life, making it more Christ-like. An important reminder to those who only think in material terms about what God has to give us.

Psalm 76 v1-12

God has clearly delivered the people of Jerusalem, but the psalmist looks beyond this to God's judgment day. Some suggest that the background may be the elimination, by an angel, of the invading army in Isaiah 37v36.

Proverbs 12 v15-17. Sadly, quick tempered action and a deceitful cover up often go together.

April 5th

Deuteronomy 28v1-68

The choice between blessing and curse; the choice as to whether to live for God or to reject His ways was up to the people. Hundreds of years later these words would ring true as God's judgment came down after several generations of persistent turning away from God and His ways.

Luke 11 v14-36

Jesus is accused of getting His power from Satan.

Others demand something to happen in the sky to prove Jesus is the Messiah. Someone else praises the mother who produced Jesus, only for Jesus to remind her that even more blessed are those who listen to, and then put into practice, God's Word.

A hint to what is going on here is found back in Mark 3 v22. The nit pickers – Scribes from Jerusalem – have landed down to investigate Jesus. This also explains some of the things Jesus then went on to say.

Psalm 77 v1-20

Derek Kidner describes this psalm as "musings in two moods." By that he means the dark mood that has engulfed the writer, which changes as the writer thinks through what God has done in the past. Kidner's headings help us work through this psalm:

V1-3 Cries of distress

V4-9 Searchings of heart

V10-15 Courage from the past

V16-20 Thunder of thy power

Proverbs 12 v18

There is sometimes a perverse pleasure in some people in being cutting in comment, as distinct from doing it unintentionally. It is contrasted with words that bring healing.

April 6th

Deuteronomy 29 v1-30v20

Moses continues to remind the people of God's deliverance in the past, and what will happen in the future when the people turn away from the Lord.

Luke 11 v37-12v7

A head on clash here, between Jesus and the Pharisees, between real change within, and ceremonial conventions in place of life changing faith.

The demand of following the Old Testament laws, with all of the added on Pharasaic rules and interpretations was indeed immense, burdensome, and robbing people of a real relationship with God.

Psalm 78 v1-25

This is a very long psalm, and the danger of reading it in parts is that we don't get an overview.

There is no specific act of cowardice on the part of Ephraim (v9). Rather, this tribe is symbolic in the psalm of the backsliding and apostacy of the people of Israel – see Hosea who has a lot of negative things to say about Ephraim in Hosea chapters 4-13.

The Psalm has been described as "From Zoan to Zion" as it retraces Israel's history from the fields of Egypt to David's reign. Derek Kidner comments on verses 17 & 18: "Evidently the more God gives, the less we appreciate it."

Proverbs 12 v19-20. As the living Bible puts it, "truth stands the test of time."

April 7th

Deuteronomy 31 v1-32v29

The handover to Joshua. More words of warning for a future in which people choose to live without the Lord.

Luke 12 v8-34 As Jesus warns His followers about denying him, someone buts in with a demand that Jesus settles a family argument over inheritance...hence all that follows in today's reading.

Psalm 78 v26-45 We continue this recap of history of what happened from the period in Egypt to the reign of David.

Proverbs 12 v21-23 Proverbs often make a simple or single point. Of course you and I can think of times when good people suffer, and the Bible provides illustrations. Proverbs is simply pointing out there is no long term pleasure in a life which has deceit as its basis.

April 8th

Deuteronomy 32v30-52

We are reminded of the reason why Moses is not to enter the promised land.

Luke 12 v35-59

Being prepared for the return of Jesus.

A reminder that God will judge what has been done before the Master returns.

The Gospel will be [and is] sometimes the cause of division.

The signs are there for those who ought to be aware that God is coming in judgment; as is the reminder to make peace with Him before judgment day.

Psalm 78 v46-58

The Living Bible puts the second half of verse 57 in a very telling way: "Like a crooked arrow, they missed the target of God's will."

Proverbs 12 v24 common sense once again. So why don't we heed it?

April 9th

Deuteronomy 33v1-29

Lovely that Moses finishes with blessings.

Luke 13 v1-22

The issue of why God allowed "innocent" people to suffer was one that troubled many people in those days. Some would have jumped to the conclusion that these people must have done something to be worse off than the rest of us. The matter is more fully dealt with in John 9 with the healing of the man blind from birth. Here in Luke, Jesus is more concerned with those who imagine that they must not be so bad themselves! So, Jesus turned the question back, here in Luke 13, to make people realise that they were heading for God's judgment themselves.

Agricultural illustrations are used a lot in the Gospels. Jesus made the point about the fig tree that gave no results even after three years of care.

The anger over Jesus healing a severely disabled woman on the Sabbath made Jesus point out that more thought was given by His critics to the welfare of their animals, than to this woman who had suffered for 18 years.

Psalm 78 v59-72

The dark and difficult days in which Eli's sons failed the Lord. Then we are reminded how God took David from sheep to Kingdom.

Proverbs 12v25

A call to be an encourager of God's people.

April 10th

Deuteronomy 34v1 – Joshua 2v24

There is a fantastic view from the top of Mount Nebo in modern day Jordan! Time for handover, from Moses to Joshua.

The Lord buried Moses. One of the strangest things, perhaps in the Bible, but it was essential that Moses's burial place should never become a shrine. The people of Israel needed to move on, and God had the successor already in place.

Once again spies are sent out, though just two this time. And bizarrely, today's reading introduces us to Rahab from Jericho, the prostitute who trusts God and ends up in the family tree of both David and Jesus (Matthew 1 v5)

Luke 13v23-14v6

Missed opportunities; people who will leave it too late to get right with God.

The Pharisees try to frighten Jesus with the danger of Herod (though Jesus seems to be wise enough to stay out of Tiberias, where Herod lives, hence no Gospel stories about Tiberias, where we tend to take you to stay for the Galilean part of a Holy Land trip.) Jesus is able to remind them that the real treat to his life comes from the Jewish authorities up in Jerusalem "It wouldn't do for a prophet of God to be killed except in Jerusalem." (Living Bible.)

Again the issue of healing on the Sabbath comes to the fore.

Psalm 79 v1-13

Horrific scenes as judgement comes upon Jerusalem. See also Psalm 74. Unlike Psalm 137, sung by the captives taken away (By the rivers of Babylon...) these psalms describe the scene witnessed by those left behind.

Proverbs 12v26

Paths taken show how lives have already been committed?

April 11th

Joshua 3 v1-4v24

There's quite a challenge – trust the Lord as you walk up to the water's edge, believing that, at that point, God will roll the waters back.

Luke 14 v7-35

Jesus' opening remarks are practical common sense, but they lead on to a story about those who made excuses for not coming to a party – and the excuses are hilarious – the new field, the new tractor (actually, a set of oxen) and finally the new wife. The sting of course, is this is God's heavenly feast, and God is going to bring in a lot of other people to take the places of those who have insulted Him.

Some of Jesus' other remarks include a warning of thinking through the cost of discipleship, but also a warning about being an ineffective follower, which is why the warning to count the cost is given in the first place.

Psalm 80 v1-19

This Psalm of Asaph looks back to the period when the northern tribes were carried away by the Assyrians in 722 BC. The fall of Jerusalem to the Babylonians would be much later. After 722 BC the King in Jerusalem (Kingdom of Judah) showed considerable concern for the survivors of the Kingdom of Israel. The lesson is that, in God's eyes, there is only one flock.

You could draw parallels with some of the things that Jesus says in John's Gospel:

I am the good Shepherd...

I have other sheep...

They are not of this fold...

I must bring them also...

Ezekiel, in chapter 37, also spoke of the two sticks joined into one – Judah and Ephraim reuniting.

Proverbs 12 v27-28

The immediate and ultimate results of taking the wrong path in life.

April 12th

Joshua 5 v1-7v15

The dramatic crossing has an impact on the pagan nations of Canaan. The outward sign of the covenant, circumcision, begins again, and the manna stops, now that they have entered the Promised Land.

An angel appears as the Commander of the Lord's Army.

The fall of Jericho is followed by the disaster at Ai – brought about by one of the people seizing loot at Jericho, against God's commands.

Luke 15 v1-32

The company that Jesus keeps causes concern to the Jewish leaders, so Jesus tells the stories of the lost sheep, the lost coin, the prodigal son. There is the significant and stinging end to the story of the prodigal son – the older, resentful brother.

Psalm 81v1-16 So much encouragement! They experience God, for the first time, as Redeemer – leading them out of Egypt.

Proverbs 13v1 Has anything changed?

April 13th

Joshua 7v16-9v2

Although in the next chapter the rules are changed to allow loot to be kept, the principle had been a very strong one that the war against Jericho was not about looting, but everything was to be devoted to the LORD. This command had been repeated again and again. Israel's obsession with the styles, lifestyles etc of the nations around them would remain a constant thorn.

At last Ai is defeated.

The reading out of the blessings and curses at Gerizim and Ebal would have been very dramatic – to this day the sound effects are still obvious.

Luke 16 v1-18

The parable that Jesus told here, has been either treated as a gaff on the part of Jesus, or else "reinterpreted" to take the bad look off it!!! So how do you react to this parable of an employee, who on realising he is about to lose his job (for dishonesty!) commits further dishonesty in order to win friends for himself in the world out there, as a kind of insurance for his days of unemployment which are looming ahead???

Always remember that parables are told to underline a single point. Jesus telling a story about a dishonest employee does not mean he is endorsing what the dishonest man did, in reducing the bills of others who owed his boss. Some of the possible points that Jesus was making are:

Godly people could do with a bit more wit in realising that they need friends out there!!! Jesus was conscious that many godly people can be abrasive and leave a trail of offence in the world out there, which does no good to any cause they are seeking to promote. Without endorsing the dishonesty of the employee, he did have a lot more social skills than some Christians demonstrate – verse 8 – "And it is true that the citizens of this world are more clever [in dishonesty!] than the godly are." (Living Bible.) The dishonest servant knew more about social networking, building up friendships etc than some of God's people who drop social clangers everywhere they go.

Secondly, Jesus advises His followers to look ahead and use "the mammon of unrighteousness" to make friends. Jesus was endorsing the right use of money, finances etc to further the work of the Kingdom, knowing that there would be those amongst His followers who would try to reject all of that.

In the next few verses, Jesus stresses the need for honesty, and indeed makes the point that if you have not been faithful "in the unrighteous mammon" you cannot be trusted with the true riches (v11)

There are alternative interpretations, which try to pretend the dishonest employee was really an honest employee, but they are basically a load of rubbish. Jesus makes clear he is a dishonest employee. Jesus is not endorsing the wrong doing, but wishes His followers were more socially astute in their networking and their awareness of handling finance – all to the furtherance of His Kingdom. Some of you are going to have to think long and hard on this one! Jesus does make the point that you cannot serve both God and money (v13)

The passage does end with Jesus' criticism of outward piety which is not matched by what you find within – which leads Him on to discuss marriage and divorce and the sham we often see in that aspect of life!

Psalm 82 v1-8

This Psalm has caused some puzzlement. Who are the "gods" that the one and only true God is judging. Some suggest that it is the judges who hold court in His name (just as today judges act on behalf of the crown.) Others see it as a reference to principalities and powers (see Ephesians 6 v12) all of which come under the judgement of the one and only true God.

Clearly, those who are in a position to exercise judgment and power over the lives of others need to realise that they will give an account to Him.

Proverbs 13 v2-3

Wise words tend to come from a wise heart. A wrong heart can be exposed by what comes out of the mouth.

April 14th

Joshua 9v3 – 10 v43

Who can blame the people of Gibeon? The people at fault here are the people of Israel, and their leadership, who see no need for prayer (v14,15), who assume they have the full picture and know everything, and are totally taken in. A warning to those who have been a Christian for a long time and think that they know it all and don't need to ask God about things that come along.

As for Adonizedek and the people of Jerusalem. What a change from the days when Melchizedek the godly friend of Abraham was King, and was known to be a priest of the one true God (Genesis 13.) Adonizedek rounds up some fierce warrior kings, and time literally stops until Israel has them defeated in one tremendous battle. More battles follow. The city of Jerusalem is burnt at this time (Judges 1 v8) but is not occupied as an Israelite city until the times of David – when the Jebusites had it so well fortified that they imagined they were invincible.

Luke 16 v19-17v10

This story throws up many questions. Once again we need to remember this is a parable, before we try working out too many other secondary issues from it. Jesus is making a small number of simple points, and not giving us a whole and final description that will answer our every question on where the dead are now, and what they are doing! The day of judgement has not happened, so the rich man, though he is in torment, has not actually been thrown into the lake of fire (the second death) just yet. He can see the righteous beggar in the distance, with Abraham. The rich man longs for a drop of water, but Abraham explains that he cannot send Lazarus over. The rich man asks that the beggar be sent back to warn the rich man's 5 brothers. Here now is the sting in the tale: "If they won't listen to Moses and the prophets, they won't listen even though someone rises from the dead." (v31)

Psalm 83 v1-18

Some see this psalm as referring to 2nd Chronicles 20, but others see it as referring to something much bigger, with God's people under threat in a very hostile world. Having said that, the psalmist has not lost the vision of how even these hostile forces might yet come to recognise the LORD. This is the final "Psalm of Asaph" (Psalms 50; 73-83)

Proverbs 13v4

Dissatisfied with your lot but not willing to put your back into changing things?

April 15th

Joshua 11v1-12v24

Unlike the common assumption that a blood thirsty Israel went crashing into Canaan seeking to slaughter all around, we see again that the initiative to attack comes from the pagan tribes and nations.

Before you become cynical about "giants" we are not talking about myth (Jack & the beanstalk) but about a tribe of exceptionally tall people – who incidentally were the cause of much of the fear of the previous generation who heard the reports of the 10 spies who warned of all the dangers in the land. Some believe they have found references to these people in Egyptian writings, and they are mentioned in Deuteronomy and Numbers as well.

Luke 17 v11-37

One grateful ex leper returns – and of the ten, he turns out to be a Samaritan!

Jesus' advice about fleeing when destruction comes was taken seriously – and very wisely – by the Christians when Jerusalem (AD 70) revolted against the Romans a generation later. A revolt which ended the Temple worship right down to this day.

The real day of the Lord is of course judgment day, and Jesus speaks of how on his return people shall be taken and others left. Trying to work out an exact order for all of this only distracts Christians and leads to pointless argument. Just be ready!

Psalm 84 v1-12

A beautiful picture of being at home in God's presence, worshipping Him. That's just where the worshipper wants to be. Some of us can barely spend an hour in His presence without checking our watches!

Proverbs 13v5-6 Honesty and integrity continue to be major themes.

April 16th

Joshua 13v1-14v15

Joshua is now old, and although a great deal has been achieved, the next generation will have to carry on the task of taking the Promised Land.

Luke 18 v1-17

Several issues regarding prayer:

Persistence in prayer.

A complete misunderstanding of prayer (self justification rather than repentance.)

The reading ends with Jesus having to rebuke his disciples for their dismissive attitude towards children. As someone has said, the children are very much part of the Church of TODAY, not just the Church of tomorrow.

Psalm 85

Take time to look at the themes, the teaching in this psalm. What a tremendous sense of contentment and peace in God's presence.

Proverbs 13 v7-8

Image and pretence, whatever the real motive. Some aspire to what wealth brings, and others are troubled by the problems and worries it brings. In fact the wealthy man is open to the kidnapper's threat. The poor man is not susceptible to that!

April 17th

Joshua 15 v1-63

The challenges faced by Judah. Caleb was certainly an unusual character! His daughter seemed happy enough with the outcome, and we are given the touching story of her request for some springs.

Luke 18 v18-43

A shock for anyone who imagines they have scored all the right points. Of course, as we have seen some days ago from our Old Testament reading, God takes seriously the sins of omission too! This man's wealth was also a burden to actually following Jesus completely.

The disciples don't really want to take in all this talk of what is going to happen in Jerusalem.

At least the beggar at Jericho jumps in and takes what turned out to be his last opportunity as Jesus heads through Jericho and uphill to Jerusalem – and the cross.

Psalm 86 v1-17

There is a very real sense of loneliness here, whatever it is that David is facing. The pressure is still there at the end of the psalm, but the praise is deliberate as David finds reason to thank and praise God even when the going is tough.

Proverbs 13v9-10

Light and darkness; insolence and wisdom.

April 18th.

Joshua 16v1-18v28

More of the work still to be achieved. There are problem areas, and Joshua still has to get them up and going again – getting a "second breath" in God's work is not easy, and it is not easy for the leaders trying to motivate people.

Luke 19 v1-27

A final opportunity for Zacchaeus too.

Jesus finds it is necessary to tell a story about how he is going away, but he will require evidence on His return of what His followers have achieved – the story of the talents.

Psalm 87 v1-7

A wonderful picture of Jerusalem as God's Holy city. (John Newton's hymn: "Glorious things of thee are spoken...") Sadly, it was and still is a very unholy place at times.

Proverbs 13 v11. A comment on hastily gotten wealth –one translation takes it as a reference to gambling.

April 19th

Joshua 19 v1-20 v9

There is some sadness in the story about Dan; people died in Leshem (La'ish), because Dan could not face up to the task in the territory they were given. Judges 18 records how the Danites turn away from the faith of their fathers and butcher the unsuspecting people of La'ish. The Judges account has a fair degree of disgust with the behaviour and general spirituality of the tribe of Dan in the times of the Judges. Their idolatry (the molten image) developed even further. Having a grandson of Moses (full story in Judges 17 & 18) heading the new cult meant it was difficult to combat the new heresies of Dan for a long time to come – right up until the tribe was carried away by the Assyrians, hundreds of years later. Judges, as you will soon see, is a very depressing time when a new generation arise with little knowledge or interest in the stories of how God led their people in the past.

The setting up of the Cities of Refuge was an important part of the instructions that Moses had given. One wonders what blunders of poor judgment and violent rage happened due to the delay in providing these.

Luke 19 v28-48

Prophecy fulfilled as Jesus entered Jerusalem this way. Real sadness too, at the spiritual poverty of the city. The clearing out of the temple was an important symbol. The merchants had set up their stalls where the Gentiles should have been allowed to worship, and the merchants were far from being honest men.

Psalm 88 v1-18

Deep depression here; but at least the psalm writer is turning to the One who can help.

Proverbs 13v12-14

An awareness of our emotional vulnerabilities in verse 12? Something to recognise – our emotions can see-saw and it is best to be aware of that vulnerability as we face life.

Despising and respecting God's Word bring very different outcomes.

April 20th

Joshua 21v1-22v20

The Levites are now provided for. Then some tension arose when the tribes who were going to stay on the East Bank of the Jordan River (present day Jordan) appeared to be building a break-away altar of their own. It was important to keep unity within the whole nation. As we shall read tomorrow, the monument was built with good intentions, and everyone calmed down again. Although as we shall see later, the tribes who remained on the eastern side of the Jordan river would always be vulnerable, and the territories would ultimately be lost –they were not part of the promised land.

Luke 20 v1-26

Questions about authority lead Jesus to tell a very pointed parable about those who rent a vineyard, only to kill the owner's son.

Angered, those in authority tried to get Jesus to say something they could report to the Romans. On the subject of taxes, Jesus gave a brilliant answer!

Psalm 89 v1-13

The psalm writer refers to God's promise in 2nd Samuel 7 v4-17 that David's dynasty will last forever. Clearly something disturbing has happened, and the psalmist is trying to work through this.

Proverbs 13 v15-16

Sanctified common sense for every day living.

April 21st

Joshua 22v21-23v16

The tensions are quickly dealt with. Long after this, Joshua sends again for the leaders, to remind them of the covenant they have with God. Joshua was quite right to be concerned that after his death the people who soon forget.

Luke 20 v27-47

After another trick question, Jesus raised the subject of how David spoke of a son (descendant) of his, but also spoke of this son as his Lord. Clearly the Messiah was more than just a descendant of David if David referred to him as 'Lord.'

Psalm 89 v14-37

How David's throne is to last forever is not revealed until David's greater 'son' the Lord Jesus Christ comes.

Proverbs 13 v17-19

The bad messenger may tell the truth but in such a way that he or she does immense harm.

April 22nd

Joshua 24 v1-33

Disappointing that Joshua has to ask them again to put away the idols that they never fully gave up. Just as Rachel stole her father's household gods, so they never really got rid of the final traces of the pagan past before their ancestor Abraham.

The covenant to worship the one true God is enacted again. Incidentally, I have been to see the huge stone that Joshua raised up. The local Arabs, keen to deny that the present day Jews have any connection with the place, have turned the area into a rubbish dump and are doing their best to cover the stone...but yes, it is there, a historical fact!

Joshua lived to the age of 110. The sad comment of verse 31 tells us what Joshua suspected all along:

"Israel obeyed the Lord throughout the lifetimes of Joshua and the other old men who had personally witnessed the amazing deeds the Lord had done for Israel." The implication is that it stopped soon after the death of Joshua and the others.

Luke 21v1-28 The widow knew more about sacrificial giving than many of the others who gave considerably more.

Herod's Temple building was an attempt to take away the shame of how the Temple rebuilt after the people returned from the exile was a poor replacement compared to the original built by Solomon. Approximately 40 years later all of this would be rubble again after the Jewish rebellion against the Romans.

Many other things were also ahead of Jesus' followers – false claims that He had returned – wars, insurrections, natural disasters – and persecution. And one day Jesus will return!

Psalm 89 v38-52

The psalm now comes to its point; having focussed in on God's promise to David, the psalmist is deeply troubled by what he has seen happening in his own lifetime.

Proverbs 13 v20-23

The topics change quickly in these few verses. Some of the things can seem contradictory, or at least the writer is aware of what someone may throw back at him. Certainly company does "rub off." He recognises the blessings that honesty and integrity bring. But he is also conscious of the injustice that strips an honest poor man of what should be his.

April 23rd

Judges 1v1-2v9: Yes – you have read some of this before – such as the story of Achsah, daughter of Caleb. (April 17th; Joshua 15.) The story of the angel speaking against the various treaties which the people of Israel had made was a warning about the self inflicted problems they had brought upon themselves – significant numbers of pagan people mingled in with the Israelites.

Although Jerusalem was defeated, it was not occupied permanently by the Israelites until the time of David.

If you are having trouble coping with all of this bloodshed, bear in mind that sin was now full-blown in Canaan – gross immorality, child sacrifice etc. God was removing the Canaanites, as He would one day remove His own people.

Luke 21v29-22v13

Jesus raises the matter of being able to read the signs of the times.

The religious leaders actively plot the death of Jesus, and Judas comes under Satan's control as he offers to betray Jesus.

Meanwhile, the disciples prepare for the Passover meal.

Psalm 90v1-91v16

We have 2 psalms in to-day's reading. The first of these, by Moses, brings home God's eternity compared to our frailty. It is, in the words of Derk Kidner, "chastened and sobering." The second psalm in contrast, brings home to us how we may indeed dwell in the shelter of the Most High. It would be a shame to know only the first, and not to know the second.

Proverbs 13 v24-25

The consequences of raising undisciplined children are brought home to us. Then the topic quickly changes – some interpret the verse to be asking, do we eat to live, or live to eat? What is being commented on clearly, is the unsatisfied appetites of evil people.

April 24th

Judges 2v10-3v31

Statement about what we knew was going to happen.

The first judge was Othniel (Caleb's son-in-law.) He was able to defeat their main enemy and gained 40 years of peace. The second Judge killed the Moabite King and then led the Israelites in a decisive battle that granted peace for 80 years. The third proved to be lethal against the Philistines with an ox goad which is between 8 and 10 feet long, with a metal point. The significance of this is that we will read in later stories that the Philistines deliberately disarmed their subject peoples – he probably had no other weapon to use.

Luke 22v14-34 The Lord's Supper

The right to eat and drink that the table – something which Jesus gives to His disciples.

Sadly there was also an argument over greatness.

There is a warning of what is to come to Simon (Peter) – he will indeed be shifted, and he will deny his Lord – but Jesus has prayed that his faith will not completely fail.

Psalm 92v1-93v5

"Sweet is the work, my God, my King" is a hymn by Isaac Watts based upon psalm 92. There is "tireless praise" (v1-4), contrasting with "heedless arrogance" (v5-9 – Derek Kidner's commentary) followed by a strong sense of the vitality that walking with the Lord brings (v10-15.) Psalm 93 celebrates God upon His throne – "The LORD reigns..." is the opening words of this psalm, psalm 97 and psalm 99 and occurs in verse 10 of psalm 96. Here is God in all His glory.

Proverbs 14 v1-2. Contrasts again between wisdom and folly, uprightness and deviousness.

April 25th

Judges 4v1-5v31

Leadership in the hands of a woman? So it seems – a prophetess holding court , deciding disputes, and bringing the people back to God. Having commanded a man to lead the army, Deborah finds she has to go into battle herself.

Another woman also becomes a hero that day – the enemy leader, Sisera, has a sharp tent peg driven through his skull by a woman, Jael. What a victory, celebrated in song!

Luke 22v35-54

The agony of the Garden of Gethsemane, and the actual arrest. The High Priest's house was just across the valley, and the steps up to it are still there.

Psalm 94 v1-23

God will judge and punish.

Proverbs 14v3-4

V4 is a bit puzzling. Here is how Derek Kidner explains it in his commentary on Proverbs (Tyndale, IVP page 106)

"Orderliness can reach the point of sterility. This proverb is not a plea for slovenliness, physical or moral, but for readiness to accept upheaval, and a mess to clear up, as the price of growth. It has many applications to personal, institutional and spiritual life, and could well be inscribed in the minute books of religious bodies, to foster a farmer's outlook, rather than a curator's."

(Basically the writer of Proverbs was saying that if you want nice clean sheds you won't have the oxen to plough the fields, to bring in the harvest etc!)

April 26th

Judges 6 v1-40

Things are so severe that wheat has to threshed in the bottom of a grape press so that the Midianites cannot see that there is something worth stealing(v11.)

When the angel appears, Gideon does not realise that it is an angel, at first. There is considerable caution – he is not going to be carried along by words alone. There is a healthy cynicism on his part, but that is not lack of faith. Likewise in the story of the fleece. There is a difference about refusing to act when we know something is from God, and being very cautious in the first place about making sure it is God speaking to us.

What about people today who put out fleeces (or something along those lines?) In our day though, we must always put centrally what God has already revealed to us in His Word; there is a danger that modern day folks who put out fleeces or their equivalents are actually looking for an answer different from what the Bible has already given them on an issue close to their hearts. So read your Bible, and also realise that there is no substitute for prayer when seeking God's will.

Luke 22v55-23v10

Peter's denial – and the source of this part of the story must have been Peter himself, for who else could have told it? Humbling and honest. How many of us would have ever told this story about ourselves?

Herod's interest in Jesus is far from that of a man looking for faith; perhaps that of a man looking to be entertained.

Psalm 95 v1-96v13

Psalm 95 is seen as a call to worship by many in the wider Christian Church. Meribah and Massah are references to bad times in the wilderness.

We find the words of Psalm 96 and parts of Psalms 105 & 106 repeated in 1st Chronicles 16 as it tells the story of David bringing the ark into Jerusalem. That was some day!

Proverbs 14 v5-6

Honesty, being a truthful witness, not being a scoffer – all important things that Proverbs has to keep bringing us back to.

April 27th

Judges 7v1-8v16

Once Gideon is certain that God is speaking to him he does get going, and takes on the task!

The LORD was determined not to allow the people of Israel to claim that they alone won the battle, so Gideon has the task of whittling down the army.

First of all, those who are frightened are sent home. Then they are divided into two groups according to how they drink at a stream. At this point I would add a note of caution in how we interpret things at this point. For a start, I find it difficult on rereading and rereading the passage again, to picture things exactly as some preachers have. What exactly is meant by people cupping the water in their hands, yet lapping it like a dog, and those who kneel to drink, and yet have their mouths in the spring.

Secondly, and particularly in Northern Ireland, those who drink from their hands are portrayed as some kind of elite, and the reason given is that "they did not kneel before the enemy" – but this is not in the Bible, though it may be a common interpretation. I doubt if the enemy were in view at this point.

Actually, many folk in our Province are missing the point. This is not about selecting an elite fighting band, or even a super spiritual group of men – this is about whittling down the number of men that Gideon has, so that the battle is clearly won by the hand of the LORD. (7v2)

Gideon's action in whipping to death the leaders of Succoth (Or was it dragging them over thorns and briars, or even did he thresh them to death using threshing sledges as they lay on thorns?) was a barbaric act, even in the moment of anger against a city that had played safe and refused to feed the Israelite troops. (Living Bible: "scraped them to death.")

Luke 23 v11-43

Read slowly; there is the danger of assuming we know all there is to know of the story.

Psalm 97v1-98v9

Two different sides to the coming of the LORD. Judgement upon the world, and the sheer delight of worship.

Proverbs 14v7-8 Should be common sense, yet once again the writer knows it needs to be said.

April 28th

Judges 8 v17-9v21

I had this lovely picture of brave young Gideon from my Sunday School days, but it is just about to be dented by several things that Gideon does in this passage. An ephod was usually part of the vestments of a Jewish priest, almost like a full size kitchen apron with shoulder straps, and with a back and front. To add to the confusion it seems to have played a role in seeking God's will, for we have a breastplate holding the urim and thummin. If I am beginning to lose you on this one, just bear in mind that Gideon seems to have created something which has nothing to do with the proper God appointed priesthood, with an apparent desire to somehow "find out things" and that whatever exactly it was that Gideon created, it became in practice an idol that distracted people away from having a real faith and trust in God. So while Gideon does not seem to have crossed the line in putting out his fleece, he clearly crossed the line on this one and created something which was at the very least a hindrance to true faith and a source of superstition. Otherwise, he does (v33) appeared to have acted as a brake on the full blown paganism that took over after his death.

Secondly, he had many wives. He undoubtedly bragged about his seventy sons, but his wives must have seemed more like a breeding herd than for Gideon to have had a meaningful relationship with any of them. And why did he have to have a concubine as well? We assume from the story that she was a Canaanite woman, but he paid dearly for raising her son on a very different basis from that of the rest of his family – his sons, with one exception end up slaughtered by the concubine's son. Incidentally, Abimelech's name (my father a king) betrays the truth that while Gideon refused the kingship in name, he appears to have otherwise acted like one, with the huge harem associated with the pagan kings of the region. As we will discover in the story of Samson and his involvement with Canaanite women, Canaanite society was a more matriarchal family structure – children belonged more to the wife's family than to the father's. Women remained much more with their own families, with the husband "visiting." So the whole understanding of marriage and family life was completely topsy turvey. Abimelech was destined to belong more to the culture and society of his mother's family.

We cringe further when we read of Abimelech's bodyguards or thugs being paid for out of the collection at the pagan temple. Here we have the people of Israel, blending in with the local paganism and its customs, having totally lost the plot in what it meant to be following the one true God. The heritage of Gideon, is to leave the people of Israel even further away from God.

Luke 22v44-24v12

The Romans had been very uneasy with how the Jewish authorities had blackmailed them into carrying out this crucifixion. The soldier in charge of the unit which had carried out the crucifixions may have known a substantial part of Pilate's own unease. The signs of what happened that day confirmed to the soldier that Jesus had indeed been an innocent man.

Joseph of Arimathea does the decent thing, and makes clear his own disassociation with the whole way in which the Jewish authorities conducted themselves.

The resurrection comes as one immense shock to the disciples; bear in mind that the actual death scene was immensely horrific. Victims of crucifixions did not just slip away, as many do peacefully and quietly in their sleep. Those who witnessed a death in these circumstances witnessed the full horrors and nobody ever kidded themselves that the dead person was just "sleeping."

Psalm 99v1-9

The holiness of God is brought home to us.

Proverbs 14 v9-10

There are different ways of translating verse 9, as a quick glance at several translations will show. The heart is the key to it all.

April 29th

Judges 9 v22-10v18

The awful story of Abimelech continues...think back to all the wrong steps that led to this. Both the men of Shechem and Abimelech get justice, in the end.

Others follow after this time as 'judges' of Israel.

Luke 24v13-53

As I said yesterday, bear in mind the awful, mind numbing reality of crucifixion. Those who were on the road to Emmaus were in pretty bad shape, emotionally. As of course were the others

Psalm 100 v1-5

It is still one of those pieces which has tremendous impact today.

Proverbs 14v11-12

Verse 11 states a common enough Jewish / Christian belief, but verse 12 brings home to us the self deception in which everyman seems himself as right.

April 30th

Judges 11v1-12v15

Reminds you of parts of the story of Abimelech!! It is also right up to date in the complexities of modern life with different families to the same parent in competition with one another. Probably sharing their mother's hatred of the other woman, his half brothers drive out Jephthah who turns into a bandit who then becomes the protector of the local people against the Ammonite invaders.

The rest of the story brings home to us just how much the people had departed from understanding God. Jephthah's extremely rash and wrong promise should never have been made, but living in times of great superstition it was fulfilled. Did he not understand that human sacrifice was a pagan, Canaanite thing that would never honour or please the one true God? The rash promise, followed by the killing of his only child, brought his family line to an end. The daughter, with her own very limited and poor understanding of God and what really pleases Him, submitted to the consequences, since God had given them victory.

His revenge on the Ephraimites was disturbing. Rather like the way in Northern Ireland today in which a person's religious and cultural background can be judged by how they say "h", so Jephthah made decisions as to whether to kill or release men according to whether they said "S" or "Sh" in the word Shibboleth. How many men died, deliberately saying it the other way, having misjudged who had seized them? These were dark and disturbing days.

John 14 v1-28

Be on your guard against any form of "Protestantism" that denies the divinity of Jesus.

Jesus was there from the very beginning, from creation itself. Anyone who tells you that Jesus was just adopted by God, or that he just came into existence at his birth, is denying a central Gospel truth.

John the Baptist had a much more substantial role than we often recognise.

The place described here is roughly opposite Qumran at the top of the Dead Sea. However, while Qumran is in present day Israel, the place where John was baptising at this point is in present day Jordan.

On a tour of Israel I would advise you to avoid another "baptismal site" much further up the country, at the bottom of the Sea of Galilee, where many Christian groups go to get baptised, and where some go to get baptised again, and again...a most cringe-worthy place to visit, but an obvious money spinner to the local Kibbutz.

John came to get the people ready for Jesus.

Psalm 101v1-8

Well intended; but we know that this kind of life must be lived in the power and strength that Jesus gives. To try this on our own, leads to a rather red-faced defeat.

Proverbs 14v13-14

Laughter cannot last forever; neither can it be a mask to cover reality. Avoid being superficial.

May 1st

Judges 13v1-14v20

In the Book of Acts, in chapter 21, you find that Paul was encouraged to go to the temple along with some Jewish Christians who were about to have their heads shaved – ironically, it was giving in to this pressure from Jerusalem's Jewish Christians that got Paul arrested and led to all that followed (imprisonment etc.) It seems that these Christians, in keeping with Old Testament practice, had taken a temporary Nazarite vow, and had kept their hair uncut while that time had lasted. Earlier, in Acts 18v18, we find that Paul himself had his own hair cut after fulfilling some vow.

I mention all of this, to put the story of Samson's hair into context. Back in Numbers 6 v2 if someone wanted to mark their life as being consecrated to God for a special purpose for a fixed period of time, he or she would leave their hair uncut, and abstain from alcohol - indeed from anything made with grapes.

Samson, however, was to be a permanent Nazarite from birth. Even his mother was not to take alcohol during her pregnancy.

Although Samson's long hair marked him out to dedicated to the LORD, his personal life was another thing – demanding that his parents get him a particular (pagan) Philistine girl as his wife. More of this particular weakness for Philistine girls later!

The point simply being, that for all that the long hair was meant to symbolise, Samson's life fell short of it, again and again.

John 1 v29-51

John declares that Jesus is the Lamb of God and points two of his own disciples to the Saviour. Andrew finds Peter. The next day Jesus finds Philip who in turn finds Nathanael...stories unique to John's Gospel.

Psalm 102v1-28

It is suggested that this psalm is the prayer of one of David's descendants – a king, prince or member of the royal house who has experienced the destruction of Jerusalem and being exiled to Babylon. While this is not certain, it does help us to make a lot of sense of the psalm.

Proverbs 14v15-16

Warnings about not believing anything, and not being hot-headed and reckless!

May 2nd

Judges 15v1-16v31

Having walked out towards the end of the week long Philistine marriage celebrations (just before the marriage was due to be consummated!), Samson decides, clearly some time later, to drop in on his wife for sex, only to find his father in law blocking the way. Since Samson had stormed out, everyone had assumed the marriage was over, and they had promptly given the bride to the bestman!

Samson's reaction is one of immense animal cruelty. The word used here can mean fox or jackal, which are closely related animals, and since jackals live in packs, it would have been easier to capture huge numbers of them. Tying the tails of three hundred animals together in pairs, with a fiery bundle tied to each pair, the hysterical animals were released to run terrified through the Philistine fields, setting fire to everything, even the olive trees. For revenge, the Philistines burned Samson's ex wife and her father alive. Samson then went on a murder spree, and caused so much ill feeling that 3,000 men of the tribe of Judah eventually went out to capture him.

Sadly, there is more about Samson and Philistine women. Gaza today is hardly a tourist attraction, being in the heart of Hamas territory, and in the times of Samson it was in the heart of Philistine territory, and Samson was no more welcome then than he would be today! But he spends the night with a prostitute there – and stays in bed until the following midnight when he goes out and rips the city gate posts out of the ground. Then of course we have the next Philistine woman of his life, Delilah...with her cold, heartless efficiency.

So, Samson is not exactly the Sunday school hero that you remember? Not exactly a team player either, and although he was supposedly the leader of Israel, he didn't actually lead anybody. His morals were non-existent, his attitudes towards animals and women were that they were things to be used, and the most useful thing he did in his life was to pull the Philistine temple down upon himself and the entire Philistine leadership.

If you are still reeling in shock (having never actually looked at the story of Samson as an adult) what good was achieved during his life? Samson's maverick life unsettled the Philistine domination that many of the Israelites in that part of the country seemed to be accepting. If we are mortified by Samson's life and intermarriage, and the acceptance of pagan customs and rites, we should be even more alarmed at the way in which his fellow Israelites were rapidly being assimilated into the pagan culture around them.

John 2 v1-25

The opening story is badly mishandled in many Christian circles. First of all, in our Northern Irish / Irish culture, we have a problem with alcohol, so much so that in the late 1800s, and the early 1900s, Christian circles moved to total abstinence – to the point that in the first couple of decades of the 20th century, virtually every Presbyterian Church abandoned using alcohol in the Communion services, which then led to the abandonment of the huge pewter cups which the whole congregation shared, and we went for our little individual hygienic glass cups. Nobody really thought through what it meant in terms of fellowship, or our understanding of the service.

The level of drinking in Northern Ireland produced appalling figures. Having said that, it still does not justify portraying the Bible's teaching as total abstinence. The Bible does have quite a lot of pretty strong stuff to say on the subject of drunkenness. It is also true that some of the words used for wine in the Scriptures do not necessarily mean formatted wine as distinct from grape juice. We are also living in times in which the alcoholic strength of many drinks has risen – in recent decades this has been particularly noticeable in wines.

We are also living in a highly mechanised age; the implications of even a small amount of alcohol when using machinery or driving is alarming. And for a decade or two we have had the "ladettes" - the girls who want to match the boys, and who often on the issue of alcohol go further. Having said all that, the word used here in John 2 is a word that leaves us in no doubt that this is wine as distinct from grape juice. Here was a family about to be totally humiliated, and Jesus acted, and He did make the real stuff, in huge quantities, not to promote drunkenness, but to bless a couple and their families that the greatest day of their lives did not end in humiliation. We could even, as an aside, think back to our reading on Samson and make some comparisons between the weddings!

Banquets, parties, wedding feasts are all used in the Scriptures as a picture of salvation. We don't know hunger and uncertainty over our next meal as people in those times knew, which is still true of parts of the world today. The image of a feast – a rare and treasured memory – was a strong picture of salvation. We have got to see this story at the start of the Gospel in the light of another towards the end, as Jesus lifted the cup and gave the wine a new meaning in that meal with the disciples.

What we need is a new respect for wine, not just in terms of the dangers of alcohol abuse, but also in terms of the new meaning that a cup of wine had for those who experienced Calvary. If every time we lift a glass to our mouths we are conscious of how the red wine reminds us of Christ's blood having been shed for our sins, then we will have a very different attitude towards it.

The next story is of Jesus clearing out the temple. Much has been made of the sales being conducted where the gentiles ought to have been able to worship, and of alleged over charging of money changers and sellers, though this is not stated. Those who have looked at where the other Gospel writers have placed this story (in terms of the context of the other stories they place with it) see it as primarily a judgment on the whole corruption of the temple.

Psalm 103v1-22

Today's and tomorrow's psalms very much go together. God is praised as "Saviour and Creator, Father and Sustainer..." (Kidner's commentary.) Unlike many other psalms which clearly refer to deeply disturbing incidents in David's life, we have a hymn with which we can all identify. This psalm inspired "Praise my soul, the King of heaven."

Proverbs 14v17-19

As Derek Kidner's commentary on these and yesterday's verses puts it, "there are different ways of being a fool."

In both the Old and New Testaments we have the certainty of the day that will come when "the wicked will bow at the gates of the godly." What may be hypocritical now, will one day be a reality as evil people have to give respect to the godly.

May 3rd

Judges 17 v1-18v31

Where do we begin with this story? It's crazy, you might be saying, but what is sane and normal in some homes to-day? First of all we have a serious case of theft in the family. The son is superstitious enough to hand the money back because he has heard a curse being put on the thief. (There is no real remorse for having taken it.) Secondly, we have a bizarre notion on the mother's part that she will spend part of the money on making an idol as a way of somehow impressing upon the Lord the new (improved) nature of her son. This idol is effectively a gift back to the son who stole her money in the first place. As it turns out, he already has a nice little collection of idols, and even has one of his own sons installed as priest. Should we laugh or cry? What kind of mumbo jumbo was passing, in this home, as worship of the one true God? And yet as we read about the lives of some of our celebrity figures today we realise what a load of utter rubbish is believed and practiced as alternative religion. This is god made in the image of sinful man. And it is deeply disturbing. The writer of Judges sums it all up in 17 v6: "In those days Israel had no king, so the people did whatever seemed right in their own eyes."

Anyway, a Levite comes passing through, who happens to be a descendant of Moses (18 v30.) Micah jumps at the opportunity to employ this man. Now Micah's little self made religion can have a more "authentic" touch with a real live descendant of Moses as the priest.

The next chapter brings us to more cringe worthy depths of despair. The tribe of Dan, instead of fighting off the people God had said they were to drive out of the land, decided instead to attack a peaceful and isolated group of people up in the far north. Impressed with Micah's shrine and all the trappings of his man made religion, the people of Dan decide to steal it for themselves! (As though "god" is something that we can buy, own or even steal for ourselves!) They take Micah's "priest" and idols with them, and after their genocide of the fine people of Laish, rebuild the town as Dan and set up their alternative religion. This of course, in their eyes, gave respectability to everything they had done, not that we have the slightest sympathy for Micah either who had suffered having his religion stolen from him! Unfortunately we are living in days of man-made religion in which many things are done in the name of God with some very bizarre notions about Him and what He requires of our lives. People today do "what is right in their own eyes" and they still like to think of themselves as "spiritual."

John 3 v1-22

We are familiar with the story of Nicodemus, who comes secretly to see Jesus at this point, but who will also be one of two (the other being Joseph of Arimathea) who take a stand of sorts when Jesus is dead and all is seemingly lost, by collecting the body for burial.

The important part of this of passage though is the teaching. Some would suggest that Nicodemus ought to understand the concept of "new birth" much more – indeed Jesus says as much. Nicodemus is fighting off the very concept of a complete and fresh start again from God. He is also struggling with his understanding of Jesus – he is quite content to accept the Lord as a good and moral teacher, but Jesus goes on to speak of what will happen at Calvary. And many writers – Jewish as well as Christian - are quite right in pointing out that Jews just don't accept the notion of the fall of mankind. Nicodemus imagines that he can still get to heaven through religious practice, through becoming a better person. The very idea of the depths of human sin in all of us, requiring God to do something very dramatic and life changing within us – this is uncomfortable stuff. Ironically, Nicodemus will have to have his eyes opened to what "religious" men are like without the transforming power of God within (when the Sanhedrin send Jesus to His death) before he accepts the necessity of what Jesus is saying.

Psalm 104v1-24

Once again we join in this tremendous praise of God. There is tremendous contentment here. We need more of that!

Proverbs 14 v20-21

The dangers of fair weather friends and the sin of contempt. (Kidner's commentary)

May 4th

Judges 19v1-20v48

Another illustration of times (even of our times?) when people do whatever seems right to them.

We read of the bought concubine, who is unhappy and runs away. We see the spiritual and moral state of pagan Jerusalem (remember these are in the days long before David conquers it) which is so bad that they avoid it at night time. Looking for safety, they make their way to a village belonging to the Benjamites, supposedly people of the LORD, but instead it has a gang of sexual perverts who want to abuse any stranger (brings back memories of Sodom!)

Then we have the callousness with which the girl is shoved out to be repeatedly raped all night, literally until she dies of the abuse.

As she is lying dead the next morning, with her hands digging into the threshold of the door, her "husband" tries to order her up. Her body is thrown over a donkey, and then in a very macabre fashion cut up the next day and sent with a message to every tribe. There is also the pride of the Benjamites (blood is thicker than water?) who tried to protect the gang and to face down the rest of the Israelites. Soon we have a war that virtually wipes out the entire tribe of Benjamin until only 600 men are left – women, children, even cattle slaughtered.

These are dark days. The Lord is "consulted" as to which tribe should lead the attack, and the Lord is "consulted" should the attack continue after substantial losses, but this is by means of lot using stones, not by prayer and intercession.

The man who cut up his concubine's body has to be one of the most unloving people we find in Scripture, but he lights a fire that ends in the almost total genocide of the tribe of Benjamin, and what was achieved in the brutal killings of every woman and child? They are very, very dark days.

John 3v23-4v3

Here we have the wrong kinds of loyalty. John came to prepare people for Jesus, but there are jealous disciples who resent the apparent growing popularity of Jesus. This apparent "success" also brings Jesus to the attention of the Pharisees.

Psalm 104 v25-35

The psalm writer continues to marvel at God's work.

Proverbs 14 v22-24

On verse 22, Kidner users the phrase "paid in their own coin."

May 5th

Judges 21v1-Ruth 1v22

The people of Israel build an altar and offer sacrifices, but what is their concept of God? What do they understand of real faith and trust in Him, or what He requires of our lives? Nothing!

Having virtually obliterated a whole tribe of Israel, under the oath that they would kill any who did not join in the attempted genocide, they now sit bemoaning the fact that there are only 600 Benjamite men left and they have vowed not to let them marry their own daughters.

Their solution? Wipe out the men, married women and young children of Jabesh-gilead who had failed to take part in the attempted genocide, and give the 400 young virgins they could find to the men of Benjamin. Still 200 short, they come up with the plan that the men of Benjamin should seize the young girls taking part in the dancing at the religious festival at Shiloh, and carry them off (more rape!) as a solution.

Yes, you should be shaking your head in despair – but have we not had the Holocaust, Biafra, Uganda, Rwanda, present day Zimbabwe and Sudan – I'm sure I've missed quite a few - to say nothing of what happened behind the Iron and Bamboo curtains in the post 2nd World War years?

We are in despair. What begins with a gang of sexual perverts surrounding a house in a supposedly safe area, followed by a callous "husband" who shoves his concubine out to be raped all night by the gang, leads to the almost annihilation of the tribe of Benjamin, which is then "put right" by massacring the people of Jabesh-gilead so that the survivors of Benjamin have new sexual (forced) partners by killing everybody except the young unmarried girls, followed by the capture and rape of the young girls dancing at Shiloh. Somehow, in their own bizarre way, the people tried to justify it all in terms of their very twisted understanding of God. Be scared, be very scared, when people make God in their own image, and do what seems right to them.

RUTH. We also start the story of Ruth. Ruth comes from the time of the Judges, so it is right that we already have a "flavour" of these evil times, but then we also need to see some good against the background of such utter evil and literal godlessness. The story has a bad start. A couple from Bethlehem abandon the territory which God gave them, and make their home in godless Moab. They had already given their sons pagan names, and after their father's death they find local wives. Sadly the sons die too, childless, leaving one embittered Naomi, who changes her name to Mara (bitter) returning to Bethlehem with devoted Ruth in tow – who nevertheless has more understanding of God and his ways, than the family she had married into! Ruth the Moabites will end up in the family tree of both David and Jesus, but we will get to that part of the story tomorrow. God is at work in the times of the Judges, and Ruth thankfully ends up with a very godly husband.

John 4 v4-42

Actually Jesus could have taken the longer route down the bank of the Jordan, but the only short route was through the land of Samaria. The Samaritan woman was shocked that He asked her for a drink. His discussion on living water led to a reaction from her not unlike that of Nicodemus. And like him she was capable of understanding what Jesus was saying. Like Nicodemus, she did not want to accept that the change would have to come from the power of God within her life. Which led Jesus to make the point that she was seemingly locked in an endless circle of unhappiness – having had five husbands, she had now progressed to the sixth man. She could not break free from the self destruction of her own life. She needed that power from above.

She tried to side step the discussion on her own life with a theological discussion on the Jews and the Samaritans! And when she brought up the subject of the promised Saviour, was shocked when Jesus revealed that He was Him!

Many from the village came out initially on the strength of her report, but believed for themselves, and not just because of her. First hand faith is essential!

Psalm 105 v1-15

We will find that this part of this psalm, the last couple of verses in the next, and a fair bit of Psalm 96 are also recorded in 1 Chronicles 16 when the ark is brought up into Jerusalem by David. There is a sweeping reminder of what God has done.

Proverbs 14 v25

Honesty is essential; as Kidner put it: "a man who trims the facts for you will trim them as easily against you..."

May 6th

Ruth 2v1-4v22

The whole concept of the Kinsman redeemer may be very foreign to us, but the idea was to prevent a childless family name from disappearing, and for land to remain with the family to whom it was first granted. A near relative of the dead husband was to father children by the childless widow, children who would take on the dead man's name and inherit his property.

Ruth has gone out, according to the provision made for the very poor, to pick up whatever the harvesters had left behind. The poor gleaned the fields after the harvesters had moved on. Ruth was very fortunate that she found herself working in the field of Boaz, a very godly man who assured that she, as a foreign woman, was not molested. Unknown to Ruth at this point, was that Boaz was also a potential kinsman redeemer. He of course knew all about her as the Moabitess who had come back with Naomi, and not only fed her, but even instructed his workers to deliberately drop grain for her. Throughout the barley harvest Ruth worked behind his workers.

We may laugh at how Ruth went about asking Boaz to fulfil the role of Kinsman Redeemer, but we see how a man of fine character went about doing everything right – and as the story of Ruth draws to an end, we see how Boaz and Ruth have a place in the family tree of David – and Jesus.

The story of Ruth is such a wholesome one, with people of genuine faith and utter decency that it helps to balance that terrible picture we have of these times from the Book of Judges.

John 4 v43-54 Faith to take Jesus at His word – and to then turn for home, believing that His word is enough.

Psalm 105 v16-38 The reminder of what God has already done continues.

Proverbs 14 v26-27

One translation uses "reverence" rather than fear – real faith has a marked effect.

May 7th

1 Samuel 1v1-2v21

We are still in the times of the Judges, and we continue to be alarmed by what we find even in the place of worship at Shiloh.

There is the unhappiness of Elkanah's home, with competing wives and one of them taunting the other about her childlessness. There is also the terrible picture of the priest Eli who can't even recognise silent prayer as prayer, and assumes it is drunkenness. When was the last time he witnessed intense personal prayer? And there is the appalling behaviour of Eli's sons, made all the more appalling because they are priests in their own right.

John 5 v1-23

To properly understand this story, you need to realise this is not a Jewish place of healing, but a pagan one, with pagan beliefs, right in Jerusalem. The remains of a pagan temple can be seen today. The often quoted "verse" that "God helps those who help themselves" is not from the Bible, but the pagan theology of Bethesda was very much that the first person to push, shove or throw aside others to get into the waters first was the one that would be healed. No wonder that one man had lain there for 38 years as others helped themselves, and no one helped him.

Jesus intervened in this dark and pagan place and directly healed the man, who promptly got into trouble with the Jewish authorities for carrying his mat, leading to Jesus then being harassed as a Sabbath breaker, and then to even further anger as Jesus spoke of God as His Father.

Psalm 105v39-45

The recall of God's past goodness ends with the people entering the promised land. Sometimes we do need to rehearse over what God has done in our past, so that we understand and trust Him into the future.

Proverbs 14v28-29. Verse 28, apart from the fact that it states the political obvious, may continue to puzzle you. Derek Kidner gives some insight that might help: "It is a reminder that solitary splendour is self-extinguishing. The true leader glories in the vigour of his followers." Well, I hope that helps a little!

V29, however, can be taken at face value as advice to live peaceably.

May 8th

1st Samuel 2v22-4v22

We have already been introduced to the personal greed of Eli's sons, now we see them as sexual predators stalking the tabernacle. A prophet has already spoken to

Eli, but eventually God's word of condemnation has to come through young Samuel. Incidentally, Samuel was carrying out what should have been the duty of a priest, sleeping in the temple near the ark, ready to hear if indeed God did gave a message. Nobody took the idea of God speaking seriously, or they would not have left the task to a young lad who was not even of a priestly line. God, however did speak, and one of the consequences of His judgement was that the ark of the covenant passed into pagan hands when Israel was defeated, Hophni and Phinehas killed, and Eli himself died as a result of breaking his neck when he fell with the shock. Even Phinehas's long suffering wife died in childbirth, giving her child a terrible name indicating that God's glory had departed. God's judgment had indeed come, not without warning, and not without time to repent and to make amends. God's tabernacle was in a sorry moral and spiritual state.

John 5 v24-47

The Pharisees and others knew all about the miracles. The stumbling block was refusing to hear what these events told them, and indeed what John had already told them of Jesus.

Psalm 106v1-12

Again we are reminded of the people's past dealings with God. This time though we are reminded of the fickleness of the people.

Proverbs 14v30-31

Many otherwise godly and hard working Christian people need to heed verse 30. Some need to be told to relax, and some need to be told to watch that competitive streak that disguises itself under "spiritual" zeal.

The following verse reminds us of what we should already know, but sometimes it needs to be said again.

May 9th

1st Samuel 5 v1-7v17

The Philistines, or sea peoples, were people who had travelled from Asia Minor via Crete. They were relatively recent arrivals to the shores of Canaan. (Ever been to any of the ruins / museums in Crete during a summer holiday to that island?)

Having arrived on the shores of Canaan, they appear to have absorbed the local language and probably absorbed local religions as well. They were iron age people, bringing weapons which were very advanced compared to bronze.

The Ark is taken as a captured "prize" into the temple of the god Dagon. This temple was in Ashdod, and not to be confused with another Dagon temple at Gaza where Samson would die. The first morning the idol of Dagon was lying prostrate before the ark; the second morning it was lying broken, again before the Ark. Then God sent bubonic plague. Eventually the Philistines agreed to send the Ark back, with gifts for a guilt offering, gold models of tumours and rats!

Having said that, the Philistines were concerned that they did not fall as victims to mere superstition, so they devised a means to see if it was just a coincidence that the plague etc happened while they had the Ark. However, the two cows deprived of their calves, pulled the ark along the road right into Israelite territory.

The irony is that while the Philistines were convinced of the power of God, the Lord struck down 70 Israelite men who had treated the Ark with disrespect.

It was at Mizpah that Samuel became the last of the "judges" having called the people to return to the Lord. The worship of Baal and Ashtaroth was already strong amongst the Israelites, and not just a feature of later generations. They had only too readily adopted many of the customs and gods of the land. Sadly, many of the "returns" to the Lord which we read about in the Old Testament were more to do with strong individual leaders than real conversions.

A successful battle against the Philistines kept them in check for the remainder of Samuel's life. We will read much more about them during the lifetimes of Saul and David.

John 6 v1-21

The feeding of the 5,000 was a very Jewish event, with pilgrims gathering before they travelled up in huge crowds to Jerusalem for the Passover. Look back to earlier comments when we were reading Matthew's accounts of both the 5,000 and the 4,000 in January.

When tested by Jesus, Philip's answer is that the cost will be too much; Peter's answer is that all they have is a young lad's lunch. Realistic answers yes, from a very human perspective, but also very defeatist. Probably Peter intended to use the young lad's lunch as a demonstration of how hopeless and pointless the situation was. When the people realise what Jesus is able to do, they are ready to make Him their King *by force,* such is the impact of the miracle upon the people. However, it is a "popularity" which is not from listening and living by what Jesus has been saying. Such is the emotion of the crowd that Jesus has to separate from the disciples and to take to the hills, quite literally. As we shall read tomorrow, watchful eyes spotted the disciples sailing off on their own, and could not figure out how Jesus had made it back to Capernaum. Meanwhile the disciples had the terrifying experience of the storm, followed by the terrifying experience of seeing Jesus walking on the water.

Those who were fishermen were particularly shaken by anything which showed Jesus' power over their world of fishing, boats and water.

Psalm 106 v13-31

We continue to be reminded of just how much of the story of Old Testament Israel was a story of whinging and whining and losing out on what God had for them. These are mindsets difficult to break in any Christian community or congregation, but with hindsight people will look back and realise what could have been. An entire generation, with two exceptions, perished in the wilderness following the failure to trust God and to enter the Promised Land during the lifetime of Moses.

Proverbs 14 v32-33

V32 Even in death the Righteous have a Refuge. As Job said, "I know that my Redeemer lives..."

Some minor differences in ancient versions of verse 33: The Greek (Septuagint) and Syriac translations tell us that "in the hearts of fools she [Wisdom] is not known. However, the Hebrew texts tell us that "even amongst fools she lets herself be known" (NIV) or as the Living Bible puts the entire verse "Wisdom is enshrine in the hearts of men of common sense, but it must shout loudly before fools will hear it."

Either way, you get the message!

May 10th

1 Samuel 8v1-9v27

Ironically, as a young lad Samuel had been used by God to speak to Eli about the disgraceful behaviour of Eli's sons as priests. Now it is Samuel's family who are behaving so badly that leaders of the nation have to come and confront Samuel.

Samuel though is upset at the request for a King, not because of the hurt caused by his own sons, but because he genuinely was concerned about the even greater dangers that the trappings of monarchy would bring. And monarchy has often used, abused and shaped religion for its own purposes, as British history will illustrate! Separating Religion and State led to Scottish history being particularly complex and bloody, with the whole issue of covenants being about drawing the line between what is right and what is improper territory for a King to be involved in, and also what duty the King owes to God. We will see how in the later periods of the Old Testament the demarcation has to be kept between the duties of the Aaronic priesthood, and the Kings and Princes who wanted to take the priestly role upon themselves. Samuel did not need to know the struggles of future Scottish Presbyterianism to realise what was going on in the neighbouring pagan states of his time. Religion was used to authenticate the rule of particular families, and Samuel knew enough from the history of Egypt as to how rulers take divinity upon themselves. Israel was supposed to be a theocracy in the proper sense – God as King.

From the perspective of the people, monarchy was to bring national unity rather than at times a very loosely held together tribal alliance. Humanly speaking, the tribes often went their own ways, and it was always difficult to muster armies and to bring the people of Israel together against common foes. Tribal loyalties were a hindrance to national unity. Standing armies, taxation, and even royal exploitation, was seem as a better option by many of the people.

God told Samuel to concede to the request.

Saul is God's first choice; that is confirmed even before Saul's tribe, then family, and then Saul himself is chosen by sacred lot in tomorrow's reading (how things were done in Old Testament days, before the coming of the Holy Spirit at Pentecost.) There will be many disappointments with their first king.

John 6v22-46

These people had wanted to "own" Jesus for their particular purposes. Those who sailed over the Sea of Galilee were curious about how Jesus made it home to Capernaum, for they had kept a careful watch upon the disciples. They are not interested in Jesus' true mission, nor particularly in his teaching; it's rather ironic that those who have experienced the feeding of the 5,000 have the utter cheek to demand further miracles as proof that Jesus is the Messiah. When Jesus talks about bread from heaven, they still have free lunches on their agenda, and are actually quite hostile when Jesus tries to spiritualise the conversation. Jesus was using concepts they should have understood; the point is that they didn't want to know. It is a king for the here and now, dispensing free lunches that they want. Interesting trends to reflect on, when taken together with our reading from 1st Samuel.

Psalm 106v32-48

Israel continued to "go native" taking the customs and gods of pagan Canaan.

Proverbs 14 v34-35

Present day UK has very serious problems. It has problems which in some areas of morality relegates the nation to the bottom of the heap in Europe.

May 11th

1 Samuel 10v1-11v15

I have heard some bad preaching on this passage – preaching that suggests Saul was chosen by the people, David was chosen by God. After reading today's passage, you realise just how much Saul was God's choice. Indeed there are signs given that by Old Testament standards are exceptional. All of this brings home to us deep sorrow that when things do go wrong, they go wrong badly. However, we cannot explain them away by suggesting that Saul was not called by God in the first place –there are clear signs – two men by Rachel's tomb (just outside Bethlehem, to this day) who inform Saul that the missing donkeys have been found, three men at Tabor on their way to worship (Samuel even describes in detail what they will be carrying), a band of prophets (Samuel describes their instruments and what they are doing) and finally, Saul himself will experience the Holy Spirit coming upon him, and will prophesy himself.

When Samuel calls the tribes together at Mizpah, Saul is eventually chosen by the sacred lot. They find him hiding among the baggage. One of the lovely touches is the band of Godly men who accompany Saul.

An encouraging success for the new king (who happens to be at home ploughing his father's fields when the news of the Ammonite siege of Jabesh-gilead breaks) is the decisive victory over the Ammonite army. This is then followed by a proper coronation service for Saul.

John 6 v47-71

In the aftermath of the feeding of the 5,000 (and the barbed comments of those who would have made Him King for all the wrong reasons) Jesus continues to shift the conversation from literal bread, to how He is the "living bread" and how they will need to take his flesh and blood.

The concepts were not beyond them. Jesus was not saying things that were impossible for them to understand. It was clear that he was teaching that they needed to move from an obsession with what they were going to eat and drink, to drawing spiritual nourishment from Him. Food and drink were needed for life, but eternal life would come from Him. Those who partake of Him would live because of Him. Jesus then goes on to speak to His own disciples about how they will see Him return to heaven, and how the Holy Spirit gives eternal life.

Ultimately people find this hard, because they are not willing to think it all through. Would-be disciples, who have their own agendas for a prophet who can feed thousands, soon desert.

That of course is the terrible irony that the feeding of the 5,000 leads ultimately to many turning away.

Psalm 107 v1-43

Perhaps best known (and often used) for its passage about sailors, but the psalm basically reminds us again and again of situations in which those who have foolishly turned away from God do cry out in their despair and find that He does rescue them.

Proverbs 15v1-3

A range of things are commented on here – the constructiveness of a gentle answer, the difference that a responsible utterance makes, and the realisation that God's eyes are on us.

May 12th

1 Samuel 12v1-13v23

In the opening verses of the reading, is Samuel still hurting from the realisation of just how much harm his sons have done to his own ministry?

Samuel recites some of the things that God has done in their lives, and reminds them that while God has acceded to their request for a King, they are not to forget the Lord.

Unfortunately things now go wrong in the second year of Saul's reign. Impatient to start the battle with the Philistines before any more troops slipped away out of fear, Saul takes the priestly role upon himself and carries out the sacrifice. This brings the judgment that the ever lasting dynasty will be given to another line. As we will see tomorrow, God will give victory to the Israelites, but there will be more stupidity and false spirituality out of Saul, who hinders his men's success with a stupid oath that makes men fight on empty stomachs.

John 7 v1-30

His own family who did not as yet believe in Him try to give Him PR advice on how to handle the crowds!

When Jesus does go up to Jerusalem, it is to confront the Jewish authorities through His preaching.

Psalm 108v1-13

What we have here are some verses re-arranged – verses 7-11 from Psalm 57, and verses 5-12 from Psalm 60 have been put together to form this new psalm. There had been particularly stressful situations behind the writing of psalms 57 and 60, but now these words are taken and put together in a psalm which reflects only the encouragement and the hope which David had work through in the other situations.

Taken as a new work, psalm 108 speaks to people facing challenges with God's praise upon their lips, and with a reminder of His loving kindness in their hearts.

Proverbs 15 v4

Using the tongue constructively.

May 13th

1 Samuel 14 v1-52

Saul is already messing up as King, but our reading today shows something of the character of his Son Jonathan, both in terms of bravery and personal faith.

God gives Saul a wonderful opportunity to put a complete end to Philistine domination, but Saul puts his troops under an oath / curse not to eat anything until the evening. The end result is weary troops eating raw freshly killed meat. Then there is the incident in which the troops have to rescue Jonathan from a death sentence for having eaten some honey (he was innocently unaware of the oath/curse) and in so doing the troops force Saul to break another oath made in God's name.

What we are to make of the people's understanding of God in the midst of all of this is another matter. And although the chapter portrays Saul as successful, how much greater and more permanent that success would have been if properly fed troops had been able to get on with the job of breaking the Philistine threat for good. Saul's theology is at best rather trashy. We begin to realise the immense impact that the Psalmist David (the next King) clearly has on the understanding of God by his people. It is at times difficult to reconcile the very different views of God being held during the two very different reigns.

John 7 v31-53

The crowds, the temple authorities, the Pharisees are all ignorant of the fact that Jesus was born in Bethlehem. They ridicule the crowds for their belief in Jesus, and even mock Nicodemus when he objects to the way that Jesus appears to be tried already in His absence.

Psalm 109v1-31

Some Christians choke on this psalm as David asks God to bring about these horrible things to those who seek to harm him. More and more of the character of God is being revealed as we come closer to the New Testament. I've already commented on the fact that David made a major impact on his people's understanding of God, but sometimes we realise that David himself is writing something like a thousand years before Calvary. There are positive points though we can make about what David is saying; our God is concerned with justice. We live in a day and age that will buy "peace" at the cost of justice.

There is a short section, pages 25-30 in Derek Kidner's commentary on the Psalms (Tyndale series, published by IVP) – Volume 1 (Psalms 1-72) which deals with such cries for vengeance throughout the psalms. Anyone who is having a real hang up about some of the things being said here will get a lot of help from that article.

I'll quote a couple of sentences from it:

"...it is not open to us to renounce or ignore the psalmists, part of whose function...was to make articulate the cry of 'all the righteous blood shed on earth' (to borrow our Lord's phrase). But equally it is not open to us simply to occupy the ground on which they stood. Between our day and theirs, our calling and theirs, stands the cross. We are ministers of reconciliation, and this is a day of good tidings."

Proverbs 15v5-7

More sanctified common sense. Derek Kidner's commentary on the Psalms looks at these 3 verses under three headings: Impatience of criticism, What are you storing up? and What are you spreading? Those three headings are food for thought on their own!

May 14th

1 Samuel 15 v1-16v23

Saul's obedience of God is only partial. The Amalekites were constant and deadly enemies of the Israelites, but instead of following the explicit directions he had been given, Saul's priority was more of taking cattle and sheep as loot. The Amalekite King, Agag, was confident enough to believe that he would be spared. It was Samuel who killed him. The Amalekite problem will return, with deadly potential to wipe out the people of Israel once and for all – see the Book of Esther, where Haman the Agagite almost succeeded in doing what Adolf Hitler also tried – the complete genocide of the Jews.

Although Saul will continue for many years as King – quite a long reign actually – God already has his eye on young David. It is rather ironic that David, after his anointing by Samuel, becomes the harpist who plays to calm the dark and troubled mind of Saul.

John 8 v1-20

There are many questions we would like to ask concerning the story. How much did the Pharisees and other leaders rig the whole thing? Was this a known case of ongoing adultery to which they had turned a blind eye, until it gave them something to use? Where is the man? – well there had to be one, in this story!!! And since it is most likely that she was an adulterous wife, where is the aggrieved husband, the second man who ought to be in the story?

The whole thing stinks of being a set up. Of course the woman's sin is real, but anyone with a little street sense would recognise that there is a whole lot more going on here, when neither the hurt husband, or the adulterous man are brought along. Jesus recognised, correctly, that it was a trap. We would love to know what Jesus was actually writing in the dust – was it directly relevant, revealing stuff, or something else, totally unrelated.

Of course, when the aggrieved husband is not there to bring his case, and Jesus refuses to take the trap, and remains calm and unemotional, the crowd begin to melt away, knowing themselves that nothing has been done in the right and proper way.

Briefly, let this be a warning to very "righteous" Christians how others sometimes try to exploit our indignation and our strong sense of morality to either trap us by getting us to appear to go "over the top" (which is what they were trying here) or who want us to hurt others (like the woman) for some other dark motive which has nothing to do with justice, even though what she had done was clearly wrong. History is full of emotionally charged crowds, and individuals who respond to the cries of the pack. Stand out from that, think, pray, and really seek God when others are trying to control and manipulate you through exploiting your Christian indignation. Be street wised enough, to recognise that all is not what it seems...

HOWEVER, the woman's sin was real, and Jesus does deal with it, but not the way the crowd wanted. A face to face meeting with the Son of God who tells you to "Go and sin no more" is not to be taken lightly – ever.

Psalm 110 v1-7

We find reference to this psalm in Mark 12 verse 36 and also in Acts 2 v33-35. Suddenly we realise, as Jesus pointed out, that for King David to refer to one of his own descendents as "My Lord" that descendent had to be someone very special, even more important than David. Jesus was of Davidic descent – but He is also the Son of God. How else do we explain the words of this psalm?

Proverbs 15 v8-10

God is disgusted at the insincere worshipper who sees worship, as the pagan nations often did, as merely a way of bending the god or gods to man's way of thinking, making sacrifice into nothing more than bribery. God is not bought, and there is discipline for those who leave his ways, and judgement for those who will not live according to His ways.

May 15th

1 Samuel 17v1-18v4a

The familiar story of Goliath; Saul does not seem to recognise the young shepherd boy as his harpist. There are probably those who suggest that yesterday's and today's readings are not in chronological sequence (and elsewhere I do point out that the Gospel writers did not share our modern obsession with chronology) but I prefer to see the whole issue of how David is introduced "twice" to Saul as something that is easily explained. Davis's first meeting as a harpist was when Saul was in deep depression and though he was playing away in the background, the introduction was no more than the polite pleasantries that our own royal family or other dignitaries might go through. Servants, performers and other staff are there to function with Kings/prime ministers/presidents oblivious to their presence. The slaying of Goliath, however, does bring David in (for real) into the inner circles at the palace, and is the beginning of his friendship with Jonathan. It also marks him out as someone that the disturbed and vulnerable-to-jealousy Saul will watch, carefully. Jonathan, however, recognises a truly honest and sincere young lad who will be a true friend.

John 8 v21-31

The people understood that Jesus was in some sense going to go away, and they seemed to have grasped something about His coming death. As we will see from His trial, and the events of the first Easter, the enemies of Jesus had grasped more than His disciples. It is also a complex time (v31) in which some are coming to a real faith.

Psalm 111v1-10

First of all, we have 3 hallelujah (praise the LORD) psalms (111-113)

Secondly, both 111 and 112 are "acrostics" in which lines, verses or groups of verses – see Psalm 119 for the best known example – work their way through the Hebrew alphabet. In these 2 cases, Psalms 111 and 112 each have 22 lines in the Hebrew original, one each for the letters of the Hebrew alphabet.

Thirdly, Psalms 111 and 112 are a cleverly constructed pair. As Derek Kidner puts it in his commentary, Psalm 111 tells us of God, and the next psalm tells us of the man of God. Something to bear in mind as you look more closely today and tomorrow.

Proverbs 15 v11. A warning to those who imagine that they can exclude God from knowing their thoughts.

May 16th

1 Samuel 18 v4b-19v24

Saul's jealousy and fear of David becomes obsessive. Michal's love for David was genuine, but she will be used callously by Saul, who hopes to tempt David to his death.

John 8v31-59

The debate between the Jewish leadership and Jesus continues. Their claim is that they are the true spiritual descendants of Abraham. Jesus suggests that if they were real descendants of Abraham they would not be trying to kill Him. It is obvious that Jesus claims that God is His Father. Jesus claims to have existed even before Abraham. It is His use of the "I AM" phrase that angers them the most – a direct claim to being divine.

Psalm 112 v1-10

An Old Testament picture of the man of God and his character. Godliness is a joy, not a burden. Note that this man's goodness goes out to others.

Proverbs 15v12-14

Contrasting hearts. Kidner sums up verse 14 with the heading: "Seeker and trifler."

May 17th

1Samuel 20v1-21v15

The irony is that for all of Saul's fear of David, David and Jonathan were absolutely genuine friends who would not have raised a finger against each other. The threat to Saul's rule, and his hope of a dynasty to follow, came not from David, but from Saul's own disobedience of God. David would keep his word to Jonathan, caring for the disabled son of Jonathan, Mephibosheth (2 Samuel 9.) Of course Saul suspected that Jonathan would have given way to David.

Forced to flee, David got some of the bread from the altar and collected the sword of Goliath. Out of desperation, David fled to King Achish of Gath. This of course was a dreadful mistake, and David had to fake insanity to get away from the Philistine stronghold.

John 9 v1-41

We cringe as we listen to the disciples having this debate over the man born blind. Of course that should be a warning to Christians in our times, to realise the dangers of repeating things that may be held by those all around us, but which are nevertheless so contrary to the heart of Christ. Had the time spent with Jesus already not helped them to see beyond such terrible attitudes?

Of course the man was well known, and no one doubted that his disability was genuine. The Jewish leaders even brought in the man's parents to confirm his identity. This was not a miracle that the authorities could easily deny, which meant that they had to find a way of discrediting Jesus. Somehow or other, in their determination to reject the idea that Jesus got His power from God, they would have to make out that Jesus got His power from the Devil. The healed man gives them common sense answers which frustrate their attempts to portray Jesus as evil, and found himself evicted from the Synagogue – the first of many who would be cast out.

In his discussion with the Pharisees afterwards, Jesus pointed out that since they claimed they were not blind, their guilt remained. And that is something which keeps coming through – these people had all the evidence, but in refusing to accept who Jesus is, they make every attempt to stand truth on its head.

Psalms 113 & 114

We are now into a group of psalms used in the Passover (actually mentioned in Psalm 114). In Psalm 113 God lifts the down trodden. Psalms 113 and 114 are sung before the Passover meal, and the next four psalms after it. These are the last psalms that Jesus and the disciples sang together before Calvary. Reflect on that over the next few days.

Proverbs 15v15-17

Largely sanctified common sense – "better a meal of vegetables where there is love than a fattened calf with hatred" – but a serious spiritual point too – "Better a little with the fear of the LORD than great wealth with turmoil."

May 18th

1 Samuel 22v1-23v29

Family members, and then others, begin to gather around David. Before very long, David is playing the role of a real life Robin Hood. Sadly, Doeg the Edomite reports Ahimelech for having fed David the temple bread, resulting in Saul ordering the butchery of every person and animal in the priestly city of Nob. When his own men refuse to butcher the priests, Doeg is only too willing to oblige.

Jonathan confirms to David that he will stand by David as the next King. Saul is so distracted in his hunt for David that he leaves the country open to Philistine attack. Due to the killings at Nob, David realises that staying with other people is not safe – either they will betray him, or pay dearly for having helped him. David moves down to the caves above Ein Gedi at the Dead Sea.

John 10 v1-22

Looking after sheep in Bible times was very different from methods today. There were no dogs for a start (dogs were seen as unclean animals) and shepherds did literally walk in front of their sheep, rather than driving them. It really is fascinating to watch a shepherd on his (or her) own, walking along with the sheep in a long line faithfully following. Due to the wild animals, sheep were often placed inside stone walled enclosures at night, with the shepherd literally sleeping in the gateway. Jesus was the gate and the shepherd. Jesus was making accurate comparisons between the actual methods of the day and his own commitment to be the good shepherd.

Psalm 115

We continue our reading of psalms used in the Passover meal. There are those who, when they read of the taunts of the heathen, place the origins of this psalm in the difficult days of the exile in Babylon.

Proverbs 15v18-19

Kidner, on verse 18 comments: “the point here is that quarrels depend on people far more than on subject matter.” Verse 19 reminds us that there is a fair degree of dishonesty in laziness.

May 19th

1 Samuel 24 v1-25v44

Saul’s jealousy of David, his suspicion that David will eventually succeed him as King (with Jonathan’s connivance) is such an obsession that on his immediate return from battling the Philistines he pursues David down to the wilderness area at the Dead Sea. Ironically, as Saul relieves himself in a cave, he has no idea that David and his men are hiding there in the dark. David refuses to take Saul’s life; if God has promised him this Kingdom, it will not be through David slaughtering Saul. Saul's words to David in the immediate aftermath are hollow; there was a real opportunity to be reconciled when David demonstrated how he had been capable of taking Saul's life and had refused to do so – Saul soon found another way to harm David – see the last two verses of today's reading. Saul's daughter – David's wife – is forced by Saul into another marriage. This may explain David's many shallow marriages for neither David or Michal ever recovered from what Saul did to them. The story of Nabal and Abigail is from that time when (as I commented yesterday) David played for real a "Robin Hood" type of existence. To some present day critics it may look like a protection racket, but the protection that David gave to vulnerable groups like Nabal's shepherds was real. "Nabal" or fool may be a nickname based on the real Hebrew name of Nadab; whatever the story behind the name, "Nabal" lived up to it. Abigail and her servants were wise enough to recognise that David was very much the next king-in-waiting. Not much grief for first husband though!

John 10 v22-42

This is the Jewish festival of Hanukah or Chanukah, remembering events between the times of the Old and New Testaments, when the Jewish temple had been rededicated and the Jewish state had been able to throw off foreign and extremely cruel oppression – celebrated close to our Christmas. Ironically we are more certain of the correct date for Hanukah than we will ever be of the right date for Christmas! (Hanukah refers to events in December 164 BC)

The Jewish authorities continue to demand answers to questions, answers which only lead to attempts to arrest Jesus or to stone him. For a period Jesus returns to Bethany beyond the Jordan – a place in present day Jordan opposite Qumran – where John's early ministry had taken place.

Some, however, do come to the conclusion that Jesus is indeed the Messiah.

Psalm 116v1-19

A very public (see verses 18,19) thanksgiving to God from someone who has real cause to give God thanks.

Proverbs 15v20-21.

What children can do to their parents! Verse 21 contrasts the playboy with the man that walks uprightly.

May 20th

1 Samuel 26v1-28v25

Saul is back to old form, and for a second time David spares his life. David is wise enough to move away, but travels to Gath, to work for the Philistine ruler there. However, under pretence of attacking Saul's territory, he actually raids groups that are enemies of the people back home (enemies of both the Philistines and the people of Judah.)

Saul's use of a medium just before his own death shows us the extent to which any credible faith in the one true God has gone. The story is most alarming, the only one of its kind in the Bible. Far from giving credibility to "mediums" we should note the horror of this woman when she realises that this really is Samuel – clearly this was not what she had expected. This was something beyond her control.

The King and his men eat the meal provided by the medium. Saul may well have seen the irony of it all – the overtones of a covenant with a medium, rather than a covenant with the true God. Saul departs to his death.

John 11v1-53

This family of two unmarried sisters and their brother were clearly very supportive of Jesus and had no hesitation in sending for him when Lazarus became ill. Jesus allowed Lazarus to die, and then travelled to the home. The disciples were thoroughly confused as to what Jesus was doing. (v16)

It is interesting that on this occasion Mary and Martha have reversed their usual roles. Was Mary, the one who previously stopped everything to listen to Jesus, disappointed that He in return had not dropped all to come and heal her brother? Whatever, it is Martha who comes out to meet Him, and in the conversation Jesus draws out faith in both the coming resurrection, and faith in Jesus Himself as both the Messiah and the Son of God. The resurrection of Lazarus, within walking distance of Jerusalem, cannot be dismissed as a rumour. The event comes as a major shock to the Jewish authorities who appear to dread the coming of a real Messiah out of fear of what will come from a popular uprising against the Romans. They share the common – and wrong – assumption as to what the Messiah was coming to do. Little did Caiaphas realise was the even deeper truth behind his words about letting one man die for the people.

Psalm 117v1-2

A call back to basics. Man's chief end is to glorify God and to enjoy him for ever. (Shorter Catechism question 1)

Proverbs 15v22-23

Sometimes in life there will be different sides of a case presented and not everybody is going to agree on the ultimate course of action – but at least you have been made aware, or have made yourself aware, of the different positions take on the matter, whatever it may be. However, it is a particularly sad thing if advice has been available, and the whole thing has blown up in our faces, because of our ignorance – or even worse – deliberate self inflicted ignorance, of advice that was out there all the time.

May 21st

1 Samuel 29 v1-31v13

Thankfully the Philistines themselves get rid of David, so that he plays no part in the defeat of Israel. Meanwhile David and his men discover the Amalekite raid on their own people and successfully free the captives. David wisely uses the "loot" to pay back cities that have supported him in the past. These events, however, are quickly overtaken with the death of Saul and his sons, following the defeat of Israel by the Philistines.

John 11v54-12v19

The tension is obvious, and Mary is acutely aware of what is ahead, even if the disciples are not. There is a telling comment on Judas Iscariot.

Lazarus has become such a talking point (following his resurrection) that the chief priests plan to kill him too.

We then have John's account of Palm Sunday.

Psalm 118v1-18

This is the final psalm of the small group that are sung at Passover. Remember the comment back on May 17th?

Proverbs 15 v24-26

The destiny of the wise man who listens to the Lord leads away from destruction.

The "proud" who are destroyed are contrasted with widows who are possibly their victims in exploitation.

Kidner in his commentary sums up verse 26 in the heading "troublemaking and peacemaking." It is obvious which the Lord prefers.

May 22nd

2 Samuel 1v1-2v11

This is a very foolish Amalekite who seeks to ingratiate himself with ("get in with") David. Whether or not the Amalekite had a hand in helping to finish off a badly wounded Saul, David refuses to take any pleasure in Saul's death, having on more than one occasion refused to kill Saul himself. Not only had David lost his great friend Jonathan, he had always taken seriously the fact that Saul continued to be "God's anointed" and David would not force God's timing. God's people had also suffered a humiliating defeat. If the Amalekite expected to be rewarded for bringing the trappings of Kingship to David, he foolishly bragged about his part in it all.

Hebron becomes David's first capital. Jerusalem is still a pagan city. David though is initially king only of his own tribe, while Saul's commander Abner sets up Saul's son Ish-bosheth as a king. Civil war was to follow.

John 12v20-50

Philip with a Greek name was an obvious choice for Greeks seeking to be introduced to Jesus.

Once more a voice from heaven speaks.

The idea that the Messiah will die – and somehow live forever, puzzles the crowd. Others believe but fear the Pharisees who continued the threat of excommunication which had already been applied to the man healed in chapter 9. Jesus speaks of Himself as the Light and calls upon the people to walk in that light while they still can.

Psalm 118v19-29

Verse 22 has particular significance for Christians as the stone rejected by the builders becomes the chief cornerstone. The parallels between Palm Sunday and the material in this part of the psalm are obvious.

Proverbs 15v27-28

The meaning of each line is obvious.

May 23rd

2 Samuel 2v12-3v39

A depressing and costly civil war continues. David, to be fair, has no choice – Abner was clearly the real power behind the puppet son of Saul that he had installed as king. However we see some of the personal cost in our reading.

We also read of the family life of David with all the seeds of division within a family that is actually several competing families of half brothers and half sisters thrown together.

Abner eventually negotiates his price of handing the kingdom over to David, after a row with Ish-bosheth over Abner sleeping with one of Saul's concubines. The price is that Abner is to be given the position of commander chief of David's forces – to which David adds his own demand that his first wife be taken off her new husband. Joab, brother of Aashel and the existing commander of David's forces then murders Abner. His burial was just a few yards away from the tombs of the Patriarchs in Hebron. These are dark chapters.

David wisely does everything to distance himself from all the treachery.

John 13v1-30

The Last Supper – the foot washing with Simon's protest, Jesus' expressed grief that one of the inner circle would betray him, and the favoured piece of bread dipped in the sauce given to Judas just before he went out to betray Jesus. John tells us that Satan entered Judas, but Judas was already deeply committed to the act of betrayal.

Psalm 119v1-16

Far from feeling the burden of God's Word, there is immense pleasure in walking by it.

Proverbs 15v29-30

God's "aloftness" is from sin.

Verse 30 speaks of heart warming things

May 24th

2 Samuel 4v1-6v23

The once great army of Israel is not much other than raiding bands.

David's reaction over the death of Ish-bosheth is consistent with how he reacted when the Amalekite took credit for killing or finishing off Saul. David will not be associated with treachery and murder.

David became King of all Israel and then captured Jerusalem (approx 1,000 BC) – his men climbed up through a vertical shaft leading down to the water.

David, with a united army behind him, begins to over throw the Philistine domination.

And he takes on more wives and concubines! His marriage to Michal (his first wife, retaken from her second husband) never recovers.

The bad experience over the first attempt to bring the Ark of the Covenant up to Jerusalem is a reminder to David of not being over familiar with important symbols of the Lord.

Jerusalem becomes both the political capital and the spiritual capital of the nation.

John 13 v31-14v14

Important teaching continues to be prioritised as the disciples are with Jesus for the "Last Supper" even though Judas has already departed.

Peter makes, and later regrets his rash promise that he will die for Jesus.

Meanwhile Jesus tells them of the home above – and on Thomas's prompting, explains how to get there. "I am the way, the Truth and the Life."

Psalm 119v17-35

The psalmist continues to take delight in God's Word.

Proverbs 15v31-32

Constructive criticism is not to be dismissed.

May 25th

2 Samuel 7v1-8v18

David is willing to build a splendid temple, but Nathan has to return and tell David that will be a task for the next king of David's line. However David's line is to continue into eternity. David's kingdom is also extensive in his own lifetime, with many surrounding nations subdued.

John 14v15-31

If you love me...

Jesus also teaches that He will live again.

He also brings important teaching about the Holy Spirit.

Psalm 119v36-52

God's Word continues to be central.

Proverbs 15 v33

Fear of the LORD (explained as "humility and reverence for the LORD" in the Living Bible) is crucial to have all our other thinking and understanding on a proper foundation.

May 26th

2 Samuel 9v1-11v27

David finds Jonathan's son Mephiboseth and keeps his promise to Jonathan.

David assumes that the new Ammonite king will continue his father's friendship. Instead David's messengers are sent back humiliated. Realising their mistake, the Ammonites hire many mercenaries.

The incident with Bathsheba is particularly sickening because now that David no longer leads his army and instead remains at home, he has the time on his hands that leads him into this sin. Now that David's rule is much more secure, he has dropped his spiritual guard. The whole deceit over Bathsheba, and the murder of her husband, has to be one of the low points of David's reign and spiritual life. The arrogance in which David imagines he can fool an entire nation that no one will spot how soon the birth was after his marriage to the widow ought to be a warning to all in leadership that their actions and behaviour is much more transparent than they imagine.

John 15v1-27

The teaching round the Last Supper table continues. Time is at a premium as Judas is out there betraying Jesus. Jesus takes one of the symbols of Israel as God's vine and applies it to Himself. Important teaching follows for the times ahead. Once more Jesus teaches about the work of the Holy Spirit in the days to come.

Psalm 119v53-70

Anger is expressed regarding those who have spurned God's laws either directly or in how they have tried to bring down the psalmist. This reading does of course contrast so sharply with what we have been reading of David's own behaviour over Bathsheba.

Proverbs 16v1-3

All our planning is subject to the Great Planner Himself. Schemers and control freaks need to be reminded of this. They also need to be reminded that God is not fooled by PR – He weighs up people's hearts.

May 27th

2 Samuel 12v1-31

Nathan the prophet confronts David. The death of the child is particularly hard hitting.

John 16v1-33

Jesus looks ahead to times when persecution will come and Jewish believers will be expelled from the synagogues.

The role of the Holy Spirit continues to be explained by Jesus.

Jesus also speaks of the grief to come and the joy of seeing Him again.

Psalm 119v71-80

Discipline from God is constructive.

Proverbs 16v4-5

Even the wicked will in due course be seen as having been part of God's plans in working out His purposes.

May 28th

2 Samuel 13v1-39

Another dark chapter in David's reign, and a direct consequence of the family life he had created. David's attitudes in all of this are obscure, partial and puzzling. He does not lead and guide his own family well.

John 17v1-26

Jesus prays for the disciples who no need to be kept safe in the days ahead.

Psalm 119v81-95

God's Laws remain his delight, but the psalmist has real enemies and there are real trials for the believer trying to be faithful.

Proverbs 16v6-7

V6 Genuine religion…fruits that befit repentance (Kidner's commentary.)

V7 God has the power when our ways are pleasing to Him.

May 29th

2 Samuel 14v1-15v22

Joab has of course seen how the prophet Nathan could turn David's heart with a tale with a moral behind it. Joab is no prophet, and a man of doubtful morals, who is simply manipulating David. Joab thinks he is doing the right thing. David perhaps needed to deal more directly with Absalom once he was allowed back. In the end, David has to flee his own city as Absalom leads a rebellion.

John 18v1-24

The actual betrayal, portrayed so vividly in the "Passion of the Christ." Part of the route from Gethsemane to the house of the High Priest can still be traced across the valley. Peter is a spontaneous but not consistent character. When he has time to think things through, fear takes hold, and the man who would have died for Jesus (flashing a sword around at the actual arrest) ends up swearing that he has nothing to do with Him.

Psalm 119v96-112

Determination to remain faithful.

Proverbs 16v8-9

Honesty and seeking God's leading.

May 30th

2 Samuel 15v23-16v23

David is thoroughly humiliated, but he also finds out who his true friends are.

Ziba turns out to be thoroughly dishonest and betrays the harmless Mephibosheth, knowing that David sees conspiracy on every corner, and sometimes with good reason.

Ahithophel's advice to Absalom to sleep with his father's wives so publicly - with a tent on the palace roof so that the whole population could see – was utterly despicable and Absalom was so ready to take the evil advice.

John 18v25-19v22

Peter's denials continue.

Pilate finds himself manipulated into crucifying an innocent man, and takes his own revenge by having the prisoner so obviously tortured and mistreated as a king before actually nailing the charge of being the King of the Jews above His head upon the cross. What petty revenge he exacted upon the Chief Priests.

Psalm 119v113-131

The pressures exerted by evil men continue.

Proverbs 16v10-11

God demands proper standards from the King and the business man alike.

May 31st

2 Samuel 17v1-29

Absalom is extremely vain, and appears to be able to attract people to him. But he is no leader, nor is he a strategist. Ahithophel soon realises what is going to happen and hangs himself.

John 19v23-42

Moving scenes from the cross. Jesus instructs John to take care of his mother. The Jewish leaders have a strange sense of what is holy and right, as they demand the breaking of the crucified men's legs to speed up their deaths before the Passover Sabbath. Jesus is however, already dead, and the Scripture holds – his bones are not broken.

Rather belatedly, Joseph and Nicodemus take their stand, though they are taking their stand when others have fled.

Psalm 119v132-155

"I have thoroughly tested your promises…" (v140) Here is no armchair Christian, but someone who has been out there and has trusted God through some very difficult times.

Proverbs 16v12-13

Just as Kings need to be established through righteousness, they also learn to value citizens who are also honest.

June 1st

2 Samuel 18v1-19v10a

David is unable to grasp some of the realities. Many men are prepared to die for him, his own son is determined to have him killed (having already raped a number of his own father's concubines in public, literally on the roof top) – and David pleads "deal gently with young Absalom…" This is not going to end with a father/son hug and all forgotten.

The whole problem has arisen because David never knew how to deal with the problems of his huge family of competing half brothers and sisters. David not having dealt with Amnon's sin led to Absalom's deep bitterness and David's inability to deal with all the subsequent wrong doing of Absalom.

Having said that, we see what a man of blood Joab was. He is the one who manipulated the situation to bring Absalom back in the first place, and does not hesitate to have Absalom killed when he is found hanging by his own hair.

David's subsequent grief over Absalom ignored what a courageous army had been prepared to do for David.

John 20v1-31

Resurrection joy mixed with inability to take it all in. Bear in mind that it was an extremely horrendous death in full public gaze. Thomas may be ridiculed by some, but he was concerned to have a reality check of all the talk which he was hearing. Thomas helps the faith of those who came later and who wanted to make sure.

Psalm 119v156-176

Faith is not held in isolation from the real world. The pressures are real. Nevertheless the psalmist knows to keep himself anchored daily in the Lord.

Proverbs 16v14-15

Though these verses may be taken as a warning to tread carefully with powerful people, they are also a warning about the abuse of power and authority and apply to many more than just literal kings.

June 2nd

2 Samuel 19v10b-20v13

David's official return and reinstatement brings all its problems too. There are decent people to be thanked and rewarded, but there is much dissatisfaction yet and another rebellion breaks out. Joab also takes the opportunity to murder his replacement as commander of the army.

John 21v1-25

An event which happened back at the start of the call of the disciples is virtually re-enacted by Jesus, and Jesus deals with the aftermath of Peter's denial, but all with the purpose of forgiving a genuinely sorry man, so that the disciples are reinstated in their call.

Psalm 120v1-7

This is the first of 15 psalms known as the "Songs of Ascent" – used by pilgrims on their way up to the Temple. The original circumstances in which the psalm was written are probably very different. The reference to two heathen groups and the problems they cause for godly people who strive daily to live according to their faith, was something which many of the pilgrims coming great distances from other lands in which they were a minority could identify with.

Proverbs 16v16-17

Obvious truths, so why do they have to be repeated?

June 3rd

2 Samuel 20v14-22v20

Joab deals with the traitor Sheba and leaves David unable to deal with Joab's own wrong doing – although on his deathbed David tells Solomon to have Joab killed, rather than letting him have the death of an old man (1 Kings 2v6). The story of how seven of the men of Saul's family (with the exception of Mephibosheth) are put to death to restore some sense of justice for what had happened to the Gibeonites is a difficult one. The Old Testament takes the concept of covenant most serious and a covenant between God's people and the Gibeonites went back to the days of Joshua.

Our reading closes with a beautiful psalm by David, but as we read through it, it clearly comes from earlier days in his reign, before the waters were very much clouded by David's own wrong doings, his failures within his own family, and the times in which he clearly lost control over people like Joab.

Over these last few days we have had our eyes opened to the very real failings of David. The inclusion of the psalm in this book brings our thoughts and focus back to happier times.

Acts 1v1-26

Acts is best seen as volume 2 of Luke's Gospel - Luke continues the story, as he knew it, from the ascension of Jesus. Due to his own journeys in the company of Paul the latter end of the book will come to dwell very much on Paul, but do not forget that while Paul was out working for the Lord, many others were out in the world spreading the Good News too – Thomas reached India! So Acts cannot tell the whole story of all that was being done for the Lord, but it will certainly help our understanding of many of Paul's epistles or letters. We will appreciate the insights into the early years of the Church in Jerusalem.

The selection of Matthias (by lot) to replace Judas Iscariot is the last time the Church will proceed by these Old Testament ways of doing things. Much will change after Pentecost.

Psalm 121v1-8

The hills might have seemed like a great place to hide, and some have even taken the reference to the hills as a reference to the temptation to look to the hill gods of the pagans – but Israel's hope is in the LORD Himself. Important reminders in times of great stress.

Proverbs 16v18

The wrong kind of pride brings its problems

June 4th

2 Samuel 22v21-23v23

The psalm continues with all its references to keeping God's laws, to having clean hands etc. A reminder of the past, when life may have been simpler, and David more focussed on the Lord. It was not without reason that the building of the temple was to be left until after David's own death. There was much in the latter part of his reign that leaves us disturbed.

Acts 2v1-47

Pentecost – the coming of the Holy Spirit in a new and dramatic way, and the explosion of evangelism that follows.

There are examples of the Holy Spirit coming upon people in the Old Testament, but now the Holy Spirit will be with every Christian, leading and guiding as Jesus promised in our readings from John's Gospel.

A huge crowd come to faith on that first day!

Psalm 122v1-9

A real sense of peace in being at worship in God's House.

Proverbs 16v19-20

Real happiness is often found away from the things that a materialistic world strives to get. "Blessed is he who trusts in the LORD."

June 5th

2 Samuel 23v24-24v25

The problem with the idea of having a national census was the self-sufficient pride that it could lead to; the King needed to trust in God, not statistics.

Acts 3v1-26

The healing of the well known beggar – known to be crippled from birth – has a very dramatic effect as a miracle that cannot be denied or disputed.

Psalm 123v1-4

Intensely personal as we focus our eyes on where they should be.

Proverbs 16v21-23

More wise words!

June 6th

1 Kings 1v1-53

The problems of old age!

And another conspiracy, this time on the part of Absalom's younger brother. And Joab is involved! Bathsheba has to jolt the aged David into action and Solomon is quickly installed on the throne, leaving the alternative coronation upstaged and in terror.

Acts 4v1-37

The boldness of Peter and John, in the aftermath of Pentecost, and the presence of the undeniably healed beggar, leaves the Sanhedrin wondering what to do.

Our reading ends with the story of lovely Barnabas, a generous soul in every way – but we will also see the difficulties in tomorrow's reading when others are jealous of the esteem in which Barnabas was held.

Psalm 124v1-8

If the Lord had not been on our side...a real sense of deliverance here.

Proverbs 16v24

Constructive words.

June 7th

1 Kings 2v1-3v2

Adonijah is very like his brother Absalom, and his desire to have Abishag, David's last wife is seen quite rightly as an attempt to regain some sense of legitimacy as the "rightful" successor. Adonijah should have known these things himself.

Solomon is therefore forced to execute Adonijah who clearly still has ambitions, and the priest Abiathar has to be removed from office, and Joab killed before any more plots and manipulations are hatched. Shime-i is spared but breaks his house arrest and also dies.

The alliance with Pharaoh or any other ruler often included the giving of daughters or sisters as brides to the other party, but here we have the beginnings of a long line of foreign wives who will import their pagan practices right into the heart of Jerusalem

Acts 5v1-42

The desire to look good, to be spiritual fakes – no one said they had to give the price of the field at all, but they wanted to look as good as Barnabas, and they wanted the adulation of being seen in a certain way... The sin is most serious for the damage it brings to a growing Church which has real spirituality and a marked sincerity.

The early Church had quite an impact, and the apostles are arrested and then delivered by an angel. Gamaliel's words are wise ones, but the truth is that the Gospel message is real and powerful and will not go away.

Psalm 125v1-5

Steady in the Lord.

Proverbs 16v25

Wisdom without God is flawed.

June 8th

1 Kings 3v3-4v34

Solomon asks for, and demonstrates great wisdom. His kingdom is also extensive. The bureaucracy of the kingdom also extends, and we will hear more of the forced labour later and then the actual criticisms regarding it when his son comes to reign.

Acts 6v1-15

More trouble, and the apostles have to appoint deacons so that they can get back to the primary task of the church, without abandoning the very real needs that exist. Rather ironically, it is one of these deacons that emerges as a striking and effective preacher – and becomes the first martyr.

Psalm 126v1-6

What utter joy it was when exiles were brought home again.

Proverbs 16v26-27

Hunger certainly focuses the mind. This is contrasted with the scoundrel who plots evil.

June 9th

1 Kings 5v1-6v38

Hiram proves to be a great friend and aid to Solomon, as huge amounts of timber are floated down the coast to Joppa (Jaffa.) The Temple is a magnificent building.

Acts 7v1-29

A very effective bit of preaching from Stephen.

Psalm 127v1-5

Unless the Lord… Important lessons here.

The psalmist (**Solomon**) does not mean to be insensitive to the childless; but perhaps those with children need to have attitudes changed and appreciate that the children are indeed a gift from God. We will need God's help to avoid the bad parenting we have already come across in the Old Testament!

Proverbs 16v28-30

Why do people do these things? The sinful urge that has to disturb peace.

June 10th

1 Kings 7 v1-51

The factual account of the elaborate building continues, but note the priority – the Temple first.

Acts 7 v30-50

Stephen touches on sensitive issues – the rejection of God's will and purposes that occurred so many times in the history of their nation.

Psalm 128v1-6

Make home life a blessing, not a battlefield!

Proverbs 16v31-33

Interesting comments on age, on self control and realising that God is in control. As Kidner puts it, "God, not chance, decides."

June 11th

1 Kings 8 v1-66

A tremendous day as the Temple is dedicated at last. The tabernacle has been around since the days of Moses, although we may wonder what exactly it was that

Eli and Samuel had served at in Shiloh – the tabernacle or a temple of sorts? (despite lots of diggings around Shiloh, nothing has been found yet.)

Anyway, whatever had been used to make do over the generations, the Temple was to be a fitting replacement for the tabernacle, and before his death David had been making tremendous preparations for what would be completed after his time.

There is a tremendous sense of what can be – if the people remain faithful to the LORD.

Acts 7 v51-8v13

They were deeply stung by Stephen's analysis of Old Testament history, but his vision of Jesus in heaven's glory was more than they could take. We assume that Pilate was absent from Jerusalem at this point, for the Jewish authorities ignore the rules and put Stephen to death himself – effectively doing to Stephen what they would have liked to have done to Jesus.

Paul / Saul is there at the stoning, and begins his own personal crusade against the followers of Jesus. Incidentally, Saul is his Jewish name, Paul is his Roman name, as a Roman citizen. He was not given a new name after his conversion, but did eventually switch to using his existing Roman name when working with non-Jews.

The dispersion of the Christians does lead to the Gospel being carried elsewhere – as in the case of Philip going to the Samaritans.

Psalm 129 v1-8

Some Christians find it difficult to cope with the tone of a psalm like this; be thankful you haven't been in the shoes of the psalmist, and see it as a blessing that you have never been where he has been.

On the positive side, note that Israel has survived, because of the LORD.

Proverbs 17 v1

An obvious lesson – why then do we so often opt for the house of strife?

June 12th

1 Kings 9 v1-10v29

Actually Solomon's many foreign wives would be a source of much of the paganism that would enter Jerusalem at this time. We also see the beginnings of a very demanding central government which would become such a serious resentment that the kingdom would split in two during the time of Solomon's son. People did tire of

Solomon's great building projects, and his build up of a powerful army with the latest chariots. The Queen of Sheba's visit has spawned countless yarns outside the scriptures.

Acts 8 v14-40

The Gospel reaching the Samaritans was an important step; so was the conversion of the Ethiopian.

Psalm 130 v1-8 As Derek Kidner puts it, "there is a steady climb towards assurance" in this psalm.

Proverbs 17v2-3 Joseph had already illustrated this truth, by his own rise to power in Egypt

---

June 13th

1st Kings 11v1-12v19

A further extension of the family life under which Solomon had grown up? Ever since David had been forced apart from his first wife (who was subsequently given away to someone else) David's relationships with women fell short of what they should have been, and he raised his family – or should I say families, in a deeply divided household. Here Solomon continues to collect women as though it were a stamp collection. A daughter of Pharaoh was only one of many trophies. Of course there were political/military reasons behind it all –women were often given as part of a treaty. What did he need 700 wives and 300 concubines for? He hardly knew them all by name and they filled their dreary (even if pampered lives) by reliving as much of their home culture and ways as they could – which meant a massive import of paganism with temples and shrine built for these bored women who never felt part of Israeli culture anyway.

God's protection of Solomon was gradually being lifted away. Promises made to David would be kept, so the kingdom would stay with Solomon. Our reading finishes with Solomon's son taking the wrong advice, and from this point the people split into two kingdoms, Israel in the north, and Judah, centred on Jerusalem.

Acts 9 v1-25

The stoning of Stephen was deeply disturbing – it produced the zealous Saul who was determined to stamp out the followers of Jesus completely. So great was his zeal that he planned to go as far as Damascus to arrest followers. But the testimony of those whose lives he destroyed must have had an impact too. After meeting Jesus on the way, he entered Damascus as a blind man now knowing the truth of the gospel message. "Straight street" still exists today in Damascus. We can't help feeling some pity for Ananias who was given the task of laying hands on Saul and praying for his healing. Saul's testimony was so effective that he then had to escape the wrath of the local Jews! Ironically, he had learnt the Gospel from those he had inflicted with terrible things.

Psalm 131 v1-3

Learning to be quiet and restful in God's presence. The psalmist has learnt something from watching a contented child on its mother's lap.

Proverbs 17v4-5

Verse 4 warns us of how wicked people select the evil message that confirms their own twisted worldview. Verse 5 challenges heartlessness and glee at others' sad circumstances.

June 14th

1st Kings 12v20 -13v34

Jeroboam becomes king of the break-away tribes – 10 tribes in all, with only Judah and Benjamin remaining loyal to the grandson of David.

Sadly, realising that the Temple was still in the hands of the king down in Jerusalem, Jeroboam invents a religion of his own with the creation of two calf idols.

Acts 9v26-43

Every Christian had heard of how evil Saul had been. Could he really be genuinely converted, or was it an elaborate trick? It took Barnabas to convince the others.

In the end, for his own protection, Saul had to be sent home to Tarsus (modern eastern Turkey) to protect him from some Jews who were planning to kill him.

We are then told some stories of Peter's ministry in the coastal area of Joppa (Jaffa, or the area near modern Tel Aviv)

Psalm 132 v1-18

The background is the bringing of the ark up to Jerusalem during the reign of David. Frim this point on, the newly captured Jerusalem becomes the holy City.

Proverbs 17 v6

See to the spiritual growth of your own family circle!

June 15th

1st Kings 14v1-15 v24

We continue the story of two separate Kingdoms – that of Jeroboam's in the north (Israel) and that of the line of kings descended from David, based in Jerusalem (Judah.)

Jeroboam knew that the kingdom had been given to him by God – yet he went ahead and created false gods, an alternative religion. When things became tough, he sent his wife in disguise to see the old prophet who had told him in the first place, that God was giving him the Kingdom. Punishment came for the way in which 10 tribes had been led away from the LORD.

Meanwhile, Solomon's son was not any better. Given that Solomon had imported a variety of false religions with the many wives he took (and the son now on the throne had an Ammonite mother) pagan and homosexual practices were everywhere – they became as depraved as the nations they had driven out.

It was not until the reign of Asa that moves were made against some of the evil in the land.

Acts 10 v1-23

The lovely story of Cornelius – a Roman officer just waiting to be told the Gospel. Meanwhile, God has to do something about the strong bigotries which Peter had – bigotries which might have prevented him from telling Cornelius the good news. These bigotries will surface again, unfortunately.

Psalm 133

A lovely picture of harmony!

Proverbs 17 v7-8

Depending on which translation you are using, these verses might give rise to some concern. Sometimes you have to allow for sarcasm in the Scriptures. The comment on the bribe is the attitude of the one who is offering it; for God's view on the matter see verses 15 & 23

June 16th

1 Kings 15 v25-17v24

Unlike Jerusalem, where a King from the Davidic line continues to reign, (due to the promises God made to David) the reign of Jeroboam's line is brought to an end in Israel.

Conspiracy follows conspiracy as the northern kingdom goes from bad to worse. Then we have the stories of Ahab and his wicked Baal worshipping wife, Jezebel, and the start of the stories about the prophet Elijah.

Stories of the prophet Jehu and the prophet Elijah remind us that the northern Kingdom was not left without a witness to the true faith. There is also irony that while Jezebel comes from Sidon, it is in a village outside Sidon (Zarephath) that Elijah finds a faithful woman who trusts the one true God.

Acts 10v24-48

There is special significance in the gentiles having their own "Pentecost" experience – whether it is Jews, Samaritans, or now gentiles, the saving experience of Jesus is just as authentic.

Psalm 134v1-3

Verses 1 & 2 are possibly said by the people to the priests and Levites in the Temple, and they then respond with verses 3.

The Psalm of Ascents, which began with Psalm 120, are now brought to an end.

Proverbs 17 v9-11

More observations on life!

June 17th

1 Kings 18 v1-46

God has withheld rain from an evil nation, and famine has a serious grip on the life of the people.

Obadiah has hidden 100 prophets of the LORD in the past – right under the noses of Ahab and Jezebel, the witness continues.

At Mount Carmel we have the dramatic confrontation between the followers of Baal and the followers of the LORD. Which is real – the one who answers by fire.

The significance of Elijah's words – "how long are you going to waver between two opinions..." is that many ordinary people had mixed up the beliefs of the two religions. This syncretisation (dictionary: blending together) was a more dangerous threat to faith in God than pure paganism.

Acts 11 v1-30

Peter has to defend his actions; there will be other occasions when he will feel the pressures of Jewish believers who felt that the Gospel was being made too easy for Gentiles. Some of these Jewish believers would rather have had the gentiles converted fully to Jewish practices. If they had got their way, Christianity would have been only a minority wing of the Jewish faith, and the centrality of Jesus and the Gospel message sidelined. Paul recognised this problem most seriously.

Antioch becomes an important place where large numbers of gentiles are converted, and Barnabas deliberately brings Paul back to help with this work

Psalm 135 v1-21

The experience of the real God is contrasted with empty idol worship.

Proverbs 17 v12-13 Folly, and the particular sin of repaying good with evil – which of course is exactly what both David and Bathsheba did to Uriah – and they were punished by subsequent events.

June 18th

1 Kings 19v1-21

After the killings of the priests of Baal, Jezebel goes berserk. Elijah takes the threat so seriously, he retreats not just to Judah, but to the bottom (southern) end of Judah!! Beersheba is the last big town before you reach the edge of the wilderness that runs down to the Red Sea (Eilat) and Egypt.

God deals very gently with a prophet in deep depression as a result of exhaustion. There are also spiritual issues too. Elijah at times runs around as though he is the last man in the country to believe in God. That's just not true. God states there are 7,000 men who have never compromised the faith!

God has big tasks for Elijah – to anoint the new king of Syria, and then to anoint the future king of Israel, and then to appoint his own successor – Elisha. Elisha takes the call of God so seriously, that he slays his oxen, making it impossible to go back to his former life.

Acts 12 v1-23

Herod moves against the Christians. Killing John's brother James, pleased the Jewish rulers so much, he planned to do the same to Peter, who is released by an angel. Peter turns up at a prayer meeting – where the people find it hard to believe that their prayers have been answered!!!

The James that Peter says they should keep informed is James the half brother of Jesus – the James who wrote the letter of James.

God's judgment upon Herod comes in verse 23.

Psalm 136v1-26

Loving kindness – by the time you read this psalm, you should get the message about it!

Proverbs 17v14-15

Put a lid on a situation before it gets out of hand!

Again God condemns those who stand truth on its head

June 19th

1 Kings 20 v1-21v29

The Syrian King is determined to provoke a war with Ahab – all of this is in God's plans, for Ahab is going to learn to depend on the LORD. Signs of grace even in the Old Testament? Ahab foolishly allows the King of Syria to live.

The story of how Ahab and Jezebel bring false charges against Naboth, in order to seize his very attractive vineyard, brings Elijah to speak words of condemnation to Ahab's face. Dogs will later eat the corpse of Jezebel, but Ahab's repentance over Naboth seems to have been genuine. God's judgment on this family line will be delayed until after Ahab's death.

Acts 12 v24-13v15

Interesting collection of people at Antioch! The story is important as Barnabas and Paul become the first official missionaries commissioned by the Church there. They set out for Cyprus, and find themselves confronted by a false prophet / sorcerer.

Although John Mark deserted them later in the story, he will prove to be a fine Christian in the end, although not before Paul and Barnabas have a serious row over him! (Still to come.)

Psalm 137 – are you old enough to remember Boney M, the pop group who made this psalm famous? If you are having problems with the last verse, bear in mind that when the Babylonians carried off the people of Jerusalem as captives, they marched them for something like 600 miles – one of the first things they did, was to slaughter those who would hold them back – literally smashing babies heads off the rocks. This verse reflects the agony and pain of the people who had this done to them. The whole psalm reflects on the pain of finding themselves in a strange land – very, very few, would see Jerusalem again. A particularly upsetting thing was the pleasure that the Edomites took in the destruction of Jerusalem.

Proverbs 17v16

The issue is not the person's ability, but an unteachable spirit.

June 20th

1 Kings 22 v1-53

Are believers always wise in some of the business relationships they get themselves into?

Jehoshaphat of Jerusalem was not wise in his involvement with Ahab, although it is to his credit that he wanted better relationships with the breakaway tribes of the northern kingdom. He was, incidentally, married to a daughter of Ahab. It is also to his credit that Jehoshaphat insists on hearing a prophet of the true God, not the pagan rabble who will say whatever pleases Ahab.

Ahab basically bleeds to death from his wound. His son, who became the next king of Israel, angered the LORD.

Acts 13 v16-41

Paul's sermon calling these Jewish people to faith in Jesus.

Psalm 138 v1-8

God's loving kindness again!

Proverbs 17 v17-18

Consistency in friendship, reliability in troubled times. On the other hand, be careful as to whose debts etc you stand over – standing as guarantor is not always the right thing to do.

June 21st

2 Kings 1v1-2v25

The King of Israel was badly injured after a fall. Judgment is pronounced, when he seeks advice from a false god.

Elijah is taken up to heaven, Elisha remains to carry on the work.

The waters of Jericho are cured. (Still safe to drink to this day!)

Acts 13 v42-15v7

Division over the Gospel as many from both the Jewish and Gentile communities come to faith.

Psalm 139

Everything is in God's hands!

Proverbs 17v19-21

Sanctified common sense.

"makes his door high" – pretentiousness?

June 22nd

2 Kings 3v1-4v17

This is one example of how Israel and Judah managed to pull together in some ways, due largely to the fact that the two royal families had intermarried. Spiritually, however, there is virtually no common ground. Jeroboam of Israel had curbed the worst excesses of his mother, and had torn down the Baal pillar or idol (Baal was a "foreign" imported god) but he still kept the pagan idols created by his own nation – the alternative religion of the two golden calves, to stop the people from travelling down to the LORD's Temple in Jerusalem, at the heart of the other nation, Judah.

Interesting too, that the army of Edom also joins in, and so we have a group of 3 kingdoms working together to put down the rebellion led by the King of Moab.

Meanwhile, Elisha, Elijah's servant is amongst the folk from the northern tribes. The followers of the LORD in the northern kingdom no longer have a temple to worship at, and their worship (at times virtually an underground religion) has become very much prophet led. They are of course under suspicion as people who still respect the southern King in Jerusalem as a descendant of King David, and of course the temple of their God is in his city. Elisha certainly doesn't hide his contempt for his own pagan king, and the respect he has for the more godly Jehoshaphat.

For Jehoshaphat's sake, the LORD gives the victory. The incident with the King of Moab sacrificing his son to his own pagan gods, and burning the body on the top of the city wall, brought disgust even to the pagan Israelites.

The second story gives us some insight into how the followers of the LORD in the northern kingdom of Israel organised the faith. Prophets trained in schools, and somehow or other led the people. In one sense it was as though Elisha was running a Bible College, and things were tight enough, without one of the students dying and leaving his family in poverty. The miracle of the oil saved the two sons from slavery; God does provide!

The third story is one of God blessing a couple who gave and supported His work without ever seeking something in return.

Acts 14 v8-28

One of the problems that Jesus also faced – the wrong response to a miracle, the wrong kind of faith! It was difficult to convince the crowd that they were not "gods" – sadly a few days later, Jewish opponents arrive and convince the same crowds to attack and leave Paul seemingly dead. Opposition and persecution did mean that ministry in many places was short and newly appointed elders found themselves taking real responsibility very quickly.

Psalm 140v1-13

Sheer malice, malicious intrigue are hard things for any Christian to have to deal with; David had to cope with such opposition.

Proverbs 17 v22

Obvious message, but one we sometimes need to hear, and remember, especially as try to encourage others.

June 23rd

2nd Kings 4v18-5v27

A very special gift – we can imagine what this child meant to a couple who were childless. And we can imagine the fear lest anything happen – worst fears were being realised.

All the description points to the child as being genuinely dead. This was no mere artificial respiration, but a child brought back from the dead.

The second story is from a time of famine. Trainee prophets have been at Elisha's Bible school, but they need to be fed somehow. Gathering what they could find, they manage to produce some kind of stew, but on tasting it, they realised poisonous gourds have been added to the pot. You and I would, of course, just simply throw the whole pot load out, and reach again for the cupboard or freezer – but this was a famine, and the little good food they had found was in the pot, mixed in with the poisonous stuff – this was a serious loss. Another miracle ensures that there is a meal after all.

The next meal – feeding a hundred young Bible students with 20 baps, is very much a forerunner to the feeding of the 5,000 in the Gospel story.

The story of Naaman – the little slave girl from Israel brings hope into a pagan home. The King of Israel is a pagan himself, and sees it as nothing more than the Syrians looking for an excuse for war. Elisha hears about it, and sends a message.

Naaman is a very proud man, and just like the way in which the King of Israel reacted to Naaman's arrival, so Naaman suspects political intrigue himself when he is told to wash in the local Israeli river. Obedience is the clue, however.

Gehazi's behaviour ruins the story so much.

Acts 15 v1-31

We think of Paul as one of the greatest missionaries ever, but the truth is that he had to take considerable stick not only from Jews opposed to the Gospel, but also from people who considered themselves to be Christians, who really wanted Old Testament religion with Jesus somehow or other perched on top. To be a good Christian, they argued, you had to be a good Jew. The matter went so much to the heart of the Gospel, that it was necessary to convene a special Assembly up in Jerusalem to deal with the matter. In fact, when they got there, the matter was already a big issue with some ex-Pharisees who were now Christians, who wanted all the converts to Christianity circumcised.

A position was reached; a Christian lifestyle required new Christians to live very differently regarding sexual behaviour, and they should also respect the very serious exceptions that fellow Christians from a Jewish background would take to eating meat that had been sacrificed to an idol, or killed in a particularly repugnant way that went against Old Testament teaching. However, it was made quite clear that Christians did not have to become Jews first. Circumcision was not going to be demanded; Christ's death on the Cross was the all sufficient sacrifice, and nothing would be added to that.

Psalm 141v1-10

The psalm ties in with the reading from Acts; what is needed, the psalmist sees, is a rejection of insincerity and compromise in godly lifestyle.

Proverbs 17 v23

Sounds like common sense, which of course it is, so why did it need to be said? Be wary of the culture in which bribes are a norm as to how things are done.

June 24th

2 Kings 6v1-7v20

Practicalities of building a new dormitory for the Bible students brings home how precarious – from a human viewpoint – are the lives of some of the students. An axe is a major loss. For us it may mean a quick trip to B & Q, Homebase or our nearest hardware shop, but for people in the developing world, the loss of tools may mean the loss of a livelihood. This particular axe was borrowed, not out of laziness about getting one of his own, but because even the price of an axe was beyond the student in these times of famine.

The story of Elisha being able – through Divine revelation – to tell secret after secret from the King of Syria's plans, leads to the Syrian king planning a direct attack on Elisha himself. The sight of a foreign army camped around the city alarms Elisha's servant – until his eyes are "opened" and he sees the army of heaven that is there protecting them. This passage has meant a lot to folk on the mission field in isolated and hostile areas.

It is quite funny the way in which the blinded, invading army are led into the city of Samaria and subsequently fed and sent home.

The next invasion from Syria was much more serious – cannibalism amongst the survivors. God does rescue them – again quite a funny side to the story as 4 lepers wander off to the Syrian camp, either to be fed or killed, but at least to get it over with – only to find that the LORD has created such fear in the camp that the Syrians have fled empty handed, leaving an incredible amount of loot behind – but the army officer who mocked God dies in the stampede.

Acts 15v32-16v15

Huge row between Barnabas and Paul over John Mark who had deserted last time. The good thing, if there ever is a good thing about arguments, is that in this case twice the work got done, as now there were 2 teams, going to different places (<u>not</u> in competition!!) The good news is that Paul and John Mark were great buddies later on, and John Mark really matured as a good solid evangelist and Gospel writer.

We are also introduced to Timothy. This was one occasion when Paul, to avoid unnecessary controversy whenever they were preaching to Jews, circumcised Timothy who was half Jewish anyway. This was different from fighting a battle with the Judaisers who would have forced every new Christian from a gentile background to be circumcised.

Interesting that God has his timing for different parts of the work.

The call to Greece is significant, as the Gospel moves from Asia (the Middle East, Turkey etc) to mainland Europe – and a huge change and challenge for the missionaries as they leave behind their own part of the world and get in deeper into alien territory.

Philippi was a very Roman city, but all Jews arriving in a foreign city knew to slip down to the nearest river bank on the Sabbath to see if in the area there were any Jews or even Gentile God-fearers who were sympathetic to the Jewish faith, who were looking to meet for worship. Some women were there – and so we are introduced to Lydia, who was just ripe for the Gospel message. Purple dye was extremely expensive, which gives us some clue as to the social standing of Lydia. The whole household converted and were baptised.

This sometimes raises issues for some folk reading passages like this (see also the Philippian jailer) - how do we cope with these "household" conversions? Is everybody in a household really converted?

The answer has to lie with the fact that you and I belong to a highly individualised culture, with homes deeply fragmented compared to the culture and times that we are dealing with here. Even compared to the Middle East and Far East of today, our Western culture comes across badly with its very self seeking outlook. These were genuine conversions as whole families, entire households, embraced Christ.

Psalm 142 v1-7

Linked to Psalm 57 – "in the cave" – a difficult time when David had to flee from Saul and live a rather Robin Hood type life. The two psalms reflect the very different emotional states of that experience. The promise of a kingdom must have seemed so very far away, if not actually rather mocking at times. Very hard to believe how life would move on from these lows.

Proverbs 17 v24-25

Wisdom is obvious to those inclined to look for it; but someone bent on foolishness brings despair to those nearest to him.

June 25th

2 Kings 8v1-9v15a

Finishing touches to the story of the woman whose son had been brought back to life.

Insight into the cruelty that will take place both internally in Syria, and against the people of Israel. Hazael stands warned by God of how his life is going to sink to new lows. Meanwhile there are new kings down in Judah. Elisha also anoints an army officer to lead a coup in Israel, to fulfil the judgement that God had announced against Ahab's line.

Acts 16 v16-40

Even though the demented girl was proclaiming the truth, it was done in a way which distracted from what Paul was trying to do, and probably interfered considerably with any serious consideration about the Gospel.

The casting out of the demon, however, robbed her owners of whatever wealth they made through her, leading to a mob, followed by a beating ordered by the magistrates, and then imprisonment for Paul and Silas.

The good outcome of their time in the jail was the conversion of the jailer and his household.

While on many occasions Paul led aside his rights in the interest of the Gospel, on this occasion he exercised his rights when the magistrates – who had never bothered to check out the issues, and the truth – tried to set them free. Paul pointed out that they were Roman citizens who had been beaten and imprisoned illegally.

Psalm 143 v1-12

The last of the "Penitential Psalms" (6, 32, 38, 51, 102, 130, 143) However, while verse 2 recognises that David has sinned too, much of the psalm deals with the threat of his enemies

Proverbs 17 v26 Innocent people being punished wrongly.

June 26th

2 Kings 9 v15b-10v31

The wiping out of an evil dynasty begins – and extends even to the killing of the Jerusalem king who was related to Ahab's family (and his brothers, later in the passage.)

Jezebel, who had so fanatically forced the religion of Baal upon the country, "tarts herself up" for her meeting with Jehu – painting her eyes in a way that made them look huge. The eunuchs were quite willing to toss her out of the window!

Jehu wiped out the worship of Baal, but still allowed the worship of the two gold calves to continue.

Acts 17 v1-34

Significant converts after 3 weeks of preaching – and opposition.

In Athens, Paul comes across the altar to the unknown god – so careful were the local Greeks to make sure they had covered them all! Paul takes the opportunity to preach the one true God, and the story of Jesus and His resurrection.

Psalm 144v1-15

A psalm of David which upsets many pacificists ("Blessed be the LORD, my rock, who trains my hands for war, and my fingers for battle...") Perhaps we need to talk more to those who do serve their country in the forces, and who have been in situations where a great deal has depended on their accuracy of fire. One serviceman in the congregation has told me of a particular situation in which the chaplain beside him was praying that the soldier would not miss! David has high hopes for what can be.

Proverbs 17 v27-28

Kidner's commentary sums it up – think before you speak.

June 27th

2 Kings 10 v 32 – 12v21

God reduces down the size of the northern country, Israel.

Meanwhile in the south, down in Jerusalem, the evil Queen Mother butchers her own grandchildren. It is bizarre to us, but Athaliah as a daughter of Jezebel, seemed to think she would achieve something for her own family (the family of Ahab and Jezebel) if she wiped out the Davidic line (even though they were her own grandchildren) down in Jerusalem. Getting into the mind of someone who does this to her own flesh and blood is thankfully something impossible for most of us to grasp, but we are seeing it more and more today in our lifetimes – around this time of year, in 2008, a British man was sentenced to life imprisonment for the murder of his own wife and child in America. We are seeing more and more people who deliberately harm their own children when relationships break up.

To Athaliah, the deaths of her own grandchildren left a child of Ahab and Jezebel (herself) on the royal throne in Jerusalem.

What she did not realise, that a half sister of her son – ie someone who was of Davidic descent herself, but through a different mother, had hidden away one prince in the temple – incidentally guaranteeing a good upbringing for the next six years!

The coronation of the young boy, and the immediate switching of loyalties on the part of the royal bodyguards when they realised that a prince of the Davidic line was still alive, makes dramatic reading!

The honesty and integrity of those involved in the temple repairs is also good reading!

Sadly, trusted aides were involved in the assassination of Joash.

Acts 18 v1-21

Key characters, Aquila and Priscilla at Corinth. It is quite possible that Jews were deported from Rome as a result of the troubles that Jewish agitators had attempted to bring upon the Christians there – so all got expelled – Christian Jews and Jews opposed to the Gospel. Anyway, Aquila and Priscilla were tent makers, sharing Paul's skills and able to provide him with work.

In Corinth, the Gospel split the Jewish community there, though Governor Gallio refused to get involved in the issues. Sosthenes, the new anti-Christian leader of the Synagogue even got a hammering from the mob himself, as attempts to cause trouble for the Christians only lit the fires of anti-Jewish feelings in the wider community. Which makes it all the more interesting, when his name reappears in 1st Corinthians 1 v1 as a leading Christian!!!

Paul shaving his head – you will remember that Samson was supposed to live a life of utter devotion to God (Samson could not have lived much worse if he had tried) and that one of the marks of this was that his hair would not be cut and he was supposed to stay clear of alcohol.

The practice continued amongst Jews (and Jewish Christians) right down to the times of Paul. **Specific periods** of special dedication or devotion to God might be marked in this way, with the hair cut at last when the time had come to an end.

Psalm 145 v1-21

The last of David's psalms in the Bible, and an "acrostic" one as well, like psalm 119 which had a section for each letter of the Hebrew alphabet. There are eight "acrostic" psalms, with sections, lines or verses for the letters of the Hebrew alphabet, which is very different from ours.

In this psalm, one verse, for the Hebrew letter "nun" was missing – this verse was found in amongst the texts found in the Qumran caves and is now included in most modern translations as 13b or 14a. Kidner describes the psalm as an alphabet of praise, although the "alphabetic" nature of it all is probably lost on someone reading it only in English! It still has important things to teach us about God.

Proverbs 18 v1

Inventing pretexts, looking for excuses – to avoid what is sound.

June 28th

2 Kings 13 v1-14v29

There is a partial repentance on the part of Jehoahaz of Israel as they face the might of the Syrians, but the worship of the goddess Asherah continues in the capital, Samaria.

We then have a period (not the first time) when the Kings of Israel and Judah have the same name – Joash. Joash of Judah was a godly man, while Joash of Israel threw himself into pagan worship – yet even he, in desperation, went to visit the dying Elisha. God kept his promise of deliverance from the Syrians. Joash of Israel was succeeded by Jeroboam II.

Down in Jerusalem, Amaziah succeeded Joash of Judah. He was a godly king, although once again the shrines on the hills continued. We are not entirely sure what went on in those shrines – worship of the one true God mixed up with the worship of other false gods into some kind of local folk religion? (The big word for mixing together conflicting beliefs and ideologies is syncreticism.)

Amaziah's problem was that he hankered after the great days of David, and wanted to unite the two parts of the kingdom again – his challenge to the Israeli king only weakened and humiliated his people, with the Temple and palace gold carried off, and 200 yards of the city wall pulled down. Amaziah was himself captured – see Psalm 42, which we believe was written by one of the hostages from Jerusalem, a temple singer/musician carried off to the north of Israel.

Amaziah, like his father, was also assassinated. His son Azariah managed to build Elath (present day Eilat on the Red Sea, or its Jordanian counterpart, Aqaba) extending the southern boundary of Judah.

Jonah the prophet also appears briefly in this passage – or at least many scholars believe that the two Jonahs are the one and the same. He was working in the northern kingdom.

Jereboam II was a much more successful king in military terms, but as far as idolatry was concerned, he lived up to the name of Jereboam. He was succeeded by Zechariah.

Acts 18 v22-19v12

There are two Caesareas – Caesarea Philippi, up near Mount Hermon, well inland, at the top of Israel, and there is the port of Caesarea on the Mediterranean coast. This is Caesarea on the coast – a huge port in biblical times, and for various rulers a welcome break from the heat of Jerusalem.

Apollos is a key character. Obviously the teachings of John the Baptist had spread all over the Mediterranean – and Apollos was an excellent follower of John, but he needed to have the Gospel story explained in a more complete way. Priscilla and Aquila filled him in, and Apollos became a leading Christian preacher and evangelist. In fact Paul while he was travelling through present day Turkey, discovered people similar to Apollos, who had a smattering of the Gospel, but were very much followers of John the Baptist who needed a fuller picture of the Gospel story. In fact they seemed to have known even less about Jesus, than Apollos. (Ephesus is modern Efes in Turkey).

There is quite a funny side to the lecture hall, where Paul preached daily for two years, being known as the lecture hall of Tyrannus. Was it a nickname for the teacher who owned it? (Despot, Tyrant!) Anyway, we assume that Paul was able to rent the premises during the heat of the day, when there would have been a break from the classes. So often Paul's visits to cities and towns had to be cut short – the fact that he got two years to teach daily meant that the local believers got steady teaching for a relatively long period.

Psalm 146 v1-10

As we come close to the end of the Psalms, we have, for the last 5, hymns of praise beginning and ending with Hallelujah ("Praise the LORD" in English!)

Proverbs 18v2-3

These are strong words in the Hebrew. The fool "expressing his opinion" uses a word in Hebrew, which means "displaying" found only in Genesis 9 v21, where Noah was lying naked, drunk – literally displaying or exposing himself. So the word used of the fool "displaying" his opinion, suggests "that decency itself is affronted" (Kidner in his commentary, page 127.) It is a very blunt comparison, between the drunk lying naked, and the eloquent, talkative fool.

Sadly we all know people who are great talkers, but what is going on in the mind behind the mouth is another matter, and for all the eloquence, we are struck with horror when we realise the implications of the "wisdom" they are spouting.

June 29th

2 Kings 15v1-16v20

We read of parallel kingdoms – rulers in the north (Israel) and in the south (Judah with Jerusalem as its capital) Each is judged from God's perspective.

Clearly, from the perspective of the compiler of the account, the southern kings should have known better, but we see much of the wickedness of the northern kingdom repeated in what we see happening in Jerusalem. King Ahaz of Jerusalem is portrayed as particularly wicked – burning his own son as a sacrifice to pagan gods, encouraging the hillside shrines that more godly kings had tried to discourage, and even taking silver and gold from the temple to bribe the Assyrians into attacking the northern kingdom, and possibly precipitating the whole Assyrian interest in conquering the region. He even had designs of a pagan altar reproduced in Jerusalem. Further spiritual compromise was carried out in deference to the Assyrians. What foolish flirting with a "world power." When the kings move away from dependence upon God, the outcome is extremely damaging, even if the consequences of their worldly wisdom are not immediately obvious.

Acts 19v13-41

First of all we have the group to try to use the name of Jesus without actually knowing the Saviour personally themselves. The response of the demon, "I know Jesus, and I know Paul, but who are you," is most revealing.

It did however lead to a wholescale rejection of satanic practices with a huge fortune of charms and incantations being burnt.

We read of Paul's conviction that he must go on to Jerusalem, knowing somehow that this would lead him to Rome. More about this over the next two days.

Meanwhile, the impact of the Gospel is such that the silversmiths specialising in pagan trinkets feel threatened by the success of the Gospel.

Psalm 147v1-20

More praise, with its reminders of how God has brought back the exiles to Jerusalem.

Proverbs 18v4-5

The meaning of verse 5 is obvious. There are different ways of taking verse 4 as you can see from the different translations. The Living Bible put it: "A wise man's words express deep streams of thought" whereas others see it in a more complex way: "the words of a man's mouth are deep waters, but the fountain of wisdom is a bubbling brook" (NIV.) Derek Kidner's commentary tends to side more with the second view: "the proverb is contrasting our human reluctance, or inability, to give ourselves away, with the refreshing candour and clarity of the true wisdom." To help explain what he means, Kidner quotes the poet Tennyson. "For words, Like Nature, half reveal and half conceal the Soul within." Food for thought on how to take this proverb!

June 30th

2 Kings 17v1-18v12

Hoshea tries to play off one world power against another and loses out. However, it is not just the personal foolishness of Hoshea that leads to the people of the northern kingdom being carried off into captivity by the Assyrians. The compiler of the book makes clear that the long term sinning against God has led to God's judgement being fulfilled. We are also given an explanation of how the Samaritans came about (foreigners imported who partially take on the worship of the one true God.) Meanwhile, Hezekiah comes to the throne in Jerusalem. He ends many of the pagan practices, and even destroys the bronze snake from the time of Moses because some had even started to worship it. More about Hezekiah tomorrow.

Acts 20 v1-38

Paul believes he has a particular destiny to fulfil, including imprisonment. That is reflected in the urgency and the sense of finality in many of the meetings which he holds on his journey back to Jerusalem

Psalm 148v1-14

We are going to finish Psalms with a great sense of praise and so we continue on with these themes in psalm 148.

Proverbs 18v6-7

"Talking oneself into trouble" (Kidner) just about sums it all up.

July 1st

2 Kings 18v13-19v37

The Assyrians successfully carried the northern kingdom of Israel off to captivity, and humanly speaking it looked as though they would do the same to the southern kingdom of Judah. (In actual fact it would be the Babylonians who would come later and carry off Jerusalem and its people to Babylon.) However, in desperation, King Hezekiah did his best to raise the tribute demanded by the Assyrians, to the point of taking the silver out of both the temple and the treasury, and stripping the Temple doors of the gold which had been used to overlay them.

The Assyrians were not satisfied, and sent a great army to lay siege. The Assyrian officer stood outside the walls, ridiculing Jerusalem's allies, and in particular their reliance on God. The officer deliberately spoke in Hebrew, so that the ordinary people would understand him. The Jerusalem officials pleaded with him to use Aramaic, which they would understand, but he deliberately continued his ridicule in Hebrew, and in particular of their faith in God.

Deeply upset and clearly personally humiliated, King Hezekiah went to the temple, where Isaiah pronounced God's judgment on the Assyrians, and in particular on King Sennacherib who was murdered by two of his own sons who subsequently fled into eastern Turkey.

What is interesting to discover in this passage, is that the common people still spoke Hebrew, and Aramaic was a language understood by the courtiers and presumably the better educated. By the times of the New Testament, Hebrew will still be the language of the Temple and Synagogue, but Aramaic will be the language widely spoken throughout the region – the language that Jesus would have spoken at home.

Acts 21v1-17

What should Paul have done? Local believers in Tyre warned him that he should not go on to Jerusalem. The warning was repeated by Agabus. As John Stott put it in his commentary on Acts, "Are we to blame Paul for his obstinacy or admire him for his unshakeable resolve?"

Paul had claimed earlier that he was compelled by the Spirit to go to Jerusalem, and yet these warnings came of what would happen if he went ahead. Most people who have looked at these passages have concluded that Paul was to go, knowing what would happen.

Humanly speaking, as we shall see later, the Jewish Christians in Jerusalem unwittingly precipitated the whole matter of Paul's arrest by demanding that he prove his "Jewishness" by taking part in some temple rites with fellow Jewish Christians who were fulfilling vows. Did the folks in the Christian community back in Jerusalem not realise how much of a controversial figure Paul had become, not just in the far flung Greek speaking world, but also in Jerusalem itself? What is difficult to accept is why they persisted in Paul taking a high profile, for what was largely PR purposes, given the warnings we read of here. (Even if it does fulfil God's designs as to how he will use Paul in the future.) More about that later.

Psalm 149v1-9

Praise and worship, combined with a call to God's people to move forward with confidence.

Proverbs 18v8

How people are so hooked on gossip!

July 2nd

2 Kings 20v1-22v3

Hezekiah was one of our more hopeful kings in Jerusalem and the miracle of the shadow going backwards on the sundial was an exceptional miracle given to strengthen a king who felt the burden of responsibility very heavy at times. He was, however, very naive in showing the Babylonian ambassadors everything. Foolish Hezekiah imagined that because Babylon was so far away it would be no threat to Jerusalem – if only he knew what a world power Babylon was about to become, threatening even Egypt in a few decades. Hekeziah's response to Isaiah explaining what the Babylonians would do was also very short sighted – as long as the problems were not in his time Hezekiah did not care! A dangerous attitude that can come with age and which is particularly damaging when we find it in Church Committees and other bodies who will not take the long term view of what they are doing in God's work.

Note the mention of how Hezekiah brought water inside the city – an Israeli guide once asked me why we wanted to see Hezekiah's water tunnel when it is not even mentioned in the Bible! Actually, there is at least one other reference too.

Manasseh who followed was one of the really evil kings – every pagan superstition that he could introduce, Manasseh seems to have gone and done so. His long reign was particularly destructive, and his son's assassination avoided a repeat of more of the same. Manasseh's little grandson Josiah came to the throne at the age of eight and was a very godly ruler, undoing decades of spiritual damage.

Acts 21v18-36

Here we have the "brilliant" PR idea that the Jewish Christians come up with – an idea of how Paul can prove his "Jewishness" to a suspicious Jewish population, not realising that they (the local Jewish Christians) were triggering the events which would lead to Paul's imprisonment and all that followed. Sometimes we need to think if we are so busy appeasing one group, that we actually end up damaging the Lord's work overall.

Psalm 150v1-6

We finish the Book of Psalms with every instrument blazing out His praise. Not quite the “Presbyterian” image of the psalms?!

Proverbs 18v9-10

Slackers, wreckers and where real security lies

July 3rd

2 Kings 22v4-23v30

Always a risky business, when accounts are not kept; nevertheless, here was exceptional honesty found amongst those who were in charge.

The rediscovery of an important part of the Old Testament in the Temple has an immediate impact. It does bring home to us, though, how badly matters had deteriorated that an important section of God’s Word had to be rediscovered in His Temple. The utter ignorance of God’s Word has its parallels in our secular society. Sadly Josiah lost his life in a battle that was really between the two superpowers of his day.

Acts 21v37-22v16

The commander has not got a clue as to who he has arrested. Paul begins explaining his life to his Jewish audience in Hebrew.

Proverbs 18v11-12

Wealth can fail as our defence.

July 4th

2 Kings 23v31-25v30

With Josiah gone, the Kings who follow are as godless as any of the others who had gone before. It was a very difficult time for the land of Judah, as they were now clearly becoming the battleground between the superpowers of their time, and as Egyptian and Babylonian power grew and waned, the kings of Judah often played the field badly. King Zedekiah’s rebellion against Babylon resulted in a violent reaction, with the walls of Jerusalem ripped down, the Temple looted and some of the people carried off into captivity. The subsequent killing of the governor appointed by the Babylonians meant that a significant number of people fled to Egypt. The Bible does see all that happens at this time as the fulfilment of God's judgment after generations of very persistent sinning.

Acts 22v17-23v10

Ironically, the people are prepared to listen to Paul's testimony until he specifically mentions God's call to evangelise the Gentiles. Clearly there were those who would have tolerated Christianity as a mere sect within Judaism but for its commitment to bring non-Jews to faith.

The Roman commander cannot understand Hebrew and decided to beat a confession out of Paul – who promptly used his Roman nationality to prevent the beating.

Naively the commander orders the Jewish council to convene in the hope that this will resolve something. Paul managed to split the council by making clear his own belief in the resurrection, which led to the Pharisees supporting him!

Proverbs 18v13

Advice given, decisions made – all before the facts are known!

July 5th

1st Chronicles 1v1-2v17

A useful recap of the generations down to David, his brothers and sisters.

Acts 23 v11-35

By the next morning, however, a significant number of Jews were planning Paul's death. Paul's nephew brought word of the plot, and Paul was subsequently rushed off to Caesarea on the coast, beginning a long period of imprisonment which would frustrate Paul and lead to his subsequent call to have his case tried in Rome.

Proverbs 18 v14-15

People can cope with physical breakdown but a broken spirit is another matter ("When courage dies…" – Living Bible.) Verse 15 is critical of closed minds that will consider nothing new.

July 6th

1st Chronicles 2v18-4v4

For us, these verses can help us put together an overall picture of how individuals and families fit together in the Old Testament, but it also served to give Jewish people sitting as captives in far away Babylon a sense of belonging and of identity, so don't be quite to dismiss it all!

Acts 24v1-27

Although Paul defends himself quite well, he is left in jail for a variety of reasons; Felix hoped to be bribed, and it also suited him to leave Paul imprisoned when he was succeeded by Festus, so as not to offend the Jewish authorities. Opportunities to witness to Felix and his Jewish wife were taken, but, as commented yesterday, the frustration of being left there sitting in prison had its impact upon Paul.

Some background:

Tertullus tried to win Felix over by making compliments. In reality, Felix was known for his brutality, not his reforms. However, given that he had been particularly violent to the Jews, anything that had them trotting out such wonderful flattery would serve him well at some point. "Long may it continue" may have crossed Felix's mind! And not without reason. According to Josephus, Felix was recalled to Rome to explain a particularly brutal reaction to a Jewish / Syrian dispute in Caesarea itself.

Drusilla was the youngest daughter of Herod Agrippa I and therefore a sister of King Agrippa II and of Bernice. (All very interesting connections!) Drusilla had already been married when she was seduced by Felix and she was his 3rd wife – which explains, as Stott points out in his commentary, why Paul preached on "righteousness, self control and the judgement to come" and indeed had some impact upon Felix!

Proverbs 18v16-18

More common sense comments. V17 warns against forming hasty opinions. Although verse 18 speaks of "casting lots" the point is about seeking God's leading.

July 7th

1st Chronicles 4v5-5v17

The family trees continue – all important to a people who needed to keep their identity and who had to prove their links when they returned years later, from captivity.

Acts 25v1-27

Appeasement of the Jewish authorities continues to be a major issue when Festus takes over. In his frustration Paul makes the legal move of appealing to Caesar – asking for his trial to be taken to Rome. Festus, who has been content to appease the Jewish authorities with some sort of trial, now realises that he has no real evidence to make the charges stick.

Proverbs 18v19

A sad truth.

July 8th

1st Chronicles 5v18-6v81

Our recap of Old Testament history continues.

Acts 26v1-32

Paul did an excellent job of evangelising Agrippa! (Strictly speaking Agrippa II who was rumoured to be in an incestuous relationship with his sister Bernice.) The King, governor and others gathered realised that Paul's imprisonment was for theological matters. Agrippa's comment that the only thing keeping Paul in prison was his own appeal to Caesar, was in one sense true – no provincial judge would invade what was now the emperor's territory (Stott's commentary on Acts in the Bible Speaks Today series.) Having said that, Paul's imprisonment was continuing on and on for reasons of political expediency, and though he made sincere and impressive defences of the Gospel, Paul was beginning to understand that he was at times only providing "amusement" as an interesting prisoner when important guests came! Agrippa II was perhaps just as intrigued by Paul as his great uncle Herod Antipas had been with Jesus (the Herod of Jesus' trial.)

Proverbs 18v20-21

Although words can "satisfy the soul" the next verse warns how the tongue can kill or nourish life. Interestingly, the Hebrew word for "satisfied" can also mean "sated" – obviously opening up a different meaning which the next verse expands - care needs to be taken with our words.

July 9th

1st Chronicles 7v1-8v40

The story continues.

Acts 27v1-20

Paul's transport to Rome is organised so late that the journey becomes quite dangerous. The other prisoners may have been people already condemned to death, being sent to Rome for some "sport" in the arena (Stott page 386.) Paul is already an experienced traveller around the Mediterranean (his home town of Tarsus was in Cilicia, never mind the huge "mileage" already under his belt as a missionary.) Paul's advice not to sail any further in verse 10 was ignored because of the unsuitability of the harbour at Fair Havens to spend the winter in. As a general rule, all sailing in those times had to stop by the start of November (Stott p388.) A quick look at a map of the times shows how the ship was blown about the Mediterranean.

Proverbs 18v22

Kidner (page 130) in his commentary makes the point: "It is implicit here, and explicit in eg 19v13,14, that not any and every wife is in mind: see by contrast 14v1; 21v9."

July 10th

1st Chronicles 9v1-10v14

Now we have the returning families listed.

Suddenly we are catapulted back in time. The jump will not make much sense with our western ways of thinking. It may just blow your mind that one moment we are reading about people coming back from captivity in Babylon, and then suddenly we are reading about Saul's final battle with the Philistines.

There is a reason for this – in listing the families of Jerusalem, the Chronicler is conscious that the family of Saul also belonged to Jerusalem, and indeed there are twelve generations after Saul listed, so in a strange way, the Chronicler does not want to pass over that family's place.

The writer of Chronicles then tells the story of Saul and David from an interesting perspective, of how the Kingdom is transferred from Saul to David. Bear with us!

Acts 27v21-44

Paul emerges as a leader on board the ship, ensuring that everyone reaches the shore of Malta safely.

Proverbs 18v23-24.

There are very real lessons to be learnt about the meaning of "friendship."

July 11th

1st Chronicles 11v1-12v18

We are reminded that David began his rule in Hebron and then captured Jerusalem. We are told how Joab became the commander in chief. David was to seriously regret Joab's appointment, even if he was very efficient at what he did. Today's reading suggests it was a rash decision from the beginning.

We are also told something of the other brave men who were part of David's inner circles.

A close reading of our passage will reveal that there were tensions because some of them were related to Saul, or came from tribes associated with Saul.

Towards the end of our reading though, we realise that at least some of these men had a strong spiritual commitment – the Holy Spirit came upon Amasai.

Acts 28v1-31

The incident of the poisonous snake fastened to Paul's hand was initially taken by the locals that Paul was indeed some hideous convict who having escaped the sea, was not going to escape justice. Then they swung to the other extreme when he did not die or fall down ill.

After spending the winter in Malta, they eventually made it to Italy. Christians, who had never met Paul, made a point of going out to meet him at two points on the overland journey to Rome.

Paul made a point of addressing Jewish leaders in Rome, who at this point had received nothing from the leadership in Jerusalem against Paul.

Paul spent about 2 years in Rome, and then it is believed he resumed his travels for another 2 years before being re-arrested, retried, condemned and executed in AD 64.

Acts though, ends with Paul's arrival in Rome, because Luke can see the significance of the Gospel radiating out from Rome into the known world of their times.

Proverbs 19 v1-3

Verse 1 is obvious in its meaning. Kidner sums up verse 2 with the heading "getting nowhere, fast" and verse 3 with the phrase "Always God's fault" giving us further cause to reflect on these verses.

July 12th

1st Chronicles 12v19-14v17

The writer is stressing the support which came from the various tribes and regions. It is important, for the returning refugees, that in their history they can see their part in it all.

The incident regarding Uzzah was particularly sad but it revealed problems in David's own spiritual understanding. Selman (Tyndale Old Testament commentaries) makes the point "that to be in possession of the ark was no unqualified guarantee of divine blessing." David then decided to leave the seemingly dangerous ark where it might do more harm to the Philistines, but instead Obed-edom the Gittite had 3 months of blessing.

We read of David's good relationship with King Hiram of Tyre and of David's success against the Philistines. We also read of his multiple marriages and we already know the long term damage caused by the family life that David gave his offspring.

Romans 1v1-17

Romans is a major letter by Paul, written to a Church he has never visited (yet) and therefore had not been directly involved in its founding. This brings a different tone to the letter.

Romans though, is a major writing whose influences throughout Christian history has been so profound that some comment needs to be made before we get any further into the book.

It has been described as a Christian manifesto (Stott's Bible Speaks Today commentary.) It had a major impact on Augustine (4th century) Luther (16th century) John Wesley (18th century)...Calvin wrote "the main subject of the whole Epistle...is that we are justified by faith." (Quoted by Stott p24.)

The time of writing is probably during the 3 months spent in Corinth (see Acts 20v2f) It is a time of concern for the believers back in Jerusalem who have passed through financial difficulty (Romans 15v25ff), and a time when Paul hopes to then visit Rome on his way to evangelise the gentiles in Spain. So he has both Jewish believers and the opportunities to witness to non Jews very much in his mind. There is also real debate within the Christian Church about the nature of the Gospel, with a significant number of Jewish believers still seeing themselves as Jews first, and not entirely comfortable with how Paul so easily welcomed the Gentiles into faith. There were believers back in Jerusalem who would have been content for Christianity to remain as a sect within the Jewish faith, whereas Paul and others had seen major breakthroughs out in the non-Jewish world. So what are the centralities of the faith? Paul dealt with these essential debates about the Gospel in his letter to the Christians in Rome who were probably best placed to understand the themes which were so dear to Paul's heart.

So there was a real longing to come to the very place which was at the heart of the Roman Empire and where these very issues were being worked out – in closing the letter, Paul referred to 26 named individuals in Rome who represented the very real diversity of backgrounds in the Christian faith. But let's start at the beginning...

Proverbs 19v4-5

Warnings on fair weather friends and perjury.

July 13th

1st Chronicles 15 v1-16v36

Again, the long lists of names are important to people returning from captivity who can recognise that this is all part of their personal heritage. We also need to recognise the considerable organisation that went into the Lord's work and realised the skills being brought together in the service of God. We also read of the Ark being brought at last into Jerusalem.

Romans 1v18-32

It is a very accurate picture of a sinful, godless world that deserves God's judgment.

Proverbs 19v6-7

More on fair weather friendships.

July 14th

1st Chronicles 16v37-18v17

Well, they say you learn something new every day. I must admit I was unaware of the overlap (16v39) of the two tabernacles. Admittedly there is a lot missing in our knowledge of what happened to the Tabernacle Tent in the aftermath of the people's wanderings in the wilderness with Moses and Joshua. We know about Eli and Samuel at Shiloh, (and just what kind of structure was there?) and now some decades on, the old tabernacle is at Gibeon while the Ark is clearly inside a new tabernacle (1 Chronicles 16v1) that David has prepared. So here in the middle of chapter 16 we have 2 tabernacles functioning simultaneously! In fact sacrifices to the

Lord appear to continue in various places, and although this does not seem to be an immediate problem, it will become one as beliefs and practices develop in years to come which are not faithful to what they have been taught about God.

The story of Nathan and the message that David is not to build the Temple is important to the Chronicler. Some sermons are bad on this point, because they take David's statement in 1 Chronicles 28 v3 *but God said to me*, 'you must not build a temple to honour my name, for you are a warrior and have shed much blood' as though that is what God did say through Nathan here in 1st Chronicles 17 (see also 2nd Samuel 7 – which we read on 25th May), when God didn't say any such thing!!!

I realise this is going to floor some people who have been brought up to believe that the reason for David not building the temple was the blood on his hands, but that is not what was said in today's passage. Some commentaries just simply refuse to deal with the issue; I prefer to see the whole thing as David in later life looking too deeply into why God would not allow him personally to build it – and I come across far too many Christians who have that little bitter corner in their hearts, instead of accepting that something is not for them, and they should just move on.

So what did God actually say in today's reading? The brakes are being put on the idea of a permanent building because this is a major shift in how God has related to His people from the very beginning of mankind. What God actually said was this:

"I have never lived in a temple, from the day I brought the Israelites out of Egypt until now. My home has always been a tent, moving from one place to another. And I have never once complained to Israel's leaders, the shepherds of my people. I have never asked them, 'Why haven't you built me a beautiful cedar temple?"

God is going to allow it a generation from now, but David must not lose the understanding of God dwelling amongst His people, in a personal relationship with them.

David's conquests of the surrounding nations were quite an achievement.

Romans 2 v1-23

Paul is now tackling this central issue of the "Law" and why God gave the "Law" to the Jews and what it is supposed to do, as distinct from how many of his fellow Jews saw it. In the chapters ahead, Paul will bring home to us the point that was being made to David, of the essential nature of a personal relationship with the Lord, and how Temple rituals and elaborate codes of what you can and cannot do cloud that essential nature of what it really means to have a relationship with God. Sin is everywhere, and the "Law" merely brings home our need, not our means of salvation. Both those with the written law, and those who have only a God given conscience are aware of what is wrong between God and themselves. Paul demolishes the ideas of those who think that they are God's elite, for sin is everywhere, even in those elite circles who are so proud of their Jewish spiritual heritage.

Proverbs 19v8-9

V9 – perjury again! Kidner's title for verse 8 is "sense pays its way."

July 15th

1st Chronicles 19v1-21v30

David's friendship towards Nahash had been genuine and so the attitudes of the new King of Ammon and his advisors was exceedingly hurtful. Nahash and David had been friendly since both had Saul as an enemy, but David had subdued neighbouring Edom and Moab, and from the perspective of the Ammonites, David's apparent thankfulness to the people of Jabesh-gilead for their kindness to Saul's family was seen as an unfriendly act to the Ammonites. It sounds complex, but David had no idea how these people, to whom he had genuine friendship, were beginning to see him. The deliberate humiliation of David's ambassadors led to a series of wars before David took the Ammonite crown.

There is a lot of detail here about how David's extended kingdom was established. The Chronicler spares us the details of the Bathsheba incident which has all of this as its background, although he does refer to the fact that in these battles David now stayed at home, which was much of the root cause of how he came to be tempted by another man's wife, while her husband was away on battle duties.

The census (chapter 21) caused offence to both God and Man – even Joab, far from being a spiritual man, recognised that David should not attempt to number God's people. As Selman put it, in his commentary: "he seems to have forgotten that the people were not his but God's."

Romans 2v24-3v8

Jewish people were probably quite offended by what Paul said here, but salvation was not a matter of being born into the family of Abraham, or through being circumcised. Paul was not, however, saying that the law was irrelevant – he always took sin seriously, and not how some of his opponents portrayed him.

Proverbs 19v10-12

Several different themes here. Kidner, for verse 10, suggests that while God in His grace wishes to bless, "he has no pleasure in a misfit." (p132) Kidner sums up verse

11 in one word "magnanimity." Verse 12 has lessons for both the King and others: one can learn to control that temper, and "subordinates may learn tact..."

July 16th

1st Chronicles 22v1-23v32

David continued to make preparations for the Temple. It was an obsession with David, his intentions were good, but remember what God actually did say in yesterday's reading.

Romans 3v9-31

The basis of salvation is faith and trust in Christ. Full-stop! Some Jewish Christians struggled with the idea of "in Christ alone."

Proverbs 19 v13-14

Comments on home life!

July 17th

1st Chronicles 24v1-26v11

That's a lot of commitment, organisation and hard work – all for the Lord!

Of course the Chronicler is also showing, in detail, the connection between the work then, and those who in his day were returning to Jerusalem. Spiritual heritage is important.

Romans 4v1-13

The intense and detailed discussion on Abraham, David etc might lose some, but the basic argument is that it is through faith and trust, not circumcision or whatever, that people are made right with God.

Proverbs 19v15-16

Laziness leads to hunger; despising God's laws can lead to death.

July 18th

1st Chronicles 26v12-27v34

If only we had these people to choose from today! It is a detailed picture of how everything in the Kingdom was highly organised. It was even more so under Solomon, but then under his son, things became rather unstuck, with the people beginning to resent the demands of central government. We may marvel at the rapid establishment of an empire from a loose federation of tribes, but problems were ahead.

Romans 4v14-5v2

The argument continues:

"So now, since we have been made right in God's sight by faith in His promises, we can have real peace with Him because of what Jesus Christ our Lord has done for us."

Some from Jewish backgrounds just could not bring themselves to give Christ central place. Paul was dealing with real crunch issues here.

Proverbs 19v17 There are Christian groups who encourage a "prosperity" gospel in which they expect like for like – that giving to God receives financial blessing in return. That's a dangerous philosophy, often used by those who are trying to exploit a willing heart. How God blesses the cheerful giver is up to Him, and often sacrificial giving is precisely that.

Getting back though to our verse from Proverbs, the point is simply that God is well aware when we give to or support the person who can never repay. "It promises faithful recompense, not necessarily one's money back." (Kidner p134)

July 19th

1st Chronicles 28v1-29v30

Here we have David's claim that it was because he was a man of blood!

The Chronicler gives us a lovely account of the handover to Solomon. From our earlier study of 2nd Samuel, we know the human factors that plotted and planned – and failed – to make things otherwise.

Romans 5v3-21

The issue of problems and trials is an important one; some people have this idea that the Christian life is to be pain and suffering free. However, as one person said, his troubles only began when he became a Christian!

That's not entirely right either, but we have a God who loves us, cares for us, and is there for us in all circumstances. That can include great trials, and moments and periods in which we have to trust when we cannot see round the corner, nor indeed, the light at the end of a tunnel. But painless, stress free life would not help us to grow and develop. Endurance, strength of character and Christian growth come through facing up to difficulty.

The rest of the chapter touches on something which present day Judaism refuses to accept – the doctrine that a sinful nature was passed down through Adam. Paul contrasts Adam and Christ.

"When we were utterly helpless, Christ came at just the right time and died for us sinners." Romans 5 v6 (New Living Translation.)

Proverbs 19v18-19

Parents rightly teach their children their rights, but some do it in a way which teaches their children how to abuse their rights and exploit situations. Parents will pay in the long run for a lack of discipline. And an adult who cannot control his temper will discover the cost too.

July 20th

2nd Chronicles 1v1-3v17

The archeological evidence is there for all of this. What an empire it was! Solomon asked for wisdom, and there is no doubt that God gave it to him. Solomon had one of the finest minds in the Bible, and in Ecclesiastes, the Song of Songs and in the collection of Proverbs which he put together, Solomon made a major contribution to the "Wisdom" material which we have in the Bible. Solomon was not flawless, however, and great "academic" wisdom needs a moral and spiritual dimension to it all, and sometimes we see how Solomon did not always take his own advice. Further reading into 1st Kings will leave us wondering about the wisdom of the many marriages with the foreign altars and idols that these brought into Jerusalem, or the wisdom which could not see what his son would inherit in terms of resentment. 1st Kings 11 specifically speaks of how Solomon failed to listen to the Lord, and he warned that his kingdom would be curtailed to one tribe – as it was in his son's reign.

Romans 6v1-23

Bonheoffer – a German theologian executed under Hitler coined the phrase "cheap grace" to describe the abusing attitude that some people have towards God's grace – rather like the wayward youth who always expects Dad or Mum to pick up the bill, once again.

God's grace is a wonderful gift, and not something we should, so to speak, wipe our feet on.

Paul seems to have dealing with one particular abuse – an attitude that further delving into sin gave further opportunity to experience God's grace. Real faith and trust in Christ, while relying on God's power and strength to live the Christian life, needs the "backbone" of a real commitment to live it.

We need to decide for real, decisively, whether we are for Christ or not.

Proverbs 19v20-21

The meaning is obvious.

July 21st

2nd Chronicles 4v1-6v13a

No expense was spared! While we sometimes have to be reminded that the Church is not the building, but the people, and that the task of the Church is mission, not maintenance, sometimes we meet great meanness towards the work of the Lord.

God did come to dwell in His earthly Temple; but He was never restricted to it. And when the Holy city became anything but holy, God was prepared to warn and then exercise judgment.

Romans 7 v1-14

Paul was still battling with a Jewish obsession that the Law of God was everything. The Law shows us our need, but does not give us our salvation. Here Christianity and Judaism were to part.

Proverbs 19v22-23

Basic truths that nevertheless need to be repeated.

July 22nd

2nd Chronicles 6v13b-8v10

Solomon's prayer celebrates the promises, but also recognises that the covenant with God brings duties and responsibilities. From the outset, the warning was always there that God would punish when the people of the covenant turned away from Him.

Romans 7v15-8v8

The old nature is striving within. And yet there is a great and wonderful sense of the burden of sin being lifted in Christ. We do need to decide though, who is to reign in our lives.

Proverbs 19v24-25

The sluggards and scorners are contrasted with the discerning who can learn even from a painful lesson.

July 23rd

2nd Chronicles 8v11-10v19

Solomon began to realise the contradiction of his foreign trophy wife with all her pagan practices so close to the Temple itself.

Solomon had poor possibilities for a significant harbour along the Mediterranean coastline, but recognised the opportunities of a port (Eilat) on the Red Sea.

The warning given to Solomon came true during the start of Rehoboam's reign. He took the advice to play even tougher than his father, and blew it.

Romans 8v9-23

Be controlled by God's Spirit! Our passage also looks forward to the resurrection body, and the even greater freedom to live as God's people. Meanwhile the Holy Spirit within is a foretaste, a promise, of that life.

Proverbs 19v26

Another insight into what it means to "honour thy father and mother..."

July 24th

2nd Chronicles 11v1-13v22

The prophet Shemaiah stopped the king from inflicting a terrible civil war on God's people. Meanwhile, Jeroboam, who was now the King of the upper part of the country (now known as Israel, as distinct from Judah, which remained loyal to Rehoboam) resented the fact that the temple was still in the hands of Solomon's son – so he invented a new religion of his own (or adapted pagan rights and beliefs) to distract the people from the Temple in Jerusalem. This of course led the priests and Levites from throughout the country having to relocate to Jerusalem to continue the worship of the one true God – so Rehoboam ended up ruling the tribe of Levi (Benjamin also remained under his rule.)

Rehoboam managed to fortify the area under his rule and became quite confident. But when he abandoned the Lord he had the humiliation of the temple and palace being stripped by the King of Egypt – Solomon's gold shields had to be replaced by bronze.

A clue to the "problem" with Rehoboam is that his mother was an Ammonite – the issue is not one of race, but of spiritual teaching. The following verse tells us "he did not seek the Lord with all his heart." Solomon, after all, had built shrines to the Ammonite gods – indeed for all his foreign wives (1st Kings 11)

The short reign of King Abijah appears to have been one of real faith in God. In his successful battle with the northern tribes, he captured Bethel, the sanctuary of the golden calf idols.

Romans 8v24-39

There are important lessons in this passage on how the Holy Spirit helps us daily in our walk with the Lord.

We must also realise that when God has forgiven, God has forgiven. And nothing can separate us from His love.

Proverbs 19v27-29

Wrong attitudes – to education, truth, respect for others…the fool soon learns the consequences.

July 25th

2nd Chronicles 14v1-16v14

Major revival seemed to be taking place. Here at last was a king who removed all the pagan shrines and practices. The first 35 years went well, but he made the mistake of taking the temple and palace gold and silver to bribe the Syrians to attack the northern tribes.

Romans 9v1-24

God has not given up on the Jews! But there is still only one way – Christ.

Proverbs 20 v1

The Bible has some hard hitting things to say on alcohol abuse.

July 26th

2nd Chronicles 17v1-18v34

Jehoshaphat ruled well and even took steps to spiritually educate his people. A foolish step (probably with the hope of reuniting the kingdom, long term), was the marriage alliance of his son and the daughter of King Ahab (as in Ahab and Jezebel – bad news!)

Romans 9v25-10v12

God has other children; they are not all of physical descent from Abraham.

Paul is trying to explain how in God's purposes the Christian Church was swelling with gentile numbers, while a significant number of Jews remained hardened against the Gospel.

Proverbs 20v2-3

Sometimes it is very important to have the wit to stay out of a fight.

July 27th

2nd Chronicles 19v1-20v37

Jehoshaphat seems to have heeded the prophet Jehu's warning about "helping the wicked and loving those who hate the Lord." (the alliance with Ahab was wrong.)

Sometime later he faced a war with the combined forces of several nations. King and people turned to God, and one of the sons of Asaph prophesied that they would not need to fight. The King led out a choir praising God the whole way – to find that their enemies had turned on each other. It took 3 days to cart away the loot!

Unfortunately, towards the end of his reign, the King went back into alliance with Ahaziah of Israel.

Romans 10v13-11v12

The preaching of the Gospel is absolutely essential – how else are people to come to faith. Paul continues to discuss the problem of Jewish unbelief.

Proverbs 20v4-6 A good proverb for farmers, but with obvious application to all. If you are too lazy to plough in the cold, you won't have a harvest.

Seeking, drawing out good advice, and recognising good and faithful friendship.

July 28th

2nd Chronicles 21v1-23v21

Now the foolishness of otherwise good King Jehoshaphat comes back upon the whole royal family.

He had arranged a marriage between his son Jehoram and the daughter of wicked Ahab and Jezebel. Jehoram wiped out his own brothers, and continued to be thoroughly wicked. His youngest son was the only one to survive an Arab raid. That son, Ahaziah, (presumably named after the former Israelite king of the same name) died in an attempt to shore up the regime in the north, which was under threat, first from the Syrians, and then from an internal rebellion by Jehu. In fact a number of the Judean royal family died as they got caught up in the coup d'état that was ongoing in the north.

Then, for whatever bizarre reasons of her own, Jehoram's widow (Ahaziah's mother, daughter of wicked Ahab of the northern kingdom) decided to butcher her own family on hearing of the death of her own son. So, no sooner was the regime of Ahab's family wiped out in the north, than the daughter of Ahab seized the southern throne from her own descendents, the Judean royal family. Ahaziah's sister, however, who was married to the priest in charge of the Lord's Temple, grabbed one of the little princes, Joash, and hid him in the Temple.

After six years, the priest took some of the army officers into his confidence, and the wicked daughter of Ahab was removed from the throne.

Romans 11v13-36

As we know from the Gospels, trees and vines were used as symbols of God's people, the Jews. Paul speaks of how some gentile branches have been grafted in; someday God in His grace will bring the Jewish branches back to Himself.

Proverbs 20v7

As Kidner puts it, "A father's best legacy..." Makes us think when we have seen the damage of a bad legacy in 2nd Chronicles.

July 29th

2nd Chronicles 24v1-25v28

It is perhaps no surprise that a prince raised in the temple in secret would be one who would restore a Temple which had been stripped of every valuable for the worship of Baal. The priest Jehoiada lived to 130 years old. After his death, some of the reforms were reversed. Zechariah, Jehoiada's son challenged the people about the way in which they were returning to idolatry, and Joash had him executed. However, after Jerusalem was defeated by the Arameans, and Joash was severely injured, his own officials took revenge for the murder of Zechariah.

Amaziah his son eventually executed those who killed his father. Many things were good about his reign, but after a war with the Edomites he adopted some of their idol worship. He also attacked Israel (where to add to the confusion, the King was known as Joash or Jehoash). Judah was defeated, part of the walls of Jerusalem pulled down, and treasures carried off from both the Temple and the palace. Although Amaziah outlived the northern king, he was eventually murdered by his own people.

Romans 12 v1-21

A call to serious living for Jesus. Paul talks of giving ourselves as living sacrifices – to use our God given gifts, to be genuine in loving God's people, to live by very different standards from the world around us.

Proverbs 20 v8-10

Kings are reminded to carefully weigh evidence; all are challenged to examine their hearts; all are reminded that God despises double standards.

July 30th

2nd Chronicles 26v1-28v27

Uzziah was in general a good King – until he arrogantly tried to take some of the duties of the priesthood upon himself, as indeed some of the pagan kings did. He was struck with leprosy for doing so. His son Jotham eventually had to act as king and was regarded as a good king when he eventually took over on the death of his father. His son Ahaz, however was a Baal worshipper who brought back some of the most hideous pagan practices into Jerusalem. At one point he sealed the doors of the Temple to prevent worship from taking place.

Romans 13v1-14

The call to be a conscientious citizen was not issued lightly given that times were not easy for Christians in many of the cities of the empire.

Christians were reminded to live in the light of the fact that Christ would one day return.

Proverbs 20v11: Character is already showing in children.

July 31st

2nd Chronicles 29v1-36

King Hezekiah reopens and repairs the Temple. The worship of the one true God recommences.

Romans 14v1-23

There were / are issues on which it was / is not constructive to offend fellow Christians, and there were matters on which Christians would have to recognise that some took a different position. Meat slaughtered in pagan markets (often in pagan temples) was one such issue.

Proverbs 20v12

Sight and hearing to be appreciated as God's gifts.

August 1st

2nd Chronicles 30v1-31v21

This is a tremendous reversal of how things had been under the previous king, with people from the northern kingdom joining in the Passover festival at the Temple.

Romans 15v1-22

Paul's hope for the kind of fellowship that might exist amongst believers from very different backgrounds.

Proverbs 20v13-15

More on the sluggard.

Is verse 14 purely a warning to the inexperienced business person or a parable of how there are things which we are too easily "talked into selling lightly"? (Kidner page 138

August 2nd

2nd Chronicles 32v1-33v13

Hezekiah's water tunnel, bringing the water supplies inside the city wall is a marvellous engineering feat and can still be visited (walked down underground) today.

We have already looked at the story of the Assyrians mocking God in 2nd Kings.

Likewise, we have already read of Hezekiah foolishly showing everything to the Babylonian envoys.

Manasseh was a particularly evil king who only learnt his lesson after being briefly deported to Babylon.

Romans 15v23-16v7

We believe that Paul did make it to Spain before his second imprisonment. (It is believed he was released after the end of the Book of Acts and then, about 2 years later re-arrested and executed.)

However, here in our reading Paul is referring to the financial support which he was to bring to the Christians in Jerusalem. Sadly, when he did get there, they would pressurise him to take part in Temple rituals which would lead to his arrest and to the fact that when he did eventually arrive in Rome it would be as a prisoner.

Proverbs 20v16-18

More sanctified common sense.

August 3rd

2nd Chronicles 33v14-34v33

Considerable amends were made by Manasseh to try and correct the spiritual damage of his early reign. His son, unfortunately reversed the good changes and was assassinated, bringing 8 year old Josiah to the throne. Today's reading brings home just how bad things had been, with a major chunk of the Old Testament, possibly the Book of Deuteronomy being rediscovered in the Temple!

Although it may seem as though a tremendous revival had taken place, it was very much under Josiah's direction that the people returned to God.

Romans 16v8-27

A lovely list of fellow workers from many different backgrounds, Jewish, Greek and Roman. However, in passing, Paul has to warn them of other divisive characters.

Proverbs 20v19

Common sense

August 4th

2nd Chronicles 35v1-36v23

Josiah was a brilliant and godly king, but his attempt to intervene in a battle between the superpowers of Egypt and Assyria led to his death. This led to a period of instability, with one son reigning for 3 months before being deposed by the Egyptians, and then the next 2 being deposed by the Babylonians, one after the other. King Zedekiah rebelled against Babylon, provoking a very harsh reaction. People were carried off into captivity until the reign of Cyrus the Persian. The captivity in Babylon was seen as God's judgment after prolonged warnings by a number of prophets. We will study all of this in greater detail in our studies of Jeremiah.

1st Corinthians 1v1-17

There are real words of encouragement in the opening sentences, but there are serious divisions and party spirit within the Church. It was quite embarrassing for people like Paul, Peter and Apollos to hear they had their rival followers.

Proverbs 20 v20-21

More on honouring parents. And also comment on quick wealth.

August 5th

Ezra 1v1-2v70

Cyrus would have had advisors who would have framed this statement for him. Here is quite a contrast with the policies of Nebuchadnezzar, who had tried to enforce uniformity, complete assimilation, and religious syncreticism (make it all the same) across his empire. In complete contrast, Cyrus is prepared to let the various peoples follow their own customs, rebuild their temples and return to the various places from which they had been uprooted. Of course we can see God's hand in all of this, but we are also aware of the challenge this will present to children and grandchildren who have grown up hundreds of miles away in Babylon/Persia. Their lives have been changed even more than they realise; as we will see later, some can no longer speak Hebrew. We are even told the exact numbers of horses, donkeys etc – emphasising the struggle it would be to rebuild a country. The genealogies are important for a people who wish to prove their links with God's people and His promises to them and to specific areas of land that had belonged to their tribes and families. It was also very important that those who claimed to belong to the priestly families and to the Levites could prove who they were.

1st Corinthians 1v18-2v5

In our times, criticism is sometimes made of how glossy multimedia hype has to be used to get the support of Christian people for Gospel projects. We can understand why the best of multimedia etc is needed to attract in to evangelistic events those who don't know the Lord – but why are those who claim to know the Lord still so dependent upon Christianity being sold to them with all the hype and gloss that is so much part of the world outside? "Big names" need to be brought in from outside etc in order to get the support of those who supposedly love the Lord.

Paul was already finding these tendencies in Corinth and elsewhere. Paul stresses the substance of the Gospel, not human oratory and showmanship.

Proverbs 20v22-23

Interesting how different issues have been put together here. First of all, in verse 22 we have the embittered person seeking revenge, who – no matter how justified his anger may be - needs to let go of his anger and to leave things to the Lord. In verse 23 we have someone who has already adopted the dishonest standards of the world around him. Is it just a coincidence that these verses are placed together, or is it a warning now righteous anger becomes a lot less righteous, and before very long we are playing the same games ourselves?

August 6th

Ezra 3 v1-4v24

In chapter 3 the Jews who have returned do their best to recreate things as they had once existed – the response is one of both joy and tears –joy that the temple foundations were now in place, but also a realisation that Solomon's temple in all its glory could not be replaced as it once had been.

Chapter 4, however, throws up the problem of how others in the surrounding area suddenly want to be included in what is happening.

Who can we – who should we, work with in Christian things? These questions are not always easily answered, and sooner or later you and I will have been on the receiving end of what it feels like to be judged by some extremely narrow group who believe that they could not possibly work with our Church or with us in particular. Some of those groups need to heed what Jesus had to say about the Pharisees, especially the bit about when they find a convert they make him twice as much a son of hell as they are themselves! (Matthew 23 v15)

In our own Province, how I wish that the energy spent by one group vaunting its "purity" over others, and in stealing members from other Churches, went into leading people to Christ who have no Church connection.

However, getting back to our passage, the Scriptures here support the decision NOT to work with these other people who, in the times of Ezra, claimed to be just as interested in the LORD as they were. Why?

Here we have the complex history of the Samaritans. First of all, ever since the break between Jerusalem and the northern tribes during the reign of Solomon's son, syncreticism – a mixing together of various religious beliefs, was a big problem in the times of Ahab, Elijah, Elisha etc – the real problem was not so much that people were choosing to worship Baal rather than the LORD, but rather that they were mixing it all up together and producing a blend. The northern tribes, who were particularly guilty of this, had been carried away into captivity by the Assyrians, several generations before the Babylonians came and carried away the people of Jerusalem. However, the Assyrians not only carried away the northern tribes, they brought people in to replace them, and these people engaged in some syncreticism of their own, blending together teachings about the LORD with their own false gods and goddesses. They also intermarried with the poor Israelites who had been left behind in the area.

Although hundreds of years later, Jesus and the early Church find Gospel opportunities amongst the Samaritans of New Testament times (and there are complex questions as to how the Samaritans of Ezra's time relate to the Samaritans of the 1st century AD) these people in Ezra chapter 4 are not seeking to convert to the Old Testament faith of God's people, the Jews, but are seeking acceptance on equal footing for their beliefs and practices. Frankly, if the Temple had meant so much to these other groups, how come they had ignored it during all the years it had remained in ruins.

The Jewish people who have just come through decades of pressure in Babylon to syncretise were not about to blend in with other groups who have gone down the road considerably far from what they had struggled to preserve in Babylon and Persia.

Chapter 4 verse 1 also describes these people as the enemies of the newly arrived exiles – far from wishing them well, these other groups in the area had a vested interest in seeing any attempt to restore Jerusalem collapse rather than thrive. There is no doubt, however, that once their requested to be included was spurned, they did everything possible to undermine the work and to prevent the temple and the city from being rebuilt.

1st Corinthians 2v6-3v4

How we read the Bible is an important issue. We need to seek God's help and leading, by the Holy Spirit, who will open our spiritual eyes, and bring it home in our hearts.

If we are not reading it from the perspective of faith and trust in Jesus, what are we going to make of it? Scriptures taken out of context are easily abused and twisted.

Paul also pleads for Christian maturity. These readers need to grow up in their faith and mature into responsible followers of Jesus.

Proverbs 20 v24-25

A challenge to be really led by the Lord – rather than the rash jumping in to a situation which then has to be reconsidered. Surprising what some will claim the Lord led them to do.

August 7th

Ezra 5 v1-6v22

Getting "a second wind" – encouraging people to start again who have been discouraged and exhausted is never easy, but here a number of prophetic leaders manage to do that.

1st Corinthians 3 v5-23

Party spirit hinders God's work.

Proverbs 20v26-27

Strong government (v26) needs a conscience (v27) lit by God's Spirit.

August 8th

Ezra 7v1-8v20

Genealogies are often dismissed (unless you are an American or Australian intent on finding your roots) and the temptation is there to just skip over these pages.

We live in an age in which people only too readily kick over the traces of their spiritual heritage. For these people, their family trees spoke of how the Bible's stories were not myth but a reality with which they had direct family links. God had been working, shaping, down through all of those generations. How conscious are we of God working down through the generations of our families, and are you praying for those generations that are following?

1 Corinthians 4 v1-21

More on this party or denominational thinking in Corinth (who was a follower of Paul, who was a follower of Apollos...)

One thing was clear, the people were no near as mature as they imagined themselves to be.

Proverbs 20 v28-30

While the writer has recognised the need for firm government, and already commented on how that must be matched by a God inspired conscience, to that he adds (v28) the need for loving kindness. Verses 29 reminds us that the generations can work together.

August 9th

Ezra 8v21-9v15

The first part of the reading brings home the scrupulous honesty that was involved in transporting back to Jerusalem all of these things that were to adorn God's House, and the very real sense of God's protecting hand with them in everything.

Sadly it contrasts sharply with the spiritual mess of the people back in Jerusalem. Intermarriage had led to many horrible examples of syncretism – worship of the one true God mixed in, blended with, pagan practices and superstitions.

1st Corinthians 5 v1-13

For all their arrogance about how mature they were, basic sexual morality was a major issue in the life of the Church, with a man living openly with his step mother. And clearly many in the Church had no problem with it. Paul disagrees strongly with that view; the life of the Church internally does matter. Paul does not mince his words. He tells them to put this unrepentant man out of the Church membership.

Proverbs 21v1-2

Again two strands woven together here. God is in control, over great kings and leaders, and yet the next verse reminds us that our motives are still weighed by God.

August 10th

Ezra 10 v1-44

These are difficult matters, and the problem was on an immense scale, involving priests and many of the leaders – and in some cases there were many children involved. None of this was easily settled. To give some balance to what you read here, Malachi chapter 2 speaks of the scandalous number of Jewish women who had been abandoned in favour of heathen women. Some of the attitudes have their parallels in today's world – "Russian babes", "Thai brides" with the implicit suggestion that these "exotic" women are somehow more erotic. The attraction of many of these foreign women in Ezra's time was that they were coming from heathen lands with fertility cults and other promiscuous practices. There are serious issues here as to what was going on in the moral life of the nation.

1st Corinthians 6 v1-20

Corinth's Christians needed to settle problems themselves rather than bringing matters before heathen judges.

Other sexual sins continue to be a very real problem in the life of the Corinthian Church.

Proverbs 21v3. As Derek Kidner puts it in his commentary on Proverbs, God cannot be bought!

August 11th

Nehemiah 1v1-3v14

Here we have an explanation of how Nehemiah arrives on the scene back in Jerusalem.

How can Nehemiah help ?– he is wine steward, not a politician or engineer – but he is a man of prayer, who also prays specifically having done his homework in getting down to details – when he receives an opportunity to speak, he has a fair idea of some of the things that are needed.

It is interesting who some of the people are who get their hands dirty, literally, in the work of rebuilding eg goldsmiths, perfume makers, Shallum and his daughters etc.

1st Corinthians 7 v1-19

Thorny questions. Which is best – single and single hearted in service, or married with companionship and mutual support? Paul also touches on the tensions of those who have become Christians, but a husband or wife has not yet followed their example. Where possible, homes are to be kept together.

Proverbs 21 v4: A reminder that the route to sin began long before the literal action.

August 12th

Nehemiah 3 v15 – 5v13

We continue with the pleasant surprise of seeing who was literally prepared to get their hands dirty in the work of rebuilding! However, the Samaritan rage at the rebuilding leads to the workers having to bring their weapons with them for protection.

Just as Ezra was deeply upset at the number of men seeking foreign brides brought up in the heathen and often very explicit practices of the nations around them, Nehemiah was upset at the extortion or opportunism going on as many ordinary people were forced to go to loan sharks. Even children had to be sold into slavery.

1st Corinthians 7 v20 -40

These were difficult times as people were struggling as to how to live for Christ in all the situations that already existed, and as some were clearly concerned about taking on new responsibilities in uncertain times.

Proverbs 21v5-7 More sanctified common sense.

August 13th

Nehemiah 5 v14-7v60

We are made conscious of the pressures that Nehemiah faced personally – suspicions that he was "doing all right" out of the job, when truthfully he was subsiding quite a lot! He literally worked on the wall himself!

We also see the psychological warfare that Sanballat and others used against him.

1st Corinthians 8 v1-13

Difficult subjects again. The meat sacrificed to idols was not going to harm a Christian. The truth is that it might have been difficult to buy meat in the local market that had not been in some sense sacrificed in the local pagan temple which doubled up as the abattoir!

Christians had to be sensitive to the fact that some of these issues were more sensitive to other Christians than themselves, and to be aware that they could upset fellow Christians who were still working through these and other matters. Although I am inclined to comment that in Northern Ireland the so called "weaker brother" uses these verses to terrorise other Christians into conformity on matters that many Christians will take different viewpoints on. Sometimes a period working abroad, in a different culture, brings home that in different parts of the world Christians have hang ups on very different matters. Be aware of how something that doesn't really bother you, may bother other Christians.

Proverbs 21v8-10

We may laugh at verse 9, but many a divorce has come out of a situation in which the couple seemed to have every material thing.

August 14th

Nehemiah 7v61 – 9 v21

The first part of the reading has a lot of detail. Genealogies may not interest you, but the mention of them has to be seen in the context of people who held on tightly to their spiritual heritage through times when to do so was costly; it reflects an active faith kept down through the generations, as families looked forward in trust to the day that God would bring them back, and new generations would take up again the duties of their forefathers in God's House and work.

The next part tells of how the people burst into tears when they heard God's Word. Some suggest that when the Levites were "explaining the Laws" they may actually have been translating for those who no longer had Hebrew as their mother tongue – but, whatever, we read of people deeply moved as the meaning of God's Word came home to them – and we read of joyful celebrations as the festivals of God's people are kept.

1 Corinthians 9 v1-19

Paul has been hurt by some of the lack of love he has experienced amongst God's people. That of course is the whole irony that we speak of "Saint" Paul and describe him as probably one of the greatest missionaries to have ever lived – but of course we say these things after his life time has come to an end. It would have been better to have shown love and support during his life than to praise him when he was no longer there!

There is more than just a hint here that Paul's ministry was not respected because he gave freely. Not having to pay for it, they did not value what he gave – but then this was a society in which their pagan philosophers and preachers charged. So there is nothing new in how some Christian people today value glossy presentations and celebrity styled "ministries" rather than depth and humility.

Proverbs 21v11-12 Actually this is one occasion when I like the way in which the Living Bible sets out the sharp contrast between those who only learn through punishment, and those who learn because their hearts really are open, listening to God.

August 15th

Nehemiah 9v22-10v39

Ezra continues to remind them of the lessons learnt the hard way in the past, but the people then go on to begin living again as the "Covenant people" – actually signing the covenant with God, and then making practical arrangements to put it into practice. Their lives were to be distinct again as God's people.

1 Corinthians 9v20-10v14

Some of the practicalities of moving from one culture to another – trying not to cause offence, being aware of the things that might upset people from a particular backgound, but never losing sight of the things that matter and understanding what are the real issues at the heart of the Gospel.

There is a warning that Christians can become complacent, imagining that they are safe from falling into particular sins. They need to be really trusting in Christ's help and strength.

Proverbs 21 v13

A parallel in many respects with the clause "forgive us...as we forgive those who trespass against us." Shutting your ears and hearts to the cries of others shows that you have not really grasped that all you have from God has been by God's grace

---

August 16th

Nehemiah 11v1-12v26

Remember that life in Jerusalem was still hard; the city had yet to regain its former glory and so volunteers were sought, and others brought in by lot to get the life and work of the city up and running again.

The details were important as the people had a real sense of beginning again with the LORD.

1 Corinthians 10v15-11v2

Paul knew that meat bought in the market place, which had probably been killed during some pagan rite in the various temples of the area would not do him harm. It was a different matter when people were actively involved in the pagan worship and effectively trying to keep a foot in both camps, the pagan and the Christian.

Christians did not need to know where the meat came from, but certainly if someone started to make an issue of it, that became a different matter. There was concern for others who might then find the whole matter difficult, either as weaker Christians, or pagans who might imagine that the Christian was endorsing much more.

Proverbs 21 v14-16

Just what do these verses mean? Wrong doing is not being endorsed here, but we are being reminded that sometimes there are very thin lines, such as the one between what constitutes a gift, and what is actually a bribe – hence the next verse with its talk of justice and righteousness, compared to evildoing.

August 17th

Nehemiah 12v27-13v31

What celebrations these were! They also bring home the extent of all the work. It has not just been about a length of wall, villages have also been rebuilt, with the temple singers, for example, deliberately building their villages near Jerusalem, and the whole spiritual life of the people has been lifted and revitalised.

This contrasts so sharply with developments when Nehemiah has to return to Babylon to see Artaxerxes. Tobiah has been an enemy of the LORD's work, and yet through his friendship with Eliashib, manages to get a temple storeroom converted into a guestroom for him. The support for the Levites and others had failed to come in, and the choir singers had been forced to return to farming to get a living. People were farming and trading on the Sabbath, and there was wide spread intermarriage into many of the surrounding pagan nations. Nehemiah was absolutely incensed to discover that one of the High Priest's sons had married into Sanballat's family. For me it is so sad that it took the constant presence of Nehemiah to keep the people on track, and ultimately this was the most depressing and exhausting aspect of the whole thing for Nehemiah.

1st Corinthians 11v3-16

Why was all of this a pressing issue? Many readers either "turn off" at this point, or get themselves into some kind of argument over the role of women today. Frankly, what head covering symbolised 2,000 years ago has little to do with hats as part of formal wear today, and I can well remember my childhood minister being exasperated with choir members who used to spend their time during the prayers of intercession adjusting their hats – so much so, that one Sunday back in the sixties, he told them to leave their hats at home!!! To be blunt, I don't think turning up at Church looking as though you are dressed for Ladies' Day at Royal Ascot makes you anymore reverent and I think it just puts up one more barrier to others coming to Church, and it feeds a certain Pharisaic streak in those who want to make themselves out to be more "spiritual" than others.

Having said that, there are no throw away passages in God's Word, and there are actually lessons to be learnt from this passage. A serious problem was the background culture from which these Greek converts were coming. Women in pagan worship had occupied roles from temple prostitution, to performing as possessed oracles. Legally women had so little standing, but they had learnt to use their sexuality aggressively in Greek society. So what would their role be in the Christian Church? What would be acceptable behaviour? What about the attitudes of men in the Church who were also coming from this crude, vulgar and amoral society? Greek culture was very sexually explicit, with little regard for marriage. Nevertheless, the Gospel was making real inroads into their society. And it all certainly put those who had been raised in the safety and the protection of the

Jewish Synagogue into one right "tizzy" as they had to work out how to handle these converts to Christianity who had none of their Old Testament background!

So, if you were dealing with converts from today's foul mouthed, crude "ladettes" – the drunken girls you see staggering down the streets in the early hours of the morning in our large cities and towns, what kind of informal guidelines would you try to have as new converts work out how to live their new Christian lives? And there are just as many problems dealing with a middle-class middle-aged group who are ultimately no more Christian in their attitudes and values.

We might skip the hats, and although we might make some suggestions as to what is more appropriate than those little black numbers that were never made for sitting in pews, **the real issues** will be changing the values of those who come in from a society so at odds with Christianity – and we have got to get it right ourselves, emphasising the things that really matter, the core values of family life, of how men and women regard each other, having come in to the Christian life from a society in which both sexes live as sexual predators.

Paul was dealing with women who were so hurt, so self abused, and abused by others, so afraid of commitment, and so aggressive as a form of defence, that some of them were incapable of sustaining a meaningful permanent relationship.

How some Christian groups interpret these verses, slapping down gifted women (and telling them to go off and make the tea) is not dealing with the very real issues that the young people in your Church/Sunday School/Youth Group are dealing with.

So forget about the hats! What kind of feminism, or masculinity, do you want to teach as a Christian norm? And what is the Biblical model of how women and men ought to treat each other, and relate together? At least I have got you thinking about real issues, which is what Paul was doing in the society of his time!

Proverbs 21v17-18

There is a contrast between finding joy and pleasure out of doing right, and trying to buy pleasure and happiness.

August 18th

Esther 1v1-3v15

I take strong exception as to how this story is taught by some Christian groups, particularly to children. Queen Vashti is made out to be evil ("Boys and girls we must learn to obey the King, King Jesus.") King Ahasuerus (Hebrew version of his name) or Xerxes (Persian version of his name) was no Christ like King. He was an impulsive, all powerful despot who could hang his favourite advisor on the gallows the next day (as indeed he does in this story) and for much of his time he was so busy/so distracted that he was ultimately manipulated by others upon whom he had to rely to interpret all the things that were happening in his Kingdom. Policies were made according to the king's whims and often with little thought as to their consequences.

Anyway, the book opens with one massive drunken party. After 7 days of heavy, mindless drinking, the King decides to "display" his wife's beauty to his nobles and to the people. How would a wife today react to the servants being sent to bring her "for display," especially in a room full of people who have been drinking continuously for a week? Though it must be pointed out, that after a week of heavy drinking herself, Vashti and her companions were in no fit shape either.

Anyway, lest women fail to obey their heavily drunken husbands, Vashti is made an example and is banished, and meanwhile beautiful girls are rounded up from around the empire for a trial night in bed with the King, so that out of the hundreds of used and discarded women (sent off to a wing of the palace, and never allowed to go home, or form another relationship) he might choose a new Queen. Not quite how you were taught this story in Sunday School???

The challenge now, is how would you teach this story to a child from a home broken by drink – a child who may very well have witnessed violence between his or her parents?

The Bible is not supporting any of this appalling behaviour, but through this evil and perverse society, God will use these circumstances to bring a girl to the position of Queen who will be able to safeguard and protect His people, and effectively counter one extremely evil and manipulative Jew-hater, Haman, who has considerable sway over the King.

1 Corinthians 11 v17-34

The Lord's Supper, or Communion, began with a fellowship meal. That was how the early Christian Church continued to celebrate it with of course a point in the meal in which everyone was reminded of the new meaning and symbolism given to the bread and wine, as they remembered Christ's body broken, and His blood shed for us. To be honest, in many respects we have lost something of that celebration and sense of fellowship in our more formal one piece of shortbread, one little glass of (non) alcoholic wine that it has become today. At least you understand why it developed into a "token" meal, for Paul was dealing with greediness, and various excesses, including drunkenness, in how the more wealthy and affluent celebrated, while others (in the same room) had a lot less to eat – in fact some had no food to bring. However we celebrate the Lord's Supper, we must make sure that we keep central its message about Calvary and what Jesus did for us – and ensure that we conduct ourselves, both at the table and in the days ahead, in a way that portrays Him in our lives.

Proverbs 21v19-20

A few interesting comments on the quality of home life – squabbling and squandering!

August 19th

Esther 4v1-7v10

As in Nehemiah, informed and specific prayer leads to action. Who would have thought that Haman would end up swinging on the gallows he built for Mordecai! In Synagogues, during the festival of Purim, this story is read in its entirety, with the kids encouraged to join in with boos, cheers etc.

1st Corinthians 12 v1-26

Most people who are young in the faith run into the problem of meeting "Christians" who make all kinds of claims as to what the Holy Spirit told them to do or say, and frankly history is full of nutters who played the religious card, making claims about messages from God.

Frankly, if you know the rest of your Bible, you will know when somebody is making a statement that contradicts or clearly does not fit in well with what you already know of the character of God. God does not contradict God.

Having said that, the Holy Spirit is not a topic to run away from. God's Spirit is given to people when they first come to faith, and He is there to lead and help us, to prompt and encourage, to equip us and to help us in Christian service.

This leads on to a discussion about gifts that the Holy Spirit brings, and the very real danger that folk with assume they have, or even fake the more unusual and more spectacular of these.

When "our gift" becomes all about us, and our status, and our prestige, it becomes even less likely to be a gift of the Holy Spirit, because God's gifts of ability are there to build up the Church, to help others in the fellowship, to encourage others in the faith – not to take us on an ego trip! May God spare us from such self-centred people for whom their entire "spiritual experience" is about self promotion. As you will notice in tomorrow's reading, Paul – without wanting in any way to deride some of the more spectacular gifts that God does give to His Church – has just about had his fill of people claiming this or that.

In today's reading the emphasis is on how the Church as the body of Christ has many parts, and there are jobs and tasks that need to done that are not very attractive, but without which the work may grind to a near halt.

Proverbs 21v21-22

These verses contradict the commonly held wisdom which fails to see personal strength in more Christ-like characteristics.

August 20th

Esther 8v1-10v3

There was a particular problem with how law worked in many of the empires – the King or Emperor had immense despotic power, but was not allowed to turn round and pass a law contradicting one he had just passed. This was understandable – imagine someone going out enthusiastically carrying out the King's orders, only to discover that while he has been doing these things, messengers have been travelling many days by horseback, bringing the news that the King has already outlawed those actions!

So having permitted the annihilation of the Jews on a certain date, the King has to find a way of ordering the Jews to defend themselves in a way that indicates to everybody that the King's real intention is to undermine the earlier law, and so everybody will actually help the Jews because it is now obvious that the King is pro-Jewish, and that harming them will bring down the King's wrath!

The outcome is that far from being annihilated, the Jews act against all those who had been looking forward to carrying out Haman's plan. For those who are shocked by the Jewish relish at this, bear in mind that what Haman had intended would have rivalled what Nazi Germany later did to the Jews in more "modern" times.

1st Corinthians 12v27-13v1

Paul continues dealing with some of the topics from yesterday's reading, and we should see all of that as background to what he has to say about faith, hope and love, and his comments towards the end of the reading about Christian maturity. Basically, a loveless Church contradicts all the claims of how gifted and spiritual its members are!

Proverbs 21v23-24

I like the Living Bible translation here: "Keep your mouth closed and you'll stay out of trouble. Mockers are proud, haughty and arrogant."

August 21st

Job 1v1-3v26

A word of warning in how you read and interpret Job. Most people cope ok with the beginning and end of the story – a godly man suffers many things, his faith is tried and in the end he is vindicated as someone who has been faithful to God all along, despite some of the most shocking things that happen to him.

How you handle the speeches of his "friends" is another thing. In fact, the "scary" thing about the bulk of the Book of Job is that you often find yourself agreeing (after reading quickly, but perhaps not thinking enough) with what Job's "friends" have just said, only to find that they are condemned at the end of the book! That's the problem with what Job's "friends" say- they repeat ideas and phrases that religious people might be expected to say, and yet we discover that in appearing to come close, they are also far away from what God actually thinks about the situation. Yet they sound pious and godly and many of us would happily set them up as Christian counsellors or have them in the pulpit, only to discover that in God's eyes they missed the mark and had no understanding of where Job was in his relationship with God. It is certainly a challenge before you walk into a situation and start handing out "Christian" advice. So, you may find yourself struggling hard to actually see what is wrong with what the "friends" are saying – didn't I just say that to someone last week?

1 Corinthians 14 v1-17

Ah, if only I had that gift, people are sometimes tempted to say! It is right to teach that God gives gifts and that He equips all of His people in one way or another for the service of His Kingdom. Gifts though, are not for putting us up on a pedestal, but to enhance and encourage God's work, to bring others to faith and to encourage the spiritual growth of those who already know the Lord. In New Testament times, and in the 1800s in particular, there were particular obsessions with the gift of speaking in tongues. Paul does not deny that there were those who had it as a genuine gift. It was not an ability to speak a modern language – that was something that clearly happened at Pentecost in Acts 2 and should be therefore put in a different category – but what Paul is describing here are utterances made during intense worship which are not in human language.

Paul is NOT denying that such things can happen for real, but the problem was that such people were often seen as more "spiritual" and even in more modern times, it has been a test in some extreme groups as to whether people are really "spiritual" or not, according to whether they have this gift. Frankly, over the last 2,000 years, people have faked it in their vanity to vaunt themselves as super spiritual people.

Coveting the gift of speaking in tongues has been a major blight on the Christian community and Paul found that some of the things that were going on in his day neither brought others to faith, nor encouraged others in their knowledge of Jesus and their daily walk with Him.

Proverbs 21v25-26. Desiring a thing and actually getting up to do, make or earn is another! The greed of the lazy is contrasted with the generosity of the godly.

August 22nd

Job 4v1-7v22

Eliphaz sounds so "Christian" in his comments – yet Job hits the mark when he replies "One should be kind to a fainting friend, but you have accused me without the slightest fear of God…" (6v16 Living Bible Translation) "It is wonderful to speak the truth, but your criticisms are not based on fact. Are you going to condemn me just because I impulsively cried out in desperation…" (6v25, 26 Living Bible translation.)

1 Corinthians 14v18-40 Paul makes clear what essential matters are when Christians meet together for worship. He is trying to allow for the fact that some people may be having a genuine spiritual experience that is being manifested in a particular way (ie speaking in tongues) and yet he is being firm that what goes on in worship must be understood and must be constructive.

Unfortunately, most people focus in on two verses in this section, dealing with the subject of women. Bear in mind that pagan Greek and Roman religion made much of the utterances of priestesses, temple prostitutes and the like in giving out "oracles." There were things in the pagan worship that were not to be mimicked in Christian meetings and Paul's comments here in these two verses were very much aimed at a society in which new and naïve converts might continue on as they had done in the lax and immodest pagan worship. Paul's problem here is the context from which many of these new Christians were coming and clearly Paul was deeply concerned about things he had already seen in Corinth.

Proverbs 21v27

Ah, what so much prayer and even giving is really about! Bribing God or attempting to flatter Him that He might come round to doing our will.

August 23rd

Job 8 v1-11v20

Two of Job's friends jump in. Bildad would have us believe that everything goes well for godly people, and Zophar would have Job repenting of sin he hasn't committed!

Be careful about your use of religious clichés!

1 Corinthians 15v1-28.

Ouch! For such a seemingly "spiritual" place, with all of those wonderful Christian people keen to have the gift of speaking in tongues (I'm being sarcastic at this point!), we discover that Paul has to deal with some very basic doctrine. Make sure you have got the basics about the Good News, about salvation in Christ, about the Saviour dying for us, and why He rose from the dead, and of the resurrection to come!

Proverbs 21v28-29. Interesting contrasts. I like how the Living Water translation put it: "A false witness will be cut off, but an attentive witness will be allowed to speak. The wicked put up a bold front, but the upright proceed with care."

August 24th

Job 12v1-15v35

We are far from comfortable with what Job himself says here, but let's at least recognise that here is a godly man trying to make sense of what has happened to him. Job has not lost his grasp on God's sovereignty and His power – indeed that is Job's problem, for he knows and believes that all things are firmly in God's hands. Job is of course speaking from the perspective of a believer living before the coming of the Saviour, but Eliphaz won't even allow Job to raise very real issues for the suffering Christian. Ultimately what Eliphaz offers is an unthinking religion, a religion that just denies that some of these issues exist. He calls Job dishonest for even raising the issue of the suffering of just and godly people. The Psalms, in contrast, are refreshingly honest.

However, Eliphaz continues to repeat the spiritual clichés of the day. In different circumstances, some of his comments might be spot on, such as "Let him no longer trust in foolish riches; let him no longer deceive himself, for the money he trusts in will be his only reward…" The point is that this is not relevant in Job's case. He has not been trusting in his wealth, he has been trusting in God all along and cannot understand what God is doing. Eliphaz is keen to defend God; and in his defence of God has to make out that Job has clearly sinned. The Lord does not need PR men like Eliphaz who crush someone like Job in their defence of God!

1 Corinthians 15 v29-58

Paul's frustrations with some of the contradictory practices and teachings he has seen and heard at Corinth continue. Paul is not defending a practice which has clearly been happening at Corinth, and which became more of a problem in the next century amongst heretical groups (being baptised for those who were dead) but he is challenging those who apparently practice such things and yet are denying the resurrection which is an essential part of Christian teaching. Many Christians today need to re-read what Paul has to say here of the coming resurrection.

His advice in the final verse is essential – it is important to be always abounding in the Lord's work – get on with the job, rather than being paralysed, confused and distracted with some of the things that the Corinthians came up with!

Proverbs 21v30-31 Be properly rooted in God for all that is ahead.

August 25th

Job 16v1-19v29

Job's friends will be clearly upset by what Job says regarding what God has done to him. They cannot face up to the real issues of how a godly person can go through such terrible things, and they continue to try to defend God by demeaning Job, who needs none of this.

With hindsight, Christians point to some things that Job says, as prophecy of the coming of Christ. "Yet even now the witness to my innocence is there in heaven; my Advocate is there on high." (16v19) "But as for me, I know that my Redeemer lives, and that he will stand upon the earth at last." (19v25)

1 Corinthians 16v1-24 - Why we have the Freewill Offering! And it is not just for the local Church – Paul is collecting together funds for Christians in need elsewhere.

He warns them to have their eyes open for spiritual danger.

Paul commends some very fine Christian leaders to them, and that includes one lovely and mature Christian lady – Priscilla!

Proverbs 22v1

Making the right choices!

August 26th

Job 20 v1-22v30

The "friends" become more frenzied in their "defence" of God. Their closed theology won't tolerate the idea that a godly man can suffer like Job, so they are relentless in making him out to be a deserving sinner. And Job points out uncomfortable truths as wicked men appear to prosper all around him. Eliphaz is determined that Job has got to repent so something which in his view lies behind all that God has allowed to happen. Job has already been searching his own heart over these matters.

How inappropriate have your words been in difficult circumstances that others are facing?

2 Corinthians 1 v1-11

What a wonderful Saviour we have. Once more Paul and Timothy want to encourage the Corinthians in their faith, but they are also very honest about the real spiritual battles they have just come through in what is now modern Turkey ("Asia") as they carried on the work of evangelising. Prayer is important. But will some of the nonsense that has been going on in Corinth prove to be a distraction from the prayer support that ought to be there?

Proverbs 22v2-4

A number of quick points are made here. Of course our study of Job gives us a more complex picture, but we are challenged by these quick reflections from the writer of Proverbs.

August 27th

Job 23v1-27v23

As I have said before, Job lived long before the coming of the Saviour – indeed there are those who argue that the book of Job is a particularly old one in the Bible – and so while Job may yearn for his Redeemer, he does not have that intimacy yet with his Saviour.

Having said that, Job's friends are still wrong!

2 Corinthians 1v12-2v8

There are still a lot of problems in Corinth, and there are those who will use clever arguments to stand the truth on its head. God does not say "yes" when He means "no!"

There are wrongs to be righted, but there is also a situation in which someone has been rightly disciplined and now needs to be forgiven and restored.

Proverbs 22v5-6

We sometimes need to recognise when people have deliberately chosen the wrong path. We also need to recognise the importance of educating our children in Gospel truth from their earliest days.

August 28th

Job 28v1-30v31 Far from seeing this as a stream of self-righteousness from Job, let us at least credit him with having done some real heart searching about his own life. Job continues to struggle with why these things have happened.

2 Corinthians 2v9-17

The need to forgive and restore is important. How terrible it would be if the Corinthians were "finally sorted" only to become hard and unforgiving.

Paul speaks of how our lives ought to be a sweet perfume for God.

Proverbs 22v7

We need to think wisely about situations which we create which then leave us obliged to others.

August 29th

Job 31v1-33v33

Job's rigorous defence will now spurn a fourth "friend" into action – Elihu. Unwittingly, he is spot on with his own description of himself as being like a wine casket with a building pressure just waiting to spurt out! Elihu's youthful froth is not going to help in the situation either!

2 Corinthians 3v1-18

New problems! Struggling with all the obvious traces of pagan worship and ways of living, a new problem is clearly that of the Judaisers who see the true destination of all new Christians to become rigorous Jews. So now these false teachers have arrived and are even questioning Paul's credentials.

Paul wants to see the evidence of lives truly changed by Christ – it will be in their faces, quite literally, for all to see.

Proverbs 22v8-9

OK, Job was struggling with the suffering of godly people, but the author Proverbs does remind us that God is very much in control. He also reminds us of practical ways in which our faith should be lived out.

August 30th

Job 34v1-36v33

Elihu's pious froth continues. It is immature, and it's unhelpful. As Francis Andersen wrote in his commentary on Job (Tyndale Old Testament Commentaries, IVP) "He is no longer reasoning with Job with a view to helping him; he is attacking Job in order to score a point…They have become an exercise in rhetoric." That is not to deny that over these chapters Elihu can make some good points. The problems begin when we lift quotes straight from these sections of Job and quote them as "God's Word" without realising that we are given these examples in the Book of Job as examples of arguments that may come close, sometimes very close – and yet miss the mark. There are flaws in all of the speeches of Job's friends, and Christians need to do some heart searching when they find it is easier to identify with the "friends" than with Job himself. Sift carefully!

2 Corinthians 4v1-12

Honesty is important in the methods used in God's work. God's Word must be handled in ways that we can stand over. And Christian work is always about making the name of Jesus known, and not about promoting us!

Paul also speaks of our own frailty into which God has entrusted His wonderful message.

We are also conscious that as Paul writes back to the Corinthians about some of the very basic issues which have arisen, he is under immense pressure as he works for the Lord in another situation. Paul needed the Corinthians to pray, and to be distracted by nonsense and immorality.

Proverbs 22v10-12: Some of the things said in these verses are very relevant to some of the distractions from the Gospel that were going on in Corinth!

August 31st

Job 37v1-39v30

God is going to answer Job, though not as Job might have expected. There is no explanation as to why Job has suffered, nor is there a list of sins to support what the "friends" have been saying.

2 Corinthians 4v13-5v11

We need to realise that it is this world which is temporary! The future is not some ghostly world, but one in which we have bodies.

Proverbs 22v13

Ah, the excuses for doing nothing!

September 1st

Job 40v1-42v17

Care needs to be taken as to how the different translators phrase 42 v6. Job regrets some of his hasty words, but he has no sins as such to repent of, as indeed God's words will show in the next few verses. Indeed if suddenly there were sins as such to repent of, the whole book would be pointless, because it is about the suffering of godly people, and the fact that they can suffer without there being any sin to show as a cause of the suffering. What we do have is Job's recognition of his status before God. As Francis Anderson put it in the Tyndale Old Testament commentary:

"As a humble suppliant, he knows his status. But, next to Job, Abraham is the righteous man of the Old Testament, and to kneel thus before God is an honour that exalts him above other men."

The sting comes towards the end of our reading, as God turns to Eliphaz and expresses His anger to him. Indeed God shocks them when He tells Eliphaz that the three of them have not been truthful in what they said about God, *as my servant Job was*! Then God warns them to bring 7 bulls and 7 rams to Job, that Job may sacrifice these on their behalf, and intercede with God so that He won't destroy them for their sin – "your failure to speak rightly concerning my servant Job."

This of course is quite a gobsmack, as we realise just how much many of their arguments throughout the book may have seemed OK to us, and perhaps we have said similar things to others ourselves.

God then restores Job, and doubles his wealth, his animals etc. Interestingly, when God gives him more children, He gives him the same number as before (not double) because in God's eyes that is double – death is not the end, and Job's earlier sons and daughters await him in eternity. One interesting thing, is the emphasis given to Job's new daughters. The three of them are named, and we are very pointedly told, included in their father's will. Hints of a new status for women?

2 Corinthians 5 v12-21

As Paul gets on with spreading the Gospel he is not worried about how others think of him. Some of the false preachers were evidently very concerned with appearance, but the Gospel is about lives being changed within. Paul wants to get on with the job of being Christ's ambassadors to a very needy world that needs to be reconciled to God through Christ.

Proverbs 22v14. Do godly people need this warning? ("The mouth of a whore is a bottomless pit" as Eugene Peterson puts it in his translation ***The Message***.) Some translations refer to the "adulteress" and some to the "prostitute." I'm afraid they do need this warning. What is shocking today are the reports coming in from many pastors and ministers of the extent of a hidden addiction to pornography, and specifically online pornography, amongst Church members.

September 2nd

Ecclesiastes 1v1-3v22

If Job was a bit of a shock to you, then brace yourself for sarcasm and black humour. Again many Christians only dip into Ecclesiastes (usually the bit about a time for this...a time for that...) as they select a text or two for evangelism, but they often run scared of much of the rest of this book.

Solomon had everything, literally from orchards to women. He even turned to wisdom and literature and had every resource at his disposal, and realised that life ends, and that so much of human activity is a "chasing after the wind..."

2 Corinthians 6v1-13

Paul is very honest about the struggles and pain of following Christ in spreading the good news of the Saviour. The Corinthians have been distracted by other things, and there is a "smallness" (Peterson's translation) or a "coldness" (Living Bible) in their lives as Christians.

Proverbs22v15 Kidner in his commentary gives this verse the heading "knocking the nonsense out"!

September 3rd

Ecclesiastes 4v1-6v12

Solomon continues to force us (particularly in our secular age) to face up to the consequences if, as some tell us, this is all there is. So basically, there are two ways of looking at life – from the perspective of "life under the sun" and from the perspective of faith.

You may not appreciate some of the illustrations he uses, but he certainly brings his point home. Who is the bachelor farmer working for, if he has no one to share his life with?

Another illustration, which comes very close to home, is that of investments turning sour.

Yes, you might not like his humour, but Ecclesiastes brings home that if you say this is all there is...well, then, this is all there is – that is, if you can't see a place for God in all of this.

2nd Corinthians 6v14-7v7

Some of the issues raised in Corinthians are not that far away from what we have just been facing up to in Ecclesiastes, and that is the whole issue of fundamentally where people stand – with a secular, godless world view, or with Christ? Which then brings us on to the whole issue of trying to partner with people who don't hold to our Christian viewpoint, who don't share our faith in Christ. Whether it is marriage, or business or whatever, the Bible is warning us "don't be teamed with those who do not love the Lord..."(Living Bible).

Clearly Paul has had to say some pretty hard hitting things to the Corinthians, and it has not been an easy relationship, as a result.

Proverbs 22 v16

Something seems to be lost in a number of translations as scholars struggle to translate the rather crypitic Hebrew original of this verse. Peterson translated it as "Exploit the poor or glad-hand the rich – whichever, you'll end up the poorer for it." And John Knox centuries ago wrote "Oppress the poor for thy enrichment, and ere long a richer man's claim shall impoverish thee."

September 4th

Ecclesiastes 7v1-9v18

Some rather cynical proverbs here, particularly when the writer is dealing "with aspects of life that anger or infuriate." (Michael Eaton in his commentary on

Ecclesiastes in the Tyndale IVP series.) The closing part of today's reading must be seen as Solomon exposing the flaws of how we see and understand things from a godless perspective.

2 Corinthians 7 v8-16: There is no doubt that the Corinthians were left smarting by some of the things that Paul said, but there has also been considerable progress too. There is nothing new about the resistance there can be to a pastor or minister teaching how things ought to be.

Proverbs 22v17-19

Continuing on from what we have been thinking about in Ecclesiastes, Proverbs tells us to make sure our foundation is in God.

September 5th

Ecclesiastes 10v1-12v14

Perfume bottles did not have a narrow neck just to make sure only a little drop came out – there was also the very real fear of what one dead fly could do to a whole batch! The point is obvious though – the most expensive container of perfume is so easily ruined by a blue bottle lying legs up in it, and a life is easily ruined by one piece of folly.

There are warnings to those in their youth who give no thought to the future. The description of old age may seem almost cruel, but the dark humour and cynicism of Ecclesiastes is meant to jolt us to our senses. There is a God, and there is a judgment coming, and the time to remember Him is in our youth, for a time may well be coming when we are no longer mentally capable of making that response. There is cold comfort for those who imagine that these are things we put off until old age.

2 Corinthians 8v1-15: The Christians in Jerusalem were going through a very difficult period and the Macedonian congregations had responded well. Paul hopes to see a similar response from Corinth. Congregations have a responsibility to support and encourage the bigger picture in Christ's work

Proverbs 22v20-21: We have what God's Word is telling us; will we listen and act by it?

September 6th **Song of Solomon 1v1-4v16**

We are getting deeper into the "Wisdom" Literature of the Old Testament, and deeper into ground that was never covered in Sunday School days. That's the whole problem of imagining that even with 10 years of regular schooling in Sunday School, that we know everything there is in the Bible! In many respects we were totally unprepared for Job with page after page of "Christian" sounding stuff that turned out to be flawed, as God rebuked Job's friends after chapters of "advice" and "spiritual" counselling, much of which we were actually slow to see what was wrong with it! And then the humour and cynicism of Ecclesiastes was hard to take. Now we come to the Song of Songs, or the Song of Solomon. There are two ways of dealing with this book. Some people take everything in this book as "allegorical," as picture language. In other words, when it talks of two lovers, it is really talking of God and His people. To be frank, that's probably a rather cowardly way to handle it, and not very honest, though there have been many, particularly in evangelical circles, who refused to take any of this stuff literally. Actually trying to treat the book that way creates problems, as some of the erotic language is not appropriate in describing the believer's relationship with Christ. The more truthful way of handling this book is to see it as a book that deals with topics that perhaps you thought the Bible had nothing to say about. God created sex for marriage, and in its proper setting there is nothing wrong with the intimacy described here. For many Christian people, this may be the first time you have read material like this. The Bible is all for the fullest expression of love when it is in its proper setting, marriage. Faithfulness has its rewards: "My darling bride is like a private garden, a spring that no one else can have, a fountain of my own." (4v12) Dare to read it in a clear modern translation! For help look at Tom Gledhill's commentary in the Bible Speaks Today Series.

2 Corinthians 8v16-24: There are solid Christian people working alongside Paul. Note though that Paul is always concerned than honesty and integrity are transparent, particularly in handling money.

Proverbs 22v22-23: Some are very vulnerable, and God has no tolerance of those who misuse that fact.

September 7th

Song of Solomon 5v1-8v14: There is no denying the shallowness of relationships in Solomon's collection of queens and concubines; that is contrasted with true happiness in a one to one relationship.

2 Corinthians 9v1-15: Important teaching on giving within the Church.

Proverbs 22v24-25: The problems of temper and the need to avoid the snares that a bad tempered companion will drag us into.

September 8th

Isaiah 1v1-2v22:

The prophets come from many different backgrounds; Isaiah comes from a royal background and ministers through a number of reigns. Some of what he says is for more immediate times, while some of our better known prophecies of Christ come in this book. Isaiah though, is concerned immediately with a nation that has turned away from God – a nation that does not know the hand that feeds it. The people need to come back to God and know the peace of sins forgiven, otherwise the day of judgment is coming.
2 Corinthians 10v1-18:

Whole commentaries have been written on the last 4 chapters of 2nd Corinthians. From chapter 10 onwards Donald Carson (From Triumphalism to Maturity, IVP 1984, page1) tells us "These chapters are among the most emotionally intense of all that the apostle Paul wrote…"There has presumably been another letter, in between the 1st and 2nd Corinthian letters that we have in our Bibles. Trying to put things right in Corinth has been emotionally draining for Paul, to say nothing of all the other problems he has had to deal with in evangelising elsewhere. And his authority has been challenged and his work ridiculed. All that Paul is seeking is to get the church back on track and to see real maturity in the lives of its members.

Proverbs 22v26-27:

Again, who are we in business with? Or is it a warning regarding our own debts? We currently live in a culture in which many have had to learn the hard way that "credit" has its payback time.

September 9th

Isaiah 3v1-5v3:

Judgment is not some distant thing. Judgment was coming in this life, and soon, to a very arrogant and godless people.

2 Corinthians 11v1-15:

The people are being led astray by more attractive false preachers. "You seem so gullible: you believe whatever anyone tells you even if he is preaching another Jesus than the one we preach, or a different spirit than the Holy Spirit you received, or shows you a different way to be saved. You swallow it all" v4 (The Living Bible translation) Are we conned by glossy presentation, by smart suits and highly polished delivery?

Proverbs 22v28-29

Two issues: moving landmarks which were boundary marks between properties is stealing. Then in verse 29 we are reminded that the quality of our work does matter.

September 10th

Isaiah 6v1-7v25:

This is a tremendous vision which Isaiah has of God on His throne. Isaiah understands the holiness of God and the contrast of sinful men – even of someone like himself being called into service as a prophet.The story of Ahaz, Rezin and Pekah: King Ahaz was basically a nervous wreck worrying over these two other kings and what they might do. God sends messages that they are of no consequence, and Ahaz should trust Him. God through Isaiah offers a sign – any sign – that might reassure Ahaz. Ahaz refuses such a sign – he basically will not trust in God. So ironically, one of the great promises of the Bible, the promise of Immanuel, born to a virgin, is given to a King who will not trust God about next week! Instead Ahaz was foolishly trusting the Assyrians for help – who will prove in due course to be enemies, not friends. Ahaz's political "wisdom" will prove to have been very wrong. He should have trusted God instead.

2 Corinthians 11v16-33

There has been real personal cost to Paul in serving the cause of the Gospel. The Corinthians though, have proved to be very gullible in being led astray by those who present a very different "gospel."

Proverbs 23v1-3 Wealthy people may use all kinds of entrapments, including the "generous" and impressive dinner.

September 11th

Isaiah 8v1-9v21

Again we have this contrast; while the King of Jerusalem won't trust God for tomorrow, we are given the glorious promise of the Saviour again in that reading which is so familiar every Christmas! Note that Israel is the northern kingdom, working very much with the Syrians, the enemies of God's people in Judah (the southern Kingdom of Judah), based in Jerusalem.

2 Corinthians 12v1-10: Visions and revelations; there was a lot of emotional manipulation going on by the false preachers who were leading the Corinthians astray. Paul has had his very emotional experiences too, but God has anchored him through some "thorn in the flesh" – some physical ailment that has kept him humble and very much dependant upon God on a daily basis. But then, it has never been

about Paul; the Gospel message is all about Christ, and people must see Him, not Paul, and not anybody else.

Proverbs 23 v4-5 The workaholic is a problem too. He or she needs to be more discerning in life. There are valuable and good things to do which bring no financial reward.

September 12th

Isaiah 10v1-11v16

Assyria is being used by God to bring His judgment upon surrounding nations, but God is also bringing His judgment on the Assyrians, who will indeed threaten Jerusalem, but not succeed, as we will see later on in this book.Judgment is coming on the royal household at a much more future date (it will actually be the Babylonians who will tear down Jerusalem.) But from the stump of the royal line there will be a shoot – once again we have one of the Bible's great promises of the Saviour.

2nd Corinthians 12v11-21Paul is very emotional, given the strain of looking after his spiritual children. There has been some dreadful immorality, as well as false teaching. We are given the impression that some in the Church valued more what they had to pay for (the false teachers) than Paul and the other Christian leaders who had cost them nothing.

Proverbs 23v6-8 The insincerity of a meal given to put somebody in their debt; there are circumstances that will leave you regretting being a guest.

September 13th

Isaiah 12v1-14v32

Babylon is the real threat to Jerusalem but Isaiah looks beyond that to God's judgment upon the mighty Babylonian empire. The Philistines will rejoice at King Ahaz's death, but his son will be a greater scourge to them.

2 Corinthians 13v1-14: This is hard hitting stuff. Wrong doing in the Church has to be stopped and punished, and people are being asked to examine themselves to see if they really are following and trusting the Saviour.

Proverbs 23v9-11   It is not that the fool lacks intelligence, but rather that he is so obstinate (ESV footnotes.) Once again boundary markers are mentioned. Orphaned farm families were clearly vulnerable and abused and cheated.

September 14th

Isaiah 15v1-18v7

Judgment comes to "great " nations that in the past have intended much harm to Jerusalem

Galatians 1v1-24

Once again we have the problem that people are falling away from the Gospel; the attraction of the Judaisers, who basically wanted to make these new gentile converts into Jews, seems to have been particularly strong. However, their "gospel" of combining the rigours of Jewish legalism with the Gospel produced a false gospel which effectively sidelined the Saviour to a lesser role. Paul points out that he was personally saved from a very extreme form of Judaism, and brought to a saving faith in Jesus. Paul also fills us in on some of the missing years between his own conversion and the start of his work as an evangelist.

Proverbs 23v12

There has to be discipline in gaining instruction. The living Bible takes this verse in a different way and talks of how criticism can be used positively. (Don't refuse to accept criticism; get all the help you can.)

September 15th

Isaiah 19v1-21v17

God's judgment continues on nations that were a terrible treat to Jerusalem.

Galatians 2v1-16:   Again Paul fills us in on the past. This is useful in itself, but also to show that some of the issues being raised by these Judaisers had already been settled, though Peter himself had been a bit of a wobbler and had to be challenged when he stopped eating with Gentile Christians. Clearly the Jewish Christian community back in Jerusalem had problems over the huge numbers of non Jews coming to faith in Christ. The key issue was, "What is the heart of the Gospel?"

Proverbs 23v13-14: Children need to be disciplined.

September 16th

Isaiah 22v1-24v23

Here judgment is pictured coming to Jerusalem, as indeed it did, several reigns later.

Judgment is also coming to Tyre and Sidon. God is working out His purposes on the world scene.

Galatians 2v17-3v7

Paul argues for the central truths of the Gospel; the death of Christ upon the cross is absolutely central, and it is through that death that we are made right with God. Many of these Judaisers are effectively treating the Lord's death as meaningless. We cannot be saved through trying to keep Jewish laws; we are saved through faith in Christ, through trusting in His death upon the cross.

Proverbs 23 v15-16

A father's joy in seeing his son succeed through wisdom.

September 17th

Isaiah 28 v14-30v11:

Still trusting in alliances, rather than in God, the rulers of Jerusalem dig holes for themselves. Their reliance on Pharaoh will backfire – seeking Egypt's help from the south west against an enemy in the North East will come to nothing – in fact it is costing quite a lot. But there is also reference to God's deliverance too.

Galatians 3 v23- 4v31:

The Jewish law as a teacher – yes, it was so useful to have that solid synagogue background, but real life is in Christ, not in slavery to full blown Judaism. There were those who sought to take the Gentile (non-Jewish) converts back into the rigours of Judaism Pharisee style – robbing them of what they had discovered through faith in Christ.

Proverbs 23v19-21: The constant problems of attractions off God's path.

18th September

Isaiah 28v14-30v11

The Living Bible puts it rather bluntly, in the opening verses of today's reading:

“You have struck a bargain with Death…and sold yourselves to the devil in exchange for his protection against the Assyrians…we are under the care of one who will deceive and fool them.”

We continue to read of the people of Jerusalem putting their trust in the wrong things. There is also the warning that there are seasons in God’s work, and there have been different approaches to how God has been speaking to them. At times the passage speaks of judgement, and at other times of blessing and restoration.

Galatians 3v23-4v31

The Old Testament Law had its purpose, to make us aware of sin and of our need – but that need is met in Christ. Paul is not suggesting that we set aside that knowledge of what God wants in our lives, but rather that we realise that salvation is in Jesus, rather than trying (and failing) to somehow or other prove ourselves to God through traditional Judaism’s attempt to keep God’s laws (and indeed many man-made additives designed to “fence” or protect us from even approaching disobedience to God’s laws.)

Those who were trying to attract new Christian converts back to the legalism of strict Judaism were taking them to a cul-de-sac that ends in failure. Salvation is in Christ, His finished work on the cross.

Proverbs 23v19-21

An interesting list of sins – yes, alcohol is mentioned – so too is gluttony, and lying on in bed while work is allowed to sit. Such lists tend to stop us pointing the finger at others!

September 19th

Isaiah 30 v12-33v12

The people’s obsession with Egypt as the saviour who would rescue them from the Assyrians runs deep. Delivery will come from the LORD.

Galatians 5 v1-12: At times Paul is rather blunt to the point that we might be shocked by his crudeness, but the determination of some to bring new Christians into the fold of extreme Judaism, with all the Jewish laws, ceremonies and of course circumcision is only sidelining Christ. Of course the attraction is ultimately of somehow or other proving ourselves to God, rather than accepting that we are sinners in need of forgiveness, and of God’s grace.

Proverbs 23v22

The writer of Proverbs has been very much wearing the guise of a parent, and in so doing is only too well aware of that contempt for the wisdom that an older generation can share.

September 20th

Isaiah 33v13-36v22:

By the middle of our reading the Assyrians are literally outside the walls – and they are streetwise crafty enough to shout their terms in Hebrew, so that the entire city will know their demands. The King is ridiculed for his belief that God can deliver. We will see tomorrow just who does come to the rescue of the people of Jerusalem.

Galatians 5 v13-26

A real need for love in this fellowship.

A real need to be open to the leading of God's Holy Spirit.

And a need to understand the very different life that God wants to lead them into.

Proverbs 23v23

"Get the facts at any price" is how the living Bible puts it –if only some of our congregational gossips would take that to heart! Others interpret the verse as recognising and valuing the truth of God's Word. Whatever way you want to take it, truth, wisdom, instruction and understanding are things to aim for in a world that often wants to be blind and ignorant on the subject of truth.

September 21st

Isaiah 37v1-38v22

The King of Jerusalem is deeply upset, but at least he goes to the temple to pray. God's answer is to create circumstances in another area altogether that force the Assyrians to withdraw their troops. As the arrogance of the King of Assyria continues, God sends some kind of plague overnight that kills 185,000 troops, and finally the Assyrian king is murdered by two of his own sons, in his own pagan temple.

We have the extraordinary story of how God reverses time – the sun's shadow is made to move backwards to prove that God will give him another 15 years

Galatians 6v1-18

Bringing someone back to God is much more preferable to a judgemental attitude that has no desire to restore someone.

There are practical pieces of advice, including an urge to get on with the Lord's work and to stop making comparisons with others, to pay their preachers / teachers, and a reminder that what you sow is what you reap.

Paul reminds them of central truths of the Gospel – it is what Jesus has done for us upon the cross that matters, when we have placed our faith and trust in Him.

Proverbs 23v24,25

Parents of teenage and adult children will appreciate this one. Perhaps others should reflect on the anguish they have caused parents at some points in their lives!

September 22nd

Isaiah 39v1-41v16

While we rejoice in how God delivered the people of Jerusalem from the Assyrians, we read of a piece of foolishness on the part of the king of Jerusalem. In a moment of personal vanity, he shows the envoys of the new and upcoming King of Babylon absolutely everything. In actual fact it would be these "new friends" who would come back at another time, in another reign, and carry everything away.

Isaiah has often dealt with things that were close in terms of timescale, (a lot of prophecy was for the here and now) but then he treats us to some wonderful verses that stretch hundreds of years into the future, to the times of John and Jesus.

Ephesians 1v1-23

Ephesus was to be a key town in the work of God's kingdom. Here Paul reminds us of central truths of the Gospel in a very fresh way, and wants us to remember the wonderful things the believer has in Christ.

Proverbs 23v26-28: The advice here is even more relevant in our present day world paying heavily in both terms of broken relationships and sexually transmitted disease.

September 23rd

Isaiah 41v17-43v13

Isaiah is now looking far ahead – beyond even the times of the Babylonians, to a righteous foreign ruler who will restore the people that the Babylonians have yet to carry away.

And then Isaiah looks even further ahead, to the Lord Jesus Christ Himself.

Ephesians 2 v1-22

Paul continues to remind us what we have in Jesus. What a contrast with our past lives!

Proverbs 23v29-35

The picture painted of alcohol abuse is so tragic. As with our reading from Ephesians, we are reminded of a life that ought to have been left behind.

September 24th

Isaiah 43v14-45v10

Although the Babylonians would be used to punish a disobedient people, God would not forget their excesses and His judgement would come upon them too.

The people continue to be warned of God's judgment, and comforted with news of his forgiveness and grace.

There is the brilliant passage which mocks idolatry – how wood for both the fire and the idol come from the same tree.

And also the closing verses which turn the argument sharply on those who would blame God for how His faithless people have turned out.

Ephesians 3 v1-21

"Secret"? Of course there is nothing "secret" about God's plan, but Paul is alluding to those false teachers who had offered "secret" knowledge. The truth is that everything about the Gospel is out in the open. Having said that, what radical news it was as salvation was and is offered to the Gentiles too.

In the last section of this reading there is a tremendous prayer for all of us, that these things may indeed be found in our lives.

Proverbs 24 v1-2

A more serious sin – and more widespread – than we often realise. Envying evil people, imagining that they have more successful lives, happier times, undermines the faith of many.

September 25th

Isaiah 45v11-48v11

Cyrus will indeed deal with the Babylonians. The people used to bring God's judgement upon Jerusalem will also be judged themselves, and that pleasure mad empire would experience the full brunt of God's judgement. The Book of Daniel gives us some idea of what it was like trying to survive under their maverick kings.

Ephesians 6 v1-16

Paul touches on a number of subjects here – how Christians ought to treat each other – and then once more we are reminded that we all have a part to play in the Body of Christ, the Church. Maturity in that body is much longed for here in this passage.

Proverbs 24v3-4

Wisdom, understanding, knowledge, common sense – are all words or phrases that come up in the different translations of these verses – underlining what the Galatians reading had to say about growing Christian maturity.

September 26th

Isaiah 48 v12-50v11

I'm not too sure how Isaiah's first readers / listeners reacted to the statement as to how important Cyrus – a pagan king after all, was in the plans of God. "The Lord loves Cyrus..."v14 – Living Bible. Yet this man would bring to an end the empire of Babylon, and replace it with his own, but in the process would open up the way for the people to return to Jerusalem. God would clearly use him, and had clear plans for him, but there would be those who would choke on this apparent endorsement of a pagan king. The message for us is that God is out there working away in a world that is often hostile to His message, yet God will have his plans fulfilled, and He is working on a canvas far greater than our imaginations ever realise. Repeatedly the message comes home that God is our Redeemer, and the passage speaks of the

"Servant" who is clearly someone far greater than Cyrus. But then we are building up to a very famous passage in Isaiah!

Ephesians 4 v17-32

Some of this is so basic in terms of morality and how Christians should treat each other that we are probably shocked that Paul felt the need to say such things. But yes, and we are living in a world which has so invaded the lives of our Christian people that basic morality can no longer be assumed – there is a real danger that the saved will live as the unsaved.

Proverbs 24v5:

This is not the first time that Proverbs makes the point that wisdom is mightier than brute force. In one way this is a piece of sanctified common sense, but at another level we will see some people in Christian circles use very worldly tactics as though all that matters is the brute force they can exert through numbers or whatever. They of course mistake this for "wisdom" in a street wise way, but the wisdom that this book speaks of begins with the fear of the Lord.

September 27th

Isaiah 51v1-53v12

The quarry from which you were mined – were you fortunate to come from a home with a solid Christian background? Yes, you are being called to think back to that spiritual heritage which you have. God is about to do great and wonderful things amongst these people, and they are being called to make themselves ready. Think of the number of little choruses based on some of the verses we have in this passage. Then we have that very moving passage of Isaiah 53. This is so clearly Jesus foreseen in the Old Testament.

Ephesians 5 v1-33

Again Paul is covering some very basic morality here, but these people were largely converts from a pagan background in which religion, far from challenging these wrong ways of living, actually endorsed them! The Greek/Roman gods and goddesses were often made in the image of their worshippers. Just about everything that was so easily accepted in the pagan world had to be challenged, from dirty story-telling to how husbands and wives treat each other. Some statistics from the US a few years ago seemed to suggest that in at least some Church circles, the rates of marriage breakdown were not any different from that in the world outside. It shocks us that Paul has to tell a Christian audience to replace their crude story telling with talk about the Lord. Just how far are you sucked into accepting what the world sees as "normal" and how far do you go in living by those standards that are accepted all around you?

Proverbs 24v6-7

Seeking out wise heads is clearly commendable – essential – in warfare. Why not the rest of the time?

September 28th

Isaiah 54v1-57v14

Isaiah had spoken of the tough times ahead for Jerusalem, especially when God's judgment would come through the Babylonians. Of course, when God's judgment comes upon a whole nation like that, the godly and innocent suffer too. There will indeed be the bitter hearts who will feel more like the wife abandoned early in her marriage – though the verses here speak more of Jerusalem the city herself as the abandoned wife who will once more know blessings beyond anything the other towns and cities of the region have.

There is though, strong emphasis on how this people need to turn to the LORD. There are key phrases which we all know: "Seek the LORD while you can find him. Call upon Him now while He is near...For just as the heavens are higher than the earth, so are my ways higher than yours, and my thoughts than yours..." and so on.

And then, we have the important point, often lost by the Jewish people, that God wants to bless the Gentiles too. We may have to wait to New Testament times to realise just how many God-fearers there were – gentiles (non-Jews) basically waiting for the Gospel message which included them. Isaiah has a strong emphasis on how God is not just concerned about a tiny corner of the Middle East (pivotal though it always has been in His plans) but wants to bring others into a relationship with Himself. It is here that we are reminded that the Temple is to be a House of Prayer for all people – and of course our thoughts jump to Jesus when he made that point so bluntly by clearing the traders out of the part of the Temple that was supposedly available for Gentiles who wanted to worship.

Then the passage goes back to the present-day of isaiah's times – to the drunkenness, the adultery and the idolatry of real life in the "holy" city of Jerusalem. Some very hideous practices have been introduced, particularly with the worship of the false god Molech.

Our passage ends though with the call to clear the road for God's people to return from exile.

Ephesians 6 v1-24

Paul's advice to children is unsurprising, but what comes in verse 4 is a real shock to many parents who expect unquestioning obedience. I quite like the tone of the King James version, which I quote from memory: "Ye fathers provoke not your children unto wrath, but bring them up in the nurture and admonition of the LORD." The commandment to "honour your father and mother..." is open to abuse by ungodly parents, or by parents who imagine that they have a blanket immunity when it comes to God's judgment upon their parenthood. Yes, we are living in times in which it is no joke being the parents of teenagers (no joke being a parent!) and we are living in times in which "elder abuse" (older relatives being abused by younger ones) is now a real issue, but we are also seeing some dreadful examples of parenthood in and around our own village. These examples may not hit the headlines, but we can only guess what we are going to reap from the way some of our children are being brought up in inconsistent and at times uncaring homes. Parents are also teaching their children how to cheat and how to make others cower and suffer, (under the guise of teaching them how to survive in a modern world, but doing it so wrongly.) Many of our children are going home from Sunday School, GB, BB – whatever – to homes that contradict virtually everything we have been teaching them.

As for Paul's comments to slaves – Christianity was not in a position then, as a minority religion in the Roman / Greek world to challenge slavery per se, but in a modern context we can take Paul's comments on an honest day's work, and fair treatment of workers, and apply them to the present day. With a bit of imagination we could think of modern day parallels to "put on all of God's armour..." – Paul is making essential points about the things that need to be in our lives daily if we are going to live for the Lord.

It is lovely to read of people like Tychicus who are there in the background giving someone like Paul (literally in chains) daily encouragement. We need to remember the people in our lives who are like that, and also be a "Tychicus" to someone else.

Proverbs 24 v8

The truth is plain. The Bible condemns the schemers (New King James version) and there are plenty of them in our congregations and outside who make snowballs for others to throw. The Living Bible goes further: "To plan evil is as wrong as doing it." I wish some of our Christian people would take that to heart when they realise what they have started but have left for other gossips or meddlers to bring to fruition.

September 29th

Isaiah 57 v15-59v21

Isaiah is continuing to speak against what was going on in his day – people were busy at their religious practices, even attending DAILY to "hear" the Scriptures being read in the Temple (now that has to be impressive) and then going out to disobey it all. Religious activity was a substitute for actually applying (living) God's Word. There is some hard hitting stuff here. Any wonder then, that "you don't know what true peace is, nor what it means to be just and good; you continually do wrong and those who follow you won't experience any peace, either." (Living Bible Isaiah 59 v8)

In fact, for all the religious activity going on – and how we must envy that fantastic temple attendance – the truth is that "anyone who tries a better life is soon attacked." (Living Bible Isaiah 59v15)

Philippians 1 v1-26

Paul was not filling their heads with flattery; he actually meant it. Oh to be a congregation that drives others to prayer with joy and thankfulness!

There are some lovely things to note in Paul's prayer for them.

Proverbs 24 v9-10

The scoffer and evil planner get their judgment, but we are perhaps taken aback by verse 24: "if you faint in the day of adversity, your strength is small" (New King James) "You are a poor specimen if you can't stand the pressure of adversity." As Christians we need to look again at how our society leaves a lot of people less resilient that perhaps generations who have gone before. People are folding under, and perhaps we could teach them better on how to deal with pressure. Having said that, our society is ruder, less respectful – and that's only the 55+ generation I'm talking about!

September 30th

Isaiah 60 v1-62v6

The call to be the light of the world.

The excitement of seeing the captives returning from Babylon.

Israel once more the crossroads of Middle East life and trade.

There is much more here, than just the literal return of the people from captivity. The theme from 60 v19 "No longer will you need the sun or moon to give you light" is picked up again in Revelation's great description of what heaven will be like as we stand around Jesus in all His glory – the last page of our Bibles, Rev 22 v5. Jesus took Isaiah 61 as his starting point when he spoke in the Synagogue in Nazareth, to announce what God the Father wanted Him to do.

Philippians 1v27 – 2v18

Paul wants to keep the good news coming!

Paul wants all divisiveness and enmity resolved within the Church, given what is challenging the faith from outside.

Philippians 2 v5-11 are regarded by some as a possible early Christian hymn. There is a good sense of rhythm here. One scholar even argues that it might be a hymn which originated in the widely spoken Aramaic language and sung at Communion. Well, whatever! These kinds of debates only make us look again at the words and marvel at what they tell us of our Lord.

Paul was very conscious that, regarding his time in prison, things were moving towards a watershed. He wants to see the work prosper beyond (if it is the case) his own death.

Proverbs 24 v11-12

The sin of doing nothing!

October 1st

Isaiah 62v7-65v25

Pray persistently and do the preparation work for what God can achieve in the future.

Chapter 63: Edom seems to have taken considerable pleasure at the destruction of Jerusalem, an attitude that God never excuses; here the LORD is seen to come from that direction, having executed His judgment. What is judgment for one nation, is tied to a tremendous sense of deliverance for another.

There is some looking back to the time in the wilderness when the people met God at Mount Sinai.

Again a familiar text: “we are the clay, you are the potter.”

Chapter 65: other nations are seeking the LORD while His own people don’t. This time, while there is more talk about judgment, there is also an acknowledgment of the faithful remnant. The passage looks far ahead to when the wolf and the lamb shall feed together – some of this is prophecy of Christ’s coming Kingdom.

Philippians 2 v19-3v3

Timothy has been an absolutely solid Christian (see Acts 16 for some background on him.) So has Epaphroditus. Lovely to be surrounded by people like that as Paul, being physically confined, continues his work by letter.

"The dangerous dogs" – those who are not satisfied with saving faith in Christ, but who want to drag the Gentile converts back into the full rigours of Judaism – circumcision and all. Not everyone realised that these people were undermining the core message of the Gospel – the all sufficiency of what Jesus did for us on the Cross.

Proverbs 24v13-14

Wisdom compared to the sweetest thing they could think of in those days!

October 2nd

Isaiah 66 v1-24

Isaiah continues to have concerns about the religious activity, which was plentiful in his own day, but which had no substance in how the people were actually living. Some of the sacrifice going on was repugnant to God because it was such a hypocritical gesture. Later on in the reading we have references to the "discreet" places you could go to eat mouse or pork, "delicacies" forbidden under the Old Testament. So there is both judgment coming soon – and deliverance after that, and hints of something far, far greater as the message is carried out to the gentiles.

Philippians 3 v4-21

Paul tackles head on the message of the Judaisers – if keeping the Old Testament laws could save anyone, he had been a zealous and exceptional Pharisee! No, says Paul, I put my trust and hope in Christ alone.

Having said that, Paul still expects us, with the help and power of the Holy Spirit, to live a life in keeping with the name of Christian.

Proverbs 24 v15-16

This book has been emphasising wisdom, but the writer is well aware of those who offer an alternative "wisdom" – that of the devious and evil schemer. The innocent righteous person will recover again and again from what others have done to him, but God will act against those who imagine themselves to be smart in their evil.

October 3rd

Jeremiah 1v1-2v30 : The personal story of Jeremiah himself brings home that when God's judgment comes upon a whole nation, there are godly people who suffer with the rest as that judgment comes. Jeremiah brought one warning message after another, but his other book, Lamentations, brings home the terrible agony of being a first hand witness to the destruction and the atrocities that came upon the inhabitants of Jerusalem.

Jeremiah's ministry began during the reign of King Josiah who came to the throne at the age of eight. Josiah was a very godly king, and quite a change after his godless father and grandfather. Josiah carried out immense reforms, which you can read about in 2nd Kings 23. As an indication of how bad things were, male prostitutes working for a pagan shrine had their quarters in part of the Temple, so it was quite a struggle for Josiah to bring the people back to anything even resembling what they once were in spiritual terms. Other prophets brought messages of coming judgment, but the prophetess Huldah declared that God would not bring the judgment during Josiah's reign. Josiah tore down even the pagan shrines that Solomon had built for his many wives. He also tore down the pagan shrines in places such as Bethel which had belonged to the northern kingdom. He died though, in battle with Pharaoh, and therein lay the problem, that the nation only "came back to God" while Josiah was around to reinforce it.

Anyway, Jeremiah's ministry began during that tremendous period, but Jeremiah was to see the godless lives of the kings that followed – Jehoahaz who lasted 3 months, but who was evil; Jehoiakim his brother was put on the throne by the Egyptians, but who initially made peace with Babylon, and then rebelled against that great superpower. His son Jehoiachin lasted 3 months on the throne, but that was still long enough for the writer of Kings to note that "he did evil in the eyes of the Lord, just as his father had done…." The Babylonians replaced Jehoiachin with his uncle whose name was changed to Zedekiah, who was also "evil in the eyes of the Lord" and it was Zedekiah who brought about the final sacking of Jerusalem when he also rebelled against the Babylonians.

That's some background, and no one expects you to remember the names of all of those kings, but it does bring home what Jeremiah was dealing with, and what kind of period he was living through. There were glimpses of what could have been during the reign of godly Josiah, but also a realisation that without Josiah about, the levels of depravity rivalled and surpassed what we have seen in more modern times. They also help you to understand the bluntness of what Jeremiah says in the opening chapters. Politically, the Kings of Jerusalem were playing many games, making alliances with various powers and then making new alliances and then fighting former "friends" – and all of this was against a background of constantly adopting immoral pagan practices from the lands around them. As Jeremiah said towards the close of today's reading, "you have as many gods as there are cities in Judah..."

Philippians 4 v1-23: Paul is finishing off his letter to the Church in Philippi. For once, the problems mentioned at the start of the chapter appear to be more a matter of personality and those are problems we should move quickly to resolve. Few problems in the letters of Paul are that simple! There are lovely quotes in this chapter. Paul must have known he was coming to the end of whatever writing material he was using, and there are plenty of "one liners" – little gems in a single line squeezed in

"Fix your thoughts on what is true and good and right..." v8

"I know how to live on almost nothing or with everything. I have learned the secret the secret of contentment in every situation..." v12

"I can do everything God asks me to with the help of Christ who gives me the strength and power..." v13. You will of course find plenty of others.

Proverbs 24v17-20

While we are told elsewhere that vengeance is to be left to the Lord, there is no excuse for gloating when God appears to be punishing someone. All have sinned and fall short of God's standards, and our glee may just be the thing that God finds he needs to correct in us.

Verses 19 and 20 warn us not to envy wrong doers. The fact that the writer of Proverbs bundles verses 17 and 18, and then 19 and 20 together suggests that our own thinking can be very fickle – envying wrong doers one minute, gloating when they appear to be suffering the next minute?

October 4th

Jeremiah 2v31-4v18

As I tried to explain yesterday, King Josiah had tried to lead a spiritual revival (more a case of imposing one) How the people lived over the next few years after Josiah's death left Jeremiah commenting that "the most experienced harlot could learn a lot from you." Jeremiah 2v33b (Living Bible.) Rough stuff!

Colossians 1v1-19

We read about godly, faithful people like Epaphras, who clearly brought the Gospel message into others parts. And isn't it lovely to read of Paul being driven to prayer by GOOD things he has heard? Paul of course wants to encourage them to stay on track, and he wants to see them grow in their faith, and as we shall see, does need

to warn them of coming dangers, such as the Judaisers who will attempt to lead them astray – but the tone of this letter is so different from some of the others we have read recently. The teaching on Christ is so important, given that others will come along who try to put Jesus over to the side, so to speak. There is no relationship with God without His Son.
Proverbs 24v21-22: Kidner sums up (with reference to 1 Peter 2v17) that good citizenship is part of Godliness.

October 5th

Jeremiah 4v19-6v14

A terrible picture of judgment, which came true.

Colossians 1v20-2v7

Everything about this passage is Christ centred! Paul needed to say it then, and the Church needs to hear it again. We need to be absolutely rooted in Jesus.

Proverbs 24 v23-25

I am writing these notes at a time when there has been much in the news of the freeing of a Libyan man convicted of bombing a plane over Scotland. Questions have arisen over what might have come out if his appeal had gone ahead (was it Libya, or was it really Iran) and then from a totally different angle, why was he being freed anyway, if he really was guilty, when he never showed any remorse or accepted responsibility for the deaths? Accusations have been made about British businesses that stand to make considerable sums in the days ahead. Whatever the exact truth of it all, serious questions about justice and fairness, and what exactly governments are up to, arise from every angle. Hopefully by the time you get round to reading these notes the world will be a little wiser as to the exact truth of it all, but it serves as an example of how little trust we have in judicial procedures when politics are involved. These couple of verses have significant things to say on partiality in judgment.

October 6th

Jeremiah 6v15-8v7

Hard hitting stuff continues. The inhabitants of Jerusalem had seen the northern tribes carried off into captivity by a previous superpower, the Assyrians. However, God had protected them and punished the Assyrians when they came to the walls and mocked the people of Jerusalem for their faith in God. These were different times, however and the people of Jerusalem were no longer what they once were, in spiritual terms. Now there was a mistaken belief that God would never allow Jerusalem to fall. People had failed to recognise that the way in which they were living had changed considerably, and prophet after prophet had brought warnings of God's judgment.

Colossians 2v8-23

Keep Christ at the centre. Paul deals with the issues that the Judaisers would raise. Claiming to be Christians themselves, they were seeking to make "good Jews" out of these new converts to Christianity. Jesus was sort off "tagged on" to a religion that was very much about laws and regulations. Paul knew that once Christ was put to the side, what was left was not Christianity.

Proverbs 24v26

October 7th

Jeremiah 8v8-9v26

The people didn't even know to blush with embarrassment.

Verse 8v20 sums it up: "The harvest is finished; the summer is over and we are not saved."

Colossians 3v1-17

Being properly focussed in our lives as Christians.

Proverbs 24v27 Good business sense!

October 8th

Jeremiah 10v1 -11v23

If sinful people imagined that they could hold God to His covenant, they needed to realise that they had broken the covenant.

Colossians 3v18-4v18

Paul was not in a position to do anything about slavery, but he could give advice to Christians, whether masters or slaves, and for that matter, whether wives, husbands or children, to live for Christ. The problems regarding marriage and family life came out of a pagan and immoral Greek society.

Proverbs 24v28-29 More on bending justice. The Lord will have none of it.

October 9th

Jeremiah 12v1-14v10

We see something of the inner turmoil of Jeremiah as the process of God's judgment unfolds.

1 Thessalonians 1v1-2v8: Here were people who listened with great interest to the Gospel story, and who responded so encouragingly. They had been a great blessing at a time when Paul and his friends had come through many difficulties. They had also become ambassadors for Jesus, carrying the Gospel into areas nearby not covered by Paul's own journeys.

Proverbs 14v11-16v15

Time and opportunity – and a livelihood – all wasted.

October 10th

Jeremiah 14v11-16v15

Jeremiah, in despair of the message he has to give, needs to hear for himself that a day of restoration will come.

1 Thessalonians 2v9-3v13

Persecution had come to the new Christians in Thessalonica, but Timothy had brought back reports of the Christians standing firm and of their faith growing.

Proverbs 25v1-5

We are introduced to a section of King Solomon's proverbs put together in the times of King Hezekiah.

October 11th

Jeremiah 16v16-18v23

Jeremiah's inner turmoil continues as he realises the consequences for his people. At the same time there are plots to get rid of Jeremiah. Other religious leaders are offering more acceptable "messages from the Lord." The image of the potter and the clay was frightening to Jeremiah because he knew what was involved as God would almost blot out their nation and start again. The others did not care about Jeremiah's message, but Jeremiah did.

1 Thessalonians 4v1-5v2a

Sexual issues were a major concern because of the godless and immoral society from which the new converts came. They also needed teaching regarding the deaths of some Christians – what about those who had died before the return of Jesus? These were questions which were live issues.

Proverbs 25v6-7

See Luke 14v7-10 as well.

October 12th

Jeremiah 19v1-21v14

The Lord's message is delivered with drama. The priest Pashhur then had Jeremiah arrested, whipped and held overnight.

Ironically, when the Babylonians declared war on Jerusalem, Pashhur was one of two priests sent by King Zedekiah to talk to Jeremiah, although Zedekiah never acted as Jeremiah advised.

1 Thessalonians 5v2b-28

The day of the Lord is coming, but if Christian people are living as they should then they have nothing to fear. Paul finishes the letter with some quick points which we should note too

Proverbs 25v8-10

The legal implications of what these proverbs say ought to be obvious, but Kidner asks "Is your tale true-kind-necessary? Interesting to look at what Jesus had to say in Matthew 5v25, 26.

October 13th

Jeremiah 22v1-23v20

Jeremiah's message is clear. But there are still the "official" prophets, like those previously in Bethel, who make up what the king and people want to hear.

2 Thessalonians 1v1-12

Teaching from the first letter is taken further.

Proverbs 25v11-14: All useful advice.

October 14th

Jeremiah 23v21-25v38

False prophets continue to be a problem.

In the aftermath of the first fall of Jerusalem (when many prominent people were taken away into captivity) Jeremiah has a vision of two baskets of figs – basically the good basket are those carried off to Babylon, while the moldy basket are those left behind in Jerusalem. Basically those who were left behind were going to infuriate both God and the King of Babylon, leading to the full sacking of Jerusalem and the destruction of the temple.

2 Thessalonians 2 v1-17

Paul has to write again; the issue of when Jesus would return was a big one for the early Church – many expected the Lord's return in their own lifetime.

Proverbs 25v15

Patience and a gentle tongue.

October 15th

Jeremiah 26v1-27v22

[Over these next few chapters things are not in chronological order. That's common in the Bible, as an obsession with chronology is a more modern thing. That's not so much a problem with today's reading, but over the next few days you may need to realise that we are sometimes moving backwards and forwards, from before the first capture of Jerusalem, to the second capture and destruction by the Babylonians, as well as having promises for the eventual return from exile.]

Jeremiah is very frank as he stands in front of the temple in Jerusalem proclaiming that God will destroy it if their wrong, sinful ways do not change. There are those who want him killed, while there are older people who remind the crowd that King Hezekiah had heard a very similar message from Micah, and rather than kill Micah, they had repented and God's judgment was postponed. We are told, however, that the prophet Uriah, working at the same time as Jeremiah, was killed for very similar preaching. The royal secretary, Ahikam, played a significant role in protecting Jeremiah. We are also told that Jeremiah repeated these warnings during the reign of Zedekiah, which would lead to the second fall of Jerusalem and the full sacking of the temple and city.

2 Thessalonians 3v1-18:

Wrong assumptions about the coming again of Jesus may have led some of the Christians into sitting around, rather than getting on with the Lord's work and their own livelihoods.
Proverbs 25v16 The advice about honey is obvious. Knowing when to stop – knowing the difference between a healthy appetite and downright greed, whatever the obsession, food or otherwise.

October 16th

Jeremiah 28v1-29v32

The false prophet very deliberately contradicts Jeremiah, and does so in God's name. Hananiah dies after two months for this very deliberate deceit.

False prophets had been unsettling those already in captivity; Jeremiah's letter was to tell them to settle down for God's judgment was by no means over on those still back in Jerusalem.

1 Timothy 1v1-20

Some letters are named after the Churches they are sent to (eg Romans or Ephesians); some by the person that sent them (eg James or Peter) whereas 1st and 2nd Timothy are named after the person that Paul was writing to. Judaisers are once again the problem, this time in Ephesus. Paul reminds us all of what the Gospel really is about: "Jesus Christ came into the world to save sinners..."

Things were clearly pretty bad regarding Hymenaeus and Alexander. Whatever the details, the situation called for strong disciplinary action.

Proverbs 25v17

Practical advice. Be a considerate friend, not a burden.

October 17th

Jeremiah 30v1-31v26

The people will one day be brought home again by the LORD.

I Timothy 2v1-15

Praying for those in authority; not easy when the state is hostile to the Gospel. Christians were to be model citizens, which then leads on to Paul's comments on the conduct of Christian men and women. The men are to be known for their prayer and their Christian character. The women are to be a complete contrast to the "ladette" culture in the world outside. As Donald Guthrie wrote in his commentary (The Pastoral Epistles, Tyndale series) Paul's directive was "designed to curb the tendencies of newly emancipated Christian women to abuse their new-found freedom by indecorously lording it over men. Such excesses would bring disrepute on the whole community, as it had probably happened at Corinth, and called for firm handling."

Proverbs 25v18-19

The real damage of slander and the real damage of putting confidence in the wrong person.

October 18th

Jeremiah 31v27-32v44

Blessing to come when the LORD brings the people back to Jerusalem.

Chapter 32 brings us to the year 588/7 BC. Jerusalem is in starvation and riddled with plague. Jeremiah is in prison. The city will fall in months, but Jeremiah has strong convictions as to what God will do in the future – and so he buys farmland.

1 Timothy 3 v1-16

Sadly, the office of elder, and even that of the Committee (the Biblical deacons) can be sought after for all the wrong reasons. Standards are set out here, and sometimes ignored by congregations, with a negative impact upon the life of the local congregation for decades.

Proverbs 25v20-22

Kidner sums up verse 20 as "heartless jollity." Verses 21 & 22 are a radically new way of dealing with enemies.

October 19th

Jeremiah 33v1-34v22

Further messages from God in those final months of imprisonment as Jerusalem is about to fall and be destroyed. (The Babylonians were particularly furious with the rebellion by the King of Judah who was seen as breaking his promises to those who had put him on the throne – their devastation would be particularly thorough and their punishment of him meant to send a signal to all.)

Some of the messages are Messianic, speaking of the One who would occupy throne of David. 34v8-22 refer to a brief period when the Egyptians threatened the invading Babylonian army (early or mid 588 BC: Kidner in the Bible Speaks Today series.) It seems that during the famine the rich and powerful, faced with extra mouths to feed, were happy to start doing things as the scriptures said, freeing Hebrew slaves. (Suddenly it was in their interests to be "scriptural"!) However, once the Egyptian intervention led to a break in the siege, suddenly they took their slaves back. God was going to punish this, and most strongly. The treatment of their fellow Jews was a very direct breach of God's covenant.

1 Timothy 4v1-16: Some of the false teaching that would soon come. The people needed to be well taught in real Christianity.
Proverbs 25v23-24: How not to go about relationships!

October 20th

Jeremiah 35v1-36v32

We are back again in the reign of Jehoiakim. (I did warn you that chronology did not matter in ancient times the way it does in more modern days – though I think we are used today to novels and films that use "flashback.")

We have the righteous Rechabite clan who maintain everything their founder had set out for his descendants; if only the rest of the nation were as committed to the faith of their forefathers.

We have the story of how at one point Jeremiah's message was written down by Baruch. The King burnt it, piece by piece. It was rewritten, in an expanded form.

1 Timothy 5v1-25

Respect and welfare provision within the fellowship. Families were not to neglect their responsibilities.

Older widows of good and consistent character might go on a list – some think they were a kind of Church worker. Younger widows were to be encouraged to remarry rather than live lives of idleness on the funds of the Church. These are of course very different times, but we can at least understand the concerns here.

There are instructions on how to regard those in leadership.

Verses 22-25 Verse 23 butts into the flow of the rest – in verse 22 we are told the danger of being too quick to ordain, and then suddenly in verse 23 we have the advice to Timothy to cease up on his total abstinence, given that the water quality was wrecking his health. Verses 24 and 25: In advising Timothy not to be too quick to ordain, Paul warns that both good and evil in some people may be only gradually revealed. As Guthrie put it in his commentary: "hasty action relies on first impressions, but these impressions are often deceptive. Unworthy men might be chosen, whose moral culpability lie deeper than the surface; and worthy men, whose good actions are not in the limelight, might easily be overlooked. The whole situation demands extreme caution." (p109)

Proverbs 25v25-27

Several different points are put together. The contrast between suspense and relief; the damage done by a righteous man compromising his principles, and having too much of a good thing, or getting carried away, dwelling on our honours.

October 21st

Jeremiah 37v1-38v28

We are given some background, perhaps a little belatedly! It is explained how Zedekiah became the king, rather than the rightful heir (though Zedekiah was of the Davidic line, being a king's son.)

We also read of how Jeremiah ended up in prison. During the Egyptian threat to the Babylonian army, Jeremiah tried to use the lifting of the siege to visit the property he had bought in the territory of Benjamin. Falsely accused of trying to desert to the Babylonians, he was whipped and imprisoned.

There is an interesting insight into Zedekiah – who actually asks Jeremiah if there is a message from God, and who in a rather guilty fashion shows some kindness to him. On the other hand, the king gives way to those who want to harm Jeremiah, and who imprison him in a muddy cistern in the yard, where he sinks in the mud, only to be rescued by a prominent Ethiopian in the palace.

Once again Zedekiah asks Jeremiah for a message from God. The message is given, but Zedekiah is too frightened to act upon it, when Jeremiah assures him that surrender now means he will live. In his fear, Zedekiah makes the wrong choice.

1 Timothy 6v1-21

A number of different issues are dealt with in the passage:

Our standard of work should not cause the Gospel to be laughed at;

Paul expresses his concerns about false teaching; Godliness and contentment ought to go together. There is a very personal "charge" to Timothy to "fight the good fight of the faith." Specific warnings to the rich. Final encouragement to Timothy. Proverbs25v28: What more is there to add? The meaning is obvious.

October 22nd

Jeremiah 39v1-41v18

Crunch time! King Zedekiah had ignored the advice from God through Jeremiah. That advice had basically been to make his peace with the Babylonians, whom God was using to punish Jerusalem and its people. Zedekiah should have realised that staging a revolt against the Babylonians, who had already defeated Jerusalem and carried off a portion of its more important residents some years previously, really was asking for a very heavy handed response from Babylon. Nebuchadnezzar, an emotional despot, (we know from the book of Daniel) was going to take things very personal because he had actually put Zedekiah on the throne.

Although on occasions Zedekiah seems to have wanted Jeremiah's messages, he never had the courage to stand up to his advisors…now you have just read, or are about to read, how Nebuchadnezzar's captain made Zedekiah watch as his children and nobles were butchered, and then Zedekiah's eyes were gouged out before he was bound to be taken away to Babylon.

In contrast, Jeremiah was released and was one of the few to be left behind while the bulk of the population were deported.

Gedaliah was appointed as Governor by Nebuchadnezzar, and was then subsequently murdered. A large group then panicked, and fled to Egypt. You will read tomorrow how they forced Jeremiah to go with them, against God's command

2 Timothy 1v1-18

The background on Timothy is useful and a reminder to all of how important it is to pass on our faith to the next generations.

Paul was involved in Timothy's ordination.

Paul encourages Timothy to live out his faith, to not be afraid to tell others about Jesus and reminds him of the central truths of the Gospel.

As we read, Paul is currently imprisoned and feeling deserted. We sometimes forget that he was as susceptible to depression and exhaustion as much as the rest of us. We also fail to realise how in his lifetime not every Christian stood behind Paul and gave him the support that they should have. Some of the Christians back in Jerusalem always had doubts about the way that Paul was making it "too easy" for gentiles like us to become Christians. There is no doubt that some so called "Christians" were quite glad to have him out of the way. The Judaisers were probably quite gleeful to see him imprisoned. In sharp contrast, someone like Onesiphorus was an absolutely consistent Christian.

Proverbs 26v1-2

Don't promote fools! Don't give in to superstition!

October 23rd

Jeremiah 42v1-44v23

The people's disobedience of God would have serious consequences. While Nebuchadnezzar would not have blamed them for the governor's death, he would go berserk about them joining Pharaoh his enemy. With great sadness we read of how they accused Jeremiah of lying when he spoke on God's behalf, and were quite blunt about how they would continue burning incense and making sacrifices to the "Queen of heaven."

No repentance at all. In fact, a belief that they were in bother for not keeping up the worship of this false goddess.

2 Timothy 2 v1-21

Paul encourages Timothy to be a good soldier for Jesus. He also draws comparisons with the discipline of an athlete, and then with farming. Although salvation is by God's grace and mercy, we don't just sit around taking God's tremendous gift through Calvary. While we can't earn it, we should live out our gratitude in service.

He reminds Timothy of essential doctrines – we need to hold together both the humanity and the divinity of Jesus, and we must defend the resurrection.

Sadly Timothy also faces problems from those who harm the Lord's work.

Proverbs 26v3-5

These verses will leave you quite puzzled, especially verses 4 and 5 which seem to contradict each other, and according to Kidner, left some Jewish rabbis wondering about the whole book of Proverbs, and whether it should be in the Bible at all! However, Kidner in his commentary makes these very wise comments (page 162):

Verse 3: "…this proverb...is written for us in two capacities: as people dealing with fools, and as potential fools ourselves."

Verses 4 & 5: "These twin sayings...bring out the dilemma of those who would reason with the unreasonable..."

October 24th

Jeremiah 44v24-47v7

Judgment will follow them to Egypt. We vthen have a number of messages which God gave Jeremiah at different times.

2 Timothy 2v22-3v17

Important advice to a young Christian worker: pick carefully where you put yourself in terms of influences. Avoid foolish arguments – yet at the same time Timothy is expected to engage courteously with people who are confused over central truths of the Gospel. Satan will distract people away using many different methods: personal pride, a need to be at the centre and to put others down (v3) shallow friendships (v4) even going to Church with no desire to learn (v5). There will be false teachers who will specifically target people with more time on their hands than sense (v6, 7.)

For those of you wondering why Paul appeared to be "targeting" women in verses 6 and 7, it was not Paul who was "targeting" them - the truth is that these women, still in a very mixed up state from their pagan pasts were actually very vulnerable and were being exploited by false teachers, some of whom taught at one extreme, self denial, while others taught the extreme opposite of all sorts of sins being acceptable. Neither group of false teachers was teaching Gospel truth. Their victims, however, had a lot to put behind them from their past, and although the past is forgiven and forgotten by God, some of these people probably were still struggling with consequences of how they had lived.

Proverbs 26v6-8

Fools in the wrong positions.

October 25th

Jeremiah 48v1-49v22

God's punishment to other nations.

2 Timothy 4v1-22

Convinced that matters are moving towards a climax in his own trial and imprisonment, Paul gives advice to Timothy to stand firm. Having said that, he still expects Timothy to arrive with his coat and to bring Mark too. We realise that Paul is under immense pressure. Nevertheless, there is an urgency in preaching the Word. Proverbs 26v9-12: More on the fool; though there is something worse. A more able man blind in his own conceit can do even more harm.

October 26th

Jeremiah 49v23-50v46

Although God has been using Babylon to punish other nations that does not excuse Babylon, who will in turn experience God's wrath to the full.

Titus 1v1-16

Those southern beaches on Crete – with their black sand – are the region where much of Paul and Titus's work took place. Titus had a lot to iron out, particularly in leadership. The Judaisers were a problem here too and were clearly extreme in the way they were leading people away from the Gospel.

Proverbs 26v13-16

The sluggard can't even see what he is.

October 27th

Jeremiah 51v1-53

There is immense detail here. Babylon may have been allowed to deliver God's judgment on Jerusalem, but others will repay Babylon. Cyrus is mentioned – his reign will prove crucial to the return of the people to their homeland.

Titus 2v1-15

Older folk are often keen to hand out advice to a younger generation – interesting that Paul deals with the older folk first!

Paul was not in a position to do anything about slavery per se, but Christian slaves could behave in ways that were constructive to the Gospel. While clearly salvation is

God's free gift, Christians were being urged to live and speak in ways that show the new life to the world. Christians are not merely sitting around for Christ's return – they are living self-controlled, upright and godly lives.

Proverbs 26v17

What a perfect picture of the meddler as someone who grabs a strange dog by the ears!

October 28th

Jeremiah 51v54-52v34: Jeremiah has more to say on Babylon, but then chapter 52 takes us back to the story of Zedekiah. We have already read part of this story before; we read of how Zedekiah made a break for Jericho, only to be caught by the Babylonians. We read of the systematic tearing down of Jerusalem, and of the items taken from the temple. Individuals such as the Chief Priest and his assistant were among those executed.

It was a sad end. Having said that, Jehoiachin, the original king of Jerusalem languished in prison for 37 years, in Babylon. This was very harsh, given that Jehoiachin had only reigned for three months.

For some reason, the new Babylonian king brought Jehoiachin out of prison and treated him with some favour. Why, we don't know. Perhaps – and this is only a wild guess – individuals like Daniel were already proving their worth back in Babylon – Daniel having been taken all those years ago amongst the first batch of captives. That's purely wild speculation on my part. Truthfully, we don't know the human forces behind the sudden improvement in Jehoiachin's treatment. At least Jeremiah's book ends with grace!

Titus 3v1-15

More on good citizenship; and the motivation for it – what Christ has done for us.

Proverbs 26v18-19

Pretending it was all a joke – if only because he or she was caught out is thoroughly condemned.

October 29th

Lamentations 1v1-2v19

This is Jeremiah's second book - and reflects the deep distress concerning what he witnessed in the aftermath of the fall of Jerusalem. Jeremiah had known – for years – that this was coming, but he still loved his own people, and felt it all deeply.

Philemon 1v1-25

The letter is to Philemon, but it is about Onesimus – the runaway slave who got converted and who was now heading back to his Christian master. There is nothing to suggest that Philemon had been cruel, but rather that Onesimus had somehow funded his getaway through what he took (v18).

Onesimus is now returning, considerably more useful and much more mature and now a brother in Christ as well. It is a cleverly written letter, but I believe Paul does have a genuinely high view of Philemon who is clearly a key Christian worker himself, and Onesimus has clearly proved himself since his conversion.

Proverbs 26v20

Gossip!

October 30th

Lamentations 2v20-3v66

Jeremiah is in deep distress and of course his faith is being challenged by what he has witnessed.
Hebrews 1v1-14 As you have seen – repeatedly through a number of the New Testament epistles – the Judaisers are an immense problem. Here Paul is writing to Jewish Christians (hence the title: Hebrews) and immediately he sets out how central Jesus is in everything. He makes clear what it means to call Jesus God, God's Son, Lord etc. A good passage to counter many of today's false teachers who won't give Jesus His full place in God the Father's tremendous plan.

Proverbs 26v21-22 As Kidner puts it: "It is the whisperer or quarreller himself, not (as he would claim) the truth, that feeds the fires; for his mind refashions facts into fuel."

October 31st

Lamentations 4v1-5v22

Jeremiah's anguish continues. Clearly the last part of the siege led people to do some terrible things – I've often wondered if being imprisoned had actually protected

Jeremiah from seeing some of those things – but the aftermath of defeat has only added to the terrible things that had already taken place. People are still in shock over the "allies" that had failed to help, and the neighbouring nations who took some pleasure in seeing Jerusalem fall.

Hebrews 2v1-18

I know that Billy Graham wrote a book on angels – which I have never read, but I'm sure it is properly balanced and scripturally correct given who wrote it, but even as a child I was aware of some who would have been quite obsessed with angels in a way that pushes Jesus into the background. The Victorians clearly had a fixation about angels, but in a way that often ignored the Gospel. As Paul says in verse 3: "what makes us think that we can escape if we are indifferent to this great salvation announced by the Lord Jesus himself, and passed on to us by those who heard him speak?" (Living Bible.)

Here Paul has to deal with Jews, or Christians from Jewish backgrounds, who are so obsessed with angels that they think of Jesus as another angelic being. Paul is defending the combined nature of Jesus – fully divine, fully human. Some of these Jewish Christians would continue having problems over these issues, to a point when we eventually have to question if they were really Christians at all, for the full consequences of the Gospel message have failed to sink in.

Proverbs 26v23

Gloss, glaze, veneers – all covering up the real thing underneath. The heart below it all is another matter.

November 1st

Ezekiel 1v1-3v15

Ezekiel was a priest who would never be able to fulfil his calling to serve in the Temple, since he was far away in Babylon, having been taken there with the first (huge) batch of prisoners when the Babylonians had captured Jerusalem for the first time. He will of course continue to have a ministry amongst the exiles, but as a prophet, rather than as a priest offering up sacrifices in the Temple. One of the issues he will have to deal with is the fact that many godly people were in exile with him, while a callous and unbelieving group were still in control in Jerusalem, moving towards further rebellion against Babylon. You and I shake our heads with disbelief at how those still in Jerusalem could not read the signs of the times and work out that what people like Ezekiel and Jeremiah were saying was "sanctified common sense." There is no doubt that some in Jerusalem had stood truth on its head, imagining that they were the “good ones” and that the first group of exiles were the “bad ones.” There is no doubt that some of the deeply troubled exiles wondered about that themselves.

Little did the current exiles realise, just what their exile was going to protect them from. You and I have the hindsight of having read Jeremiah and Lamentations, and therefore know all about the second fall of Jerusalem, with its systematic destruction of both the city and its Temple, but we need to put ourselves in the sandals of those who would like to be back home in Jerusalem, but who have to be told that God's judgment is far from over on what is still going on at home.

Poor King Jehoiachin has only been in prison for five years – remember from the end of Ezekiel that Jehoiachin will actually spend 37 years in prison before the next Babylonian king will let him out! The exiles were in for the long haul, which is always a problem for people of faith who hope to see quick solutions.

Ezekiel has visions, and the first one should be obvious. God is not restricted to a geographical area – in the vision he comes from the north, not Jerusalem to the south. The angelic beings around the throne have four sides, four faces and they can move in any direction without having to turn. Even the throne of God is on casters, and does not have to turn like a cart or chariot, but can move in any direction. You can compare Ezekiel's vision “of the appearance of the likeness of the glory of the Lord” with that of Christ in the opening chapter of Revelation. Ezekiel will not, of course, say that he has seen God, only the “appearance of the likeness of the glory of...”

At this point I probably do need to warn you that there was a Scandinavian who wrote a book (serialised in the late sixties in one of the Sunday papers) claiming that this chapter was describing a flying saucer! It was a best seller. But no, this is not a flying saucer, but a vision of God, His throne and the angelic beings around Him, unlimited to any geographical area or direction. Basically, those who were in exile needed to stop thinking that they could only know God back in the Holy Land, or that God was confined to that part of the world. Clearly the exile, with its trek of literally hundreds of miles, had come as quite a shock to a people whose world was comprised of Jerusalem and its hills. You can know God in Babylon too.

And clearly, there were many of the exiles who had deserved God's punishment, and who had work through the consequences of their sin, their anger against God etc.

Hebrews 3v1-19

Now Paul has to deal with another stumbling block to Jews and to Jewish Christians – their obsession with Moses. Paul is able to apply some of those stories of the wilderness experience to a current hardness of heart against the central truths of the Gospel.

Psalm 95 features in quotes and references in chapters 3 and 4 of Hebrews.

Proverbs 26v24-26

More on spiritual veneers and what may lie underneath, if the truth be known.

November 2nd

Ezekiel 3v16-6v14

The concept of a watchman for God: Some of Ezekiel's preaching used drama – the "imprisoned" prophet, the large brick to represent Jerusalem, cooking his food over a fire made from dried dung (as inhabitants of Jerusalem run out of any other fuel)... Hebrews 4v1-16: Even the whole concept of the Sabbath was becoming an obstacle to the Gospel as people focussed on anything but the Gospel. Paul is able to apply the concept of Sabbath rest to entering an even greater "rest" that God has for his people- the peace and assurance of knowing God through Christ. There are parallels too in coming into the Promised Land and coming into the presence of God as we come into faith in Christ. There are complex arguments in this chapter; it is sad to see how the whole wealth of spiritual inheritance which Jewish people had was being turned by some into obstacles to full blown faith in Christ. Unlike them, however, your problem is probably lack of knowledge of the Old Testament, whereas they sought to take refuge in it from the full consequences of the Gospel.

Proverbs 26v27

Your insincerity may recoil on you. (Kidner.)

November 3rd

Ezekiel 7v1-9v11

Ezekiel has a terrible vision of how open the paganism of Jerusalem is, even in the temple itself. Ezekiel's listeners would have found his description shocking and possibly offensive in its bluntness. Having said that, we know from Jeremiah how some fled to Egypt taking their pagan practices with them, even in the aftermath of the destruction of Jerusalem and its temple.

Hebrews 5v1-14

The whole concept of priesthood and sacrifice – all of this had to be understood in a fresh way, now that Jesus is both the sacrifice and the true High Priest interceding for us. In his complex argument, Paul takes us back to a priesthood that preceded even that of Aaron – right back to the early chapters of Genesis, when there was a Priest-King of Jerusalem, called Melchizedek, whom Abraham acknowledged as Priest to the one true God. Clearly some Jewish Christians had great difficulty with “putting aside” the current (in their day) priesthood and sacrificial system that continued on in the temple.

Towards the end of our reading, Paul expresses frustration that those who should have been much more mature as Christians, were still at square 1 in their Christian growth.

Proverbs 26v28 You may be shocked by the bluntness of this verse in some translations (Flattery is a form of hatred and wounds cruelly: Living Bible.) The point is that flattery distracts from the truth, and right decisions are made on the basis of truth. (Kidner)

November 4th

Ezekiel 10v1-11v25

The Temple back in Jerusalem needs to be cleansed. We are also given an example of the false prophecy going on in Jerusalem, how the city is an iron shield etc. The current exiles will be brought back to Jerusalem, but first God must deal with the ongoing sin there.

Hebrews 6v1-20

The whole problem of people who have embraced the Gospel, and then gone back. Many of Paul’s readers were missing the ritual and the daily bondage of the Pharisees approach to Judaism.

Proverbs 27 v1-2 We were made aware of how flattery is deceitful, in yesterday’s reading. Boasting brings its problems too. Where does God fit into our thinking? Kidner in his commentary describes boasting as the “companion sin of worry. Both are rectified by an embracing of the present will of God.”

November 5th

Ezekiel 12v1-14v11

Ezekiel is to act out what has yet to happen to King Zedekiah.

More about the false prophets.

Even the current exiles need to be told to give up their idols.

Hebrews 7v1-17

More about Melchizedek, as Paul has to deal with arguments as to how can Jesus be our great High Priest if he is of the tribe of Judah, not of the line of Aaron. Melchizedek existed long before Jacob's children, so there can be a priesthood independent of the house of Levi.

Proverbs 27v3

More on fools. Some translations use "anger" and some use "provocation." Whatever – fools can get us into deep trouble.

November 6th

Ezekiel 14v12-16v42

Sin runs deep, back in Jerusalem.

Hebrews 7v18-28

Salvation is through Jesus, not the old priesthood.

Proverbs 27v4-6

The dangers of jealousy and the need for frank honesty amongst friends.

November 7th

Ezekiel 16 v43-17v24 The people in Jerusalem have proved to be spiritual sluts. We are also told how God is angered by Zedekiah's rebellion against the Babylonians, for he gave oaths of loyalty to them, oaths taken in God's name.
Hebrews 8v1-13 Old priesthood, old covenant. God has replaced these. The Cross makes all things new.

Proverbs 27 v7-9

Several concepts thrown together here. Kidner sees a parable in the full man who will have no interest even in honey – a parable about possessions and outlook. The man who has deserted his home has forfeited much. Friendly counsel is quite a contrast to being on your own. There is a lot here about chosen lifestyles.

November 8th

Ezekiel 18v1-19v14

The issue of a generation suffering for the past sins of others was a big issue amongst the refugees in Babylon. Personal responsibility is Ezekiel's message.

Hebrews 9v1-12: The failure of the old system contrasted with Christ, God's new and better way. Christ's own blood, not the blood of calves and goats

Proverbs 27v10: Value tested friends.

November 9th

Ezekiel 20v1-49

A deputation of elders comes to visit Ezekiel; God's point is that they already know how they ought to be living.

Our reading finishes with hope as we read of the day when God will restore the nation.

Hebrews 9v13-28

Christ's blood achieves all.

Proverbs 27v11

Ah, to have wise children!

November 10th

Ezekiel 21v1-22v31

The stupidity of Zedekiah's policies, making an enemy of the power that put him on the throne. Judgment is coming to a city steeped in sin.

Hebrews 10v1-17

Paul continues the argument as to how inadequate the old system is.

Proverbs 27 v12 Sensible, careful planning.

November 11th

Ezekiel 23 v1-49

Once you understand that the girls Ohalah and Oholibah are figures representing Samaria (the Northern 10 tribes that broke away from Solomon's son) and Jerusalem (the Kingdom of Judah that still followed the descendants of David) you soon get the message.

Throughout their history, the people of Judah and Israel were always looking elsewhere. Admiration of Egypt, admiration of Assyria, admiration of Babylon...and look where it led. The Assyrians carried the northern kingdom off to captivity, and the Babylonians did the same to Jerusalem a few generations later. Their cultural, political, social and religious prostitution with foreign powers and cultures was their downfall.

Hebrews 10 v18-39

What a contrast with our reading from Ezekiel! Here we have all the Old Testament imagery, but we realise that through Jesus and His shed blood the way through to God the Father is now open.

There are warnings too – of neglecting worship, of persistent and callous backsliding, fully aware of how we are turning our backs on the Saviour. Warnings for those who are deeply attracted back into a Judaism that loves ritual and custom but which has turned its back on the Saviour.

Proverbs 27 v13

More sanctified common sense. Christians need to be loving, caring, generous – but not stupid. Precious resources are not to be wasted on the con man. Be wise in reaching out into a world that needs to know Jesus. Don't harden your heart either, but don't be a fool as you seek to do good for God. Sometimes you need to stop someone from doing wrong or making a fool of himself – financing his stupidity is hardly the right way.

November 12th

Ezekiel 24v1-26v21

Ezekiel had been carried away in the first Babylonian defeat of Jerusalem. Sadly, those left behind imagined that they could muster enough strength and throw off the Babylonians. This was not based on belief in God – far from it – those who were planning to rebel were guilty of many things in God's eyes, and what was coming was a vigorous stripping away of hypocrisy, of evil, of corruption – and this would entail a thorough destruction of Jerusalem, including of its temple. Sitting in faraway Babylon, Ezekiel knew that as a priest turned prophet, he would never be able to work in the Temple. Soon it would be gone. Judgement, however, was also coming on the neighbouring nations who took so much intense pleasure in seeing these things happening.

Hebrews 11v1-16

By faith...that's how all of these famous names lived. "Living for heaven" as the Living Bible put it in v16

Proverbs 27 v14

As Derek Kidner put it in his commentary, "It matters not only *what* we say, but *how, when and why* we say it.

November 13th

Ezekiel 27v1-28v26

We remember Tyre as an ally of Solomon, a source of wood in particular for the magnificent buildings of that time. However, by the time of the fall of Jerusalem, Tyre had rejoiced, in that Jerusalem was a serious commercial competitor. The fall of Jerusalem had left Tyre with considerable control of international trade routes. (Taylor's Tyndale commentary.) Judgment will come on those who took delight in the fall of God's people; Tyre in particular was known for incredible arrogance.

Hebrews 11v17-31 "By faith..." continues to be the key phrase, both for our reading, and for our lives.

Proverbs 27v15,16

The nagging wife! To be serious, it is a description of a person "as unsteady as the wind, and as slippery as oil" (a writer called Fritch quoted by Kidner in the Tyndale commentaries.) And as Kidner himself commented "you will never tie such a person down." These are serious comments on some of the characters, male and female, who will cross our paths.

November 14th

Ezekiel 29v1-30v26

Our reading begins with a reminder that the Davidic king, the King of Jerusalem, is now in the tenth year of his imprisonment by the Babylonians. Though judgment will ultimately come upon the Babylonians themselves, they continue, for the time being, to be instruments in the hand of God who is bringing judgment on many nations.

Nebuchadnezzar's army have defeated Tyre – we have an interesting description part of the way through our reading of the Babylonian soldiers wearing their heads bald carrying the baskets of earth etc to build the ramps during the siege. The

Babylonian soldiers are going to be paid with all the promises of what they can have when they bring down Egypt as well. There is a purpose to the humiliation of Egypt: "then they shall know I am the Lord."

Hebrews 11v32-12v13

Some of the terrible things referred to here are probably references to some of the horrors in the centuries which proceeded the New Testament times. From the end of the Old Testament, to the beginning of the New, there are periods in which mighty armies ravished the Middle East.

These illustrations, however, build up to an important point:

"Since we have such a huge crowd of men of faith watching us from the grandstands, let us strip off anything that slows us down or holds us back, and especially those sins that wrap themselves so tightly around our feet and trip us up; and let us run with patience the particular race that God has set before us." (Living Bible)

We need to keep our eyes on Jesus, and be prepared for the discipline and training in his service.

Proverbs 27v17

A lovely, positive verse. If only we had more stimulating conversations that bring out the best, that bring out our creativity. Also a challenge to be the person who brings about such things!

November 15th

Ezekiel 31v1-32v32

This is quite a long passage about God's judgement coming upon the culture and kingdom of Egypt. Egypt was arrogant enough to assume it can either defeat or at least have a stalemate with the Babylonian invaders, but Ezekiel lists all the other kings and leaders that Pharaoh will meet after death – all those who have fallen under what is ultimately God's judgment, using the Babylonians for the time being, until, as we shall see in other passages, God's wrath comes upon them too.

Hebrews 12 v14-29

Warnings about carelessness that leads to straying into sin.

Also some thinking back to Mount Sinai and what it was like for a sinful people to be confronted by a Holy God. In sharp contrast, we have Jesus, and the relationship we can have with God through what Jesus has done for us. Which is all the more reason to "please God by serving Him with thankful hearts, and with holy fear and awe. For our God is a consuming fire."

Proverbs 27v18-20

Service should be rewarded.

v19 brings its problems of how exactly to interpret it; what is clear is that self knowledge is important. We should probably look at James 1v23-25 alongside this verse although I suspect that Proverbs here is looking at it from a different angle.

V20 ambition and death are never satisfied. (Living Bible)

November 16th

Ezekiel 33v1-34v31

This is a significant passage, with its description of the "watchman" who has a responsibility to sound the alarm in time of trouble. They were of course all familiar with the roles of such people on the city walls during times of trouble and war, but there are those who are also watchmen with a responsibility to shepherd God's people and to warn them of the consequences of their sins.

Continue to keep in mind that Ezekiel was amongst the first group of captives carried away to Babylon. Unfortunately lessons have not been learnt by those who are left behind, with the result that the Babylonian army will have to return and do a "proper" job next time of really wrecking Jerusalem, and this time carrying off the vast majority of the population.

Ezekiel, who had trained for the temple priesthood, and who now will never be able to serve in the Temple, serves instead as a prophet in faraway Babylon. He finds that his words are not always taken seriously; some even come for the "sport" of hearing what the prophet will say next.

God's judgment is coming upon the rebellious people and their leaders who are still in Jerusalem. There is much brash talk – some of it quoted by Ezekiel. There is a false manipulation of the Old Testament story going on:

"Abraham was only one man and yet he got possession of the whole country! We are many, so we should certainly be able to get it back!"

False shepherds, rousing sentiments such as these, are also looking after themselves, and not the vulnerable people they are leading. The thorough destruction of Jerusalem and its Temple will come soon. There is hope though – see the last parts of this reading with its references to the Messiah – still several centuries away, but surely coming!

Hebrews 13 v1-25

Much is crammed into this closing chapter. If you have time, "unpack" this chapter slowly, possibly with a notebook and pen noting all the things mentioned here.

Proverbs 27 v21-22

The praise of others can prove to be a testing; is it praise from people worth heeding, or is it praise from those who have a particular agenda of their own? Would you even want to have praise from some characters? And of course, being praised by some can bring problems from other quarters. Yes, praise itself can be testing!

Nov 17th

Ezekiel 35v1-36v38

The Edomites were "relatives" of the people of Israel – descendants of Essau, Jacob's brother. They had quickly taken on the worship of the gods and goddesses of whatever tribes Essau had married into. Relations were often tense, but here judgment is pronounced on a people who took immense pleasure on the misfortunes of the people in Jerusalem.

Israel's return to the land is repeatedly prophesied. A new heart, a new spirit – the removal of "stony hearts of sin" is promised (36v26)

James 1 v1-8

James was the book which annoyed Luther so much. Having rediscovered the heart of the gospel message, Luther would have preferred this book to be more evangelistic! I think that points to a flaw in many Christian people who want more evangelism, but who are not open to teaching themselves, especially when there are areas of their own lives that are still very immature. Preach to the unsaved, but leave us alone! James was preaching to the saved – and some of the things he saw *Christians* getting up to needed to be dealt with! Tossed *about by every wind* (who knows what pious sounding drivel some of them said) and as we shall see in tomorrow's reading, the shameful falling over themselves to accommodate (sinful) wealthy people in the Church. The awful truth is that the lives of some professing are anything but a help to the Gospel. The irony is that some tried to blame God for the failure of their lives as Christians.

Proverbs 27v23-27

Some Christians are a lot worldlier than they realise. The problems of the Presbyterian Mutual Society caused anguish for many lovely and sincere people, but there were those who needed to take stock of where their confidence and assurance lay – often in huge sums stashed away. However, today's reading is a reminder to be diligent in matters of money and property, and taking proper care of all the things that must be attended to in running any home, farm or business.

November 18th

Ezekiel 37v1-38v23

For many of his contemporaries, Israel and Judah were finished. Nothing but valleys of bones – a reminder of slaughter that must have occurred during these times. However, God can bring life once more into this nation, and we are once more told of the Messiah of the Davidic line.

There are hard and difficult times as Ezekiel looks far into the future. Speculation as to which events these refer to is not always helpful; some see references to terrible events in the period between Old and New Testament times, others in the 1960s and 70s were only too willing to read the "Cold War" and the East-West tensions into all of this. Probably others today will look at Islam and some of its extreme states. The important lesson is that God never loses control, and this seemingly unstoppable power will be stopped in the land of Israel itself.

James 1v19-2v17

Christians bursting to talk but not listening! The "unteachable" Christians again? Clearly there is a lot that is wrong in some of these Christian lives. The picture of someone who looks into a mirror (the Scriptures) sees things about their own life which need to be changed, but still do nothing about it.

Wrong attitudes towards wealthy people – did the early Christians crave the influence and social standing that such company might bring them in the world outside? Some Christian business men are anything but mature Christians. Also warnings about selecting which of the commandments we see as more important than others. Some lives had little evidence of God's mercy, or grace. Faith without works is dead. Time there was real evidence of being a Christian, not just empty platitudes.

Proverbs 28 v1

Interesting comment on how living with lies continually has its impact on people.

November 19th

Ezekiel 39v1-40v27

Here Ezekiel goes over the destruction of Gog again. God drives these forces to what will be their doom. God's Word will be fulfilled, His name vindicated and the heathen will know that they are dealing with the one true God.

The description of death and destruction is on a huge scale.

In chapter 39 v25-29 Ezekiel returns to dealing with the needs of his people in his own times. The immediate message for the exiles sitting in Babylon (the post 587 BC generation John Taylor calls them in his Tyndale commentary on Ezekiel) is that the day is coming when God will reverse the shame of the exile.

Chapter 40 marks the start of the last nine chapters of Ezekiel, and the first time reader may find the going tough over the next few days. You can get bogged down in how some will interpret these verses. Some take them very literally as a temple that will one day be built; some interpret it all very symbolically – and there are some mighty complex versions of all of this.

Put on the brakes if you are tempted down extreme and highly subjective interpretations. Remember what the Shorter Catechism taught you: "The Scriptures principally teach what man is to believe concerning God, and what duty God requires of man."

What we do learn is the centrality of worship in a right relationship with the Lord and the abiding presence of God amongst His people, and the blessings that flow out. (Taylor p253)

The Temple had an immense importance to Ezekiel personally. He had trained to be a priest in Jerusalem; it was his inheritance, born into a priestly family. There was a time when he could not have imagined any other way of serving God. Now he was sitting in a far away land, ministering as a prophet, but knowing that he would never see the Jerusalem Temple again during his earthly life. He learns to trust God knowing that glorious things are yet ahead.

James 2v18-3v18

Intellectual assent – believing with our heads is not the same thing as living by God's Word day in, day out.

We have that famous passage about the tongue, and wise words about wisdom and peacemaking.

Proverbs 28 v2. The scramble for power can be so destabilising in any country. Kidner in his commentary referred to how the northern part of the country, Israel, would go through nine separate dynasties in two centuries. Pray for present day states that are equally unstable, impacting as they do upon those who seek to do the work of God's kingdom.

November 20th

Ezekiel 40 v28-41v26

Continue hanging in there! Ezekiel's vision challenges us about the way we enter God's presence with little thought and little idea of what we are doing. Every step in Ezekiel's temple vision should make us think about what a tremendous privilege it is to come in the name of Jesus. Ezekiel's vision is of perfection with nothing out of place.

James 4v1-17

Quarrelling, fighting, and skirting around and flirting with sin, and playing very dangerously with the values and outlook of a world very much out of step with God. Do we really want to be what God wants, where He wants, doing what He wants? Our agenda, or His, in our lives? We still haven't cast off that wrong division that some Christians are called to this or that, while the rest get on with living for themselves and their own agendas while turning up at Church and paying their envelopes and living out some form of godly exterior. It is no wonder some are falling and backsliding; their hearts are really not in discipleship at all! Begin to really live for God!

Proverbs 28v3-5

I tend to favour those who back the reading that says "A POOR man who oppresses the poor..." (Some translations such as the NIV say "A ruler...") It is particularly bad when those who have faced real trial in their own lives are the very last people to have any sympathy for others who are also struggling. Use those past experiences to help others.

Interesting comments on God's laws.

November 21st

Ezekiel 42v1-43v27

Ezekiel, much earler, had a vision of God's glory leaving the Temple in Jerusalem. Central to this vision is God's glory appearing and filling the Temple. Ezekiel is overpowered with an experience of God's holiness.

James 5 v1-20 Even in Christian circles, many people have their real trust in wealth, not in the Lord. And their faith and trust is often what some would call "cupboard love" – loving God when all is well. James reminds them of Job.

He also deals with the need for your "yes" and "no" to mean exactly that. Shades of truth, white lies etc are an abomination.

The duty of elders of the Church to go and pray with the sick is clear here. As is our duty to help a fallen brother or sister to get back to the Lord.

Proverbs 28 v6-7 "Better to be poor and honest..." No prosperity gospel here, just a reminder of the life that God expects.

November 22nd

Ezekiel 44v1-45v12

The walled up eastern gate is closed because the LORD's glory entered the temple this way, in Ezekiel's vision. Those who have been to Jerusalem will be familiar with the walled up eastern gate, or golden gate, which to this day Muslim authorities are extremely sensitive about and will not even allow Christian pilgrims to go over and look at it, because of the expectation that it will be opened for the return of Christ. HOWEVER, most serious commentators on the book of Ezekiel warn against making the jump from Ezekiel and linking this passage to the much later tradition.

The objection to "foreigners": this was a feature of a number of prophets, and of Ezra and Nehemiah, in the period after the exile. The objection was to people who were not of the covenant, people who were not of the faith, being employed in the temple – which was clearly the case before the exile (see 2 Kings 11v4 – the Carites) Instead the Levites should be doing the duties which were theirs all along.

Holiness was to be a mark of the priests' lives.

Honesty was to be a mark of how everything was to be conducted in the Temple and in the land.

1 Peter 1v1-13

Peter is writing to Christians dispersed through what is largely modern day Turkey (names like Asia refer to the Roman province of Asia, not the whole continent). We are reminded of basic truths of the Gospel, that our salvation has come through the blood of Christ shed for us, and we are reminded of our hope of eternal life. It is important that Peter reminds them (and us!) of these things, and that he speaks so positively of what Jesus has brought into our lives, because he also has to speak of the coming persecution of Christians. Tomorrow's reading will deal more fully with how Christians are to meet these challenges, but begin to take note of the closing verse of today's reading.

Proverbs 28 v8-10

V8 is interesting; God is well aware of wrong doing and does act out His judgment and redress over longer periods than we realise. V9 Prayer is about a real relationship with God, not somehow or other charming a god who is unaware of what we are really doing in life. V10. Time and time again in Scripture we have this warning of judgment on those who deliberately lead others astray, particularly those who have been following the Lord.

November 23rd

Ezekiel 45v13-46v24

This is a picture of everything being done honestly and fairly in worship and life in general. The prince is to be paid properly in terms of the land's produce, and he in turn will make provision for the people at particular times during the year. The Sabbath is to be kept. All of this is in sharp contrast to being a captive in a strange and foreign land where God's people, for the time being (in Babylon) have no choice but to obey the customs that are forced upon them. Strange isn't it, how people who often broke the Sabbath before the Babylonians carried them away, now miss the rhythm of work and rest that was part of the life that God sought to give them.

There are also regulations in place so that families do not lose their property down through the generations(46v16-18.) This was a particular concern throughout the Old Testament, that no family lost what God had given them when they first entered the promised land.

1 Peter 1v14

The temptation to fight evil with evil, slander with slander...to use every dirty trick in the book to fight back. This is NOT what Peter advises.

They are to remember that they have a new life, and are not to return to the old one, not even in the guise of fighting back and "holding their own." They are to continue living lives that are distinctly different by the presence of Christ within. Everything about the Christian Church and about the Christians themselves is to be built upon Christ, the true cornerstone.

Proverbs 28v11.

Riches are no guarantee of wisdom. Some of the richest people (not all of them, I might add) that we will meet in life can be very shallow, and sometimes the poorest and least educated see right through them immediately.

November 24th

Ezekiel 47v1-48v35

I don't think this is meant to be a literal temple on earth. This stream has amazing dimensions. This is all symbolism, a picture of the blessings and restoration that God intends. God has so much to pour out upon a people ready and fit to receive His blessings.

The comparisons with Revelation 21 are obvious. The closing verse gives this heavenly city a new name **Yahweh Shammah: The Lord is there.**

1 Peter 2 v11-3v9

Remember you are only passing through this world!

Christians are to work within the constraints of the legal system as best as they can and silence their critics where possible by model citizenship. Their first loyalty is of course to the Lord, but Peter is aware of how anger can arise within the persecuted Christian community that only feeds the accusations made against them.

The comments on clothes, jewelry etc are not an attack per se on Christian women looking after their appearances, but they are a very appropriate criticism that is right up to date with our own times in which outward appearance is all that counts, and many lives are shallow and self respect is often poor when everything seems to depend on "image."

Proverbs 28v12-13

V12 is probably fairly obvious. But v13 is a reminder that concealed sin will be revealed in God's timing, whereas God always deals in terms of grace with those who genuinely repent.

November 25th

Daniel 1v1-2v23

Think of Daniel as a refugee; seized as a prisoner in his own country as a youth, he had to adapt quickly to a very different culture hundreds of miles from home. (605 BC)

The Babylonian king assumed that youths from the wider royal family and nobility might make promising civil servants and had them trained.

For Daniel and his friends, adapting to a new culture did not mean assimilation; they had to think through what was distinctive about their Jewish faith that they should retain. Food might seem a strange thing to make an issue of, but it went straight to the heart of Jewish home life, and to the fact that these were important issues from the days of Moses and the people's wandering in the wilderness all those centuries ago. Some of the Babylonian food was forbidden in Old Testament days; and some of it was probably too rich and ultimately unhealthy. Nevertheless, they sought to keep their Jewish identity without causing offence. Throughout their lives, these Jewish men would walk fine tight ropes in the Babylonian palace. They knew God's blessing through this time.

They were in the employment of a maverick king who wielded incredible power, perhaps to an extent never seen before in our world. Living by the whims of Nebuchadnezzar came home very sharply when he woke up terrified by a dream. Nebuchadnezzar was wily enough to realise that there were those in his palace who would use such dreams to manipulate him, or who would merely tell him what they thought he wanted to hear. So the king put all his astrologers and other advisors on notice that they had to tell him the dream, as well as the interpretation, or face death.

Daniel – or more precisely –Daniel's God – came to the rescue. As we shall see tomorrow, jealousy of the Jews positions will soon lead the other officials to forget just how much they owed their lives to Daniel.

1 Peter 3v10-4v6

Discipline will be needed in difficult times of pressure and persecution.

Proverbs 28v14

Firmly rooted in God.

November 26th

Daniel 2v24-3v30

God's judgment against Babylon wasn't just preached by people like Jeremiah in far away Jerusalem; it was given to Nebuchadnezzar himself through the dream and explanation.

Unlike Cyrus, many years later, who could accept diversity in his empire (Cyrus was the one who allowed the Jews to go back to Jerusalem) Nebuchadnezzar wanted to impose conformity, to enforce unity. His statute was his idea of an empire worshipping together.

There were those who gleefully reported Daniel's friends; probably they could not "touch" Daniel, at least not yet.

The whole thing backfired – the God of the Jews is shown to be all powerful and the three friends are promoted – more reason for jealousy amongst the other staff.

1 Peter 4v7-5v14

Christians are encouraged to get on with working for Christ. Suffering is coming, but make sure that if you suffer it is for the right reasons (eg not as a busybody meddling in others' business.)

Elders are called to get on with the work that God has called them to. Younger people are reminded of their calling too. All Christians are reminded of how Satan is waiting to seize opportunities.

Proverbs 28 v15-16

Warnings to those in leadership.

November 27th

Daniel 4v1-37

Nebuchadnezzar is humbled by God. There is an illness that fits the description of what he went through.

2 Peter 1v1-21

The challenge to be a growing, consistent Christian continues.

Proverbs 28 v17-18

A troubled conscience is compared to one that has nothing to fear.

November 28th

Daniel 5v1-31

A king proves flippant with the utensils taken from the temple and finds judgment declared on him. The army of Darius finds how to get into the impregnable city –

they redirect the water and walk up and in – while Belshazzar and a thousand officers drink themselves into a stupor. The Medes take over the Babylonian empire.

2 Peter 2v1-22

Warnings of false teachers who will take immature Christians and confuse and mislead them.

Proverbs 28v19-20

Comments on attitudes to work.

November 29th

Daniel 6v1-28

An efficient civil servant continues under the new administration. Daniel is fairly discrete regarding his disobedience of the king's ridiculous law – but then the law had been formulated in the hope of catching Daniel out. His prayer time was so regular they caught him.

As in the Book of Esther, we find the Persian and Median kings were constrained by one rule – they couldn't undo their own laws. The King was cornered by a law made out of his own vanity and had to give way. Daniel's survival though, shocked everyone. God protected him, and the men who plotted his death soon found themselves, with their wives and children, in the lion's den.

2 Peter 3v1-18

Scoffers are already here, and the clock is moving on to God's judgment day. Meanwhile Christians are to get on with living for Jesus and passing on the Message. Peter makes an interesting comment on how others are already attempting to ridicule Paul's letters, twisting them to mean something else.

Proverbs 28v21-22

Money earned the wrong way; showing preference and acting mean. Kidner comments on verse 22: "a grudging or grasping spirit ensures inner poverty even while the outer hoard lasts."

November 30th

Daniel 7v1-28

Daniel has a dream of vast and powerful empires to come. There are many different interpretations, many of them speculative, and have meant different things to Jews and Christians facing immense persecution. God will be Sovereign.

1 John 1v1-10

The old fisherman (John) has lived to see and hear 2nd and 3rd generation Christians speculate about Jesus as though he is a legend that we can play about with. John will have none of that – he literally saw, heard and touched. His Jesus was real flesh and blood.

John also makes clear there is no twilight zone; we either live in Christ's light or not at all.

Proverbs 28v23-24

Frankness is one thing, but verse 24 speaks of a complete lack of compassion.

December 1st

Daniel 8 v1-27

Further visions of great empires. Some terrible things did happen in the period between the last Old Testament prophet and the Gospel stories in the New Testament. The Temple was defiled, and we can certainly identify the descriptions here with those empires that did trample across the Middle East. God was aware, was in control, and was (and is) working out His purposes on a worldwide scale. To understand even that much, was quite a jump (as I commented before) for a people whose whole world was once just Jerusalem and the hills around it. God was working on a scale much more vast than many of the people ever understood.

In the context of this Bible study, it possibly is not profitable at this point to launch you into a whole explanation of the intervening history between the two testaments. The point is, that as we leave the Old Testament, with the people under the control of the Persians, and then enter the New, with the Romans dominating the known world of those times, nothing has happened unknown to, or outside of, God's knowledge and power. But yes, Daniel had good reason to be disturbed by what He saw – but he had more to see.

1 John 2v1-17

Simple but profound. John writes with immense experience of life. What he writes is perfectly understandable, if we give it time to sink in.

Proverbs 28 v25-26

Where is our trust?

December 2nd

Daniel 9v1-10v21

Daniel has had a long life, and was aware from the Book of Jeremiah that the time of the exile should be drawing to an end. Daniel is over 80 and this is 539 BC. What God shows Daniel in our passage runs the whole way into the first century AD. There is a clear reference to the death of Christ, and many believe a reference to the Roman general who destroyed Jerusalem in 70 AD, ending the sacrificial system to the present day.

We are also made aware of a spiritual battle which is ongoing.

Christians can get into some dreadful arguments over what Daniel did or did not see. Perhaps we need to listen to Daniel 10 v19: "O man greatly loved, fear not, peace be with you, be strong and of good courage." (ESV)

Daniel was an exceptional believer, and through him great insight was given, to encourage his people through centuries of difficulty, as they awaited God's great purposes.

1 John 2v18-3v6

John is also speaking of end times, but he gives simple advice to stay in fellowship with the Lord.

Proverbs 28v27-28

V27 speaks on attitudes to the poor; v28 on society and the impact of those who are in ascendancy.

December 3rd

Daniel 11v1-34

This is detailed prophecy; as noted yesterday, this is the year 539 BC – here in this chapter we are given details of kings yet to come – right down to Xerxes who invaded Greece (v2) and Alexander the Great (v3). Verse 4 even describes how Alexander's kingdom was broken up in 323 BC between his four generals. Then in verses 5 to 20 we read about kings of Egypt and Syria. The ESV footnotes comment "Many of the specific predictions of this chapter were fulfilled in striking detail." This chapter deals with things that happened during the period between the end of the Old Testament and the beginning of the New – right down to Antiochus IV who plundered the temple and killed 80,000 men, women and children – leading to the Maccabean revolt. The reference to the Kittim (v30) is to the Romans who forced

Antiochus out of Egypt in 167 BC. His anger for this, however, was directed against the Jews, and every attempt was made to exterminate the Jewish faith.

Obviously this is not the place to give you a detailed lesson in 400 years of Jewish history, but merely making the point that Daniel was able to prophesy in extreme detail. It was an extremely difficult period in Jewish history.

1 John 3 v7-24

Some people pass over these simple words, without realising that in the simplicity of what John says, there is much that is profound. John is getting beyond words, to intentions.

“Those who do what God says – they are living with God and he with them.” (Living Bible verse 24a)

Proverbs 29v1

There is a bloody mindedness that brings severe consequences; here we have someone who is unteachable.

December 4th

Daniel 11v35-12v13

What Daniel has to say about Antiochus IV is spot on – he viewed himself as a god. Daniel’s prophecy, however, is seen by many Christians to refer to someone beyond Antiochus, to the Antichrist who will arise before the end times – the opening verses of chapter 12 refer to the resurrection.

To explain things in further detail is to enter into areas that Christians have disagreed over, especially how to interpret some of the figures given.

1 John 4v1-21

John’s opening warning in this passage is important; some people are too easily impressed when people use the “right” phrases and words, and “sound Gospel,” particularly if they throw in plenty of thous and thys and sound King James.

If you are familiar with God’s Word you should be able to spot when they are denying basic teaching about the divinity and the humanity of Jesus.

It is much harder to do something about it when you recognise that the Gospel is being used for other purposes, such as personal or political advancement; it took Christian people in Northern Ireland a long time to waken up on that one, but it has severely damaged the credibility of the Gospel.

John's teaching on God's love is important because much of the travesty that passes for authentic Christianity fails on this.

Proverbs 29v2-4

We are given a set of opposites and their consequences. The utter contrasts ought to be alarming.

December 5th

Hosea 1v1-3v5

By now you are familiar with how some of the prophets compared Israel's / Judah's unfaithfulness to God to adultery – sometimes quite bluntly and even rather crudely.

The Book of Hosea takes that comparison somewhat further. We read in 1v2 how Hosea is told to go and marry a whore. While there are some commentators who take it quite literally that Hosea went down the street and found a whore to marry, it is generally assumed that Hosea is talking about a wife who turns out to be unfaithful – the first child is his, but the second and third are described as the children of whoredom. Hosea uses his own marriage as an illustration of Israel's behaviour towards the Lord. As the footnotes of the ESV study Bible put it, "The tragedy of Hosea is the tragedy of a marriage that began well but went bad. And so it was with the Lord and Israel...The book of Hosea refers to Israel's cherished beginnings."

You now understand why this is another one of those books you never did in Sunday School!

Today's reading ends with Hosea buying Gomer back for fifteen shekels and some barley. In Malawi, we did come across a man who took back an adulterous wife, after first taking her to the hospital and having her tested for aids.

Hosea's actions, were a picture of God restoring a very much fallen people.

1 John 5v1-21

John continues to put profound matters in simple terms. However, what is meant by the passage about a Christian sinning in a way that leads (or does not lead) to death? David Jackman in The Message of John's Letters (Bible Speaks Today series, IVP 1988 p164ff) explains that if faith in Jesus Christ and what He has done for us at Calvary is what leads to eternal life, then this sin that leads to death must be a rejection of all of that – a rejection of "the atoning death of the incarnate Son of God." This sin is clearly in a very different category to a believer falling back into sin and needing to be restored; this is an utter denial of everything which the Gospel is about.

While John wants to emphasise that Christians should pray for a fellow Christian who has fallen back into sinful ways, he does raise serious doubts about the reality of the Christian faith and commitment of someone who "makes a practice of sinning." (Living Bible v18) – which really brings us back to the issue of a life that is a total denial of the Gospel.

Proverbs 29v5-8

Flattery can have cynical motives. Sinful and righteous people are contrasted. Innocence is able to go on its way singing, whereas an evil man ensnares himself

---

December 6th

Hosea 4v1-5v15

A description of the people who are supposed to belong to the Lord.

"There is no faithfulness or steadfast love, and no knowledge of God in the land; there is swearing, lying, murder, stealing, and committing adultery; they break all bounds, and bloodshed follows bloodshed." (ESV 4v1b & 2)

Sadly, Judah is following what they see the people of Israel doing, and judgment is coming on both.

2 John 1v1-13

Basic Christian truths are being denied – the humanity of Jesus was under attack by false teachers

Proverbs 29v9-11

More on the fool, but verse 10 brings home that there are deadly enemies that cannot be simply dismissed as a fool.

December 7th

Hosea 6v1-9v17

Our reading begins with Hosea's hope that the people might return to God, but as our reading progresses we see there is no repentance.

3 John 1v1-15

There are lovely things for which Gaius is thanked; hospitality was and is important. This is in sharp contrast to the petty tyrant behaviour of Diotrephes. Jackman sums up this man

"Destroying unity, flaunting authority, making up his own rules to safeguard his position, spreading lies about those whom he had designated his enemies, cutting off other Christians on suspicion of guilt by association...this is what happens when someone who loves to be first decides to use the church to satisfy his inner longing for a position of pre-eminence, for his own personal aggrandisement." (page 198)

Demetrius is also the complete opposite, thankfully. Jackman raises an interesting speculation. The very mention of Demetrius, given that John seems to be writing from Ephesus, leaves us wondering can this be the same Demetrius who created so much trouble for Paul in the past (ACTS 19) – was he now converted??? Wow! If indeed it was the same man. It may be just a coincidence – perhaps the person delivering the letter is called Demetrius and so it would be pretty obvious to those standing there if or not it was the same man. Interesting thought though.

Proverbs 29v12-14

V12 – if the ruler is dishonest, then those who work under him soon learn from him.

V13 – the Lord has given both the same ability – but what contrasts in how it is used.

V14 – this may be a sweeping generalisation, but while the poor may seem insignificant, their loyalty to a just king may one day be the very thing that counts in keeping a throne.

December 8th

Hosea 10v1-14v9

We see more of God's deep hurt.

13v2 refers to those who worshipped calf idols – hence the "kissing of calves" – paying homage to their idols by kissing them. We have a pretty thorough picture of how far the people have sunk.

Jude 1v1-25

Jude is another half brother of Jesus (like the James who wrote the letter of James.) His Jewish background means he makes a lot of references to Jewish stories – some Biblical, and some from outside the Bible. This can open up quite a can of worms for some people, and can make it very difficult to preach from because people obviously want an explanation as where some of these come from, but they are best explained as Jude using and quoting (as illustrations) from writings that were well known in Jewish circles without necessary endorsing them as Scripture. So, in using some of these illustrations, what is Jude attacking? (1) People who have known salvation who have gone back on the faith . (2) He compares false teachers to fallen angels . (3) He uses the story of Sodom and Gomorrah to illustrate how far and how unnatural rebellion against God can go. These false teachers had gone pretty far;

"They are godless men, who change the grace of our God into a licence for immorality and deny Jesus Christ our only Sovereign and Lord." V4

"These men are grumblers and fault-finders; they follow their own evil desires; they boast about themselves and flatter others for their own advantage." V16

Judgment is coming on these false teachers – lust, rebelliousness, irreverence (Kidner's commentary on 2nd Peter and Jude) are some of the things of which they are accused. There is a denial of the Lordship of Jesus.

How are Christians to respond? See from verse 20 on.

Proverbs 29v15-17

From children to adults – the consequences of not confronting wrong doing.

December 9th

Joel 1v1-3v21

Joel's book is generally dated after the exile of 586 BC. As to how much after it, that's an argument in itself. However, he is clearly based in Jerusalem, and the temple is functioning. I tend to go along with those who date the book sometime after the **return** from the Babylonian exile.

The people are facing a national calamity, and Joel calls them to repent. The threat of locusts and drought are very real.

Some of the prophecy is clearly for a future that was still far away for Joel's first readers – the Day of Pentecost fulfilled the promises of 2v28. Some see direct references to God's final judgment throughout the book.

Revelation 1 v1-20

Revelation has a forerunner in the Old Testament – parts of the book of Daniel. The first few chapters are less controversial than other parts of the book.

"Asia" in the New Testament is basically what we call Turkey today – which also leads to another piece of information that you need – which is that what are now "Turkish" places, were Greek in New Testament times. It is outside the scope of these Bible notes, but basically massive movements of Greek speaking people have taken place over the centuries, so you may very well be puzzled how you can go on a holiday to Turkey and go and visit places such as Ephes or Efes (Ephesus) and see all these fantastic Greek remains.

Anyway, Revelation is addressed to 7 Churches in "Asia." John reminds us of the basic Gospel message, and then presents us with a tremendous vision of Jesus in His ascended glory – and we are reminded that He is coming again!

Proverbs 29v18 "...the dependence of public morality on the knowledge of God." (Kidner, Proverbs IVP Tyndale series, page 176)

December 10th

Amos 1v1-3v15

Amos is from Tekoa, south of Jerusalem – I remember it as a pretty arid area during a very hot summer. Amos had a hard life in agricultural work, and was called by God to cross from Judah (the southern kingdom based around Jerusalem), and to go and preach to (northern) Israel.

This was a time of relative prosperity and the various shrines and "temples" of the northern kingdom were flourishing and well attended. Indeed both kingdoms were having an economic boom and were politically stable and the Assyrian Empire was currently in a weaker position and not seen as the very real threat which it would become later.

An approx date is 760 BC. The worshippers at these various shrines (which included well known places such as Bethel) were looking forward to the "Day of the Lord," expecting God's judgment to pour down on their enemies and rivals, and were oblivious to the fact that in the "Day of the Lord" God would judge them too – indeed they were in a very sorry state spiritually, and their constant religious activity hid the truth of a nation who were morally in a mess and far from God. The official prophets gave the messages that the king and his advisors wanted the people to hear – which were the messages the people wanted to hear anyway. Amos was clearly out of step with the "appointed" (Royally approved) prophets.

As you will have read, Amos began with various tirades against some of their enemies. All of this went down well – and then Amos really began with those who claimed to belong to the Lord. From tomorrow's opening words, you'll begin to see just how close to the bone Amos could go.

Revelation 2v1-17

Now we have specific messages for Churches in this region. The congregation at Ephesus certainly had its good points, but its love for Jesus was cooling. Smyrna was, and would, suffer persecution for their faith and trust in Jesus Christ. The Church at Pergamos was working in a difficult area with much Satanic worship going on in the pagan population. Antipas had lost his life sat the hands of opponents of the Gospel. Yet there was false teaching that saw no problem with sexual sin.

Proverbs 29 v19-20 Verse 19 may be puzzling, "A servant cannot be corrected by mere words; though he understands, he will not respond." It is mentality that some adopt today in our society – "unresponsive, irresponsible" (Kidner.)

December 11th

Amos 4v1-6v14

Ouch! The cows of Bashan were not pedigree cattle, but the wealthy pampered women. Amos certainly got his message home, to be followed up with some deep sarcasm:

"Come to Bethel and transgress; to Gilgal, and multiply transgression; bring your sacrifices every morning, your tithes every three days..." ie what was going on in places like Bethel and Gilgal was a sickening show of insincere religious hypocrisy, but what a religious show they could put on!

God's judgement was coming on both Israel (Samaria) and Judah (Jerusalem.)

Revelation 2v18-3v6

The Church in Thyatira had its good points, but tolerated a false prophetess who taught sexual immortality and compromise with idolatry. The Church at Sardis still had some faithful Christians, but the bulk of the congregation were complacent – as Michael Wilcock put it, in the Bible Speaks Today Series (1975, page 52) "Convenience and circumspection, rather than whole-hearted zeal."

Proverbs 29v21-22 The wrong management of people brings its problems.

December 12th

Amos 7v1 – 9v15

Our reading begins with near disasters (God's way of bringing judgement) which were averted when Amos interceded for the nation.

Amos however, now sees that judgement averted has done nothing in terms of bringing the nation to repentance. Once God gives Amos a vision of a plumb line, Amos knows not to intercede this time.

Amaziah, the priest of Bethel, now thought it was time to act against Amos. When Amos denied being a prophet, he was denying belonging to any "school" or guild of prophets. Amaziah was so spiritually "gone," to be quite frank, that he could not see Amos as a real authentic God-sent prophet, but could only see him as an intruder from some southern (Judean) guild in competition with their own Royally appointed prophets. Yes, that is precisely how far gone things were. Prophets were useful tools in the hands of the rulers if they could keep them under control. A nice well paid occupation under royal pay in both kingdoms. Amos was anything but one of these prophets.

Judgement was definitely coming! And then suddenly, in the middle of chapter 9, Amos began to talk about the restoration of Israel. He spoke of the restoration of David's line – fulfilled in Jesus. He spoke about things which were only properly fulfilled in the New Testament when non-Jews – Gentiles – came to faith in Christ. Chapter 9 v11, 12 was quoted in Acts 15 v16-17 as evidence of God being very much in the work of Paul, Barnabas and the others who were bringing the Gospel to the gentiles. If the Judaisers, who opposed Paul had been given their way, Christianity might have stayed a small cult within Judaism. Instead the early Church saw (Amos's) prophecy being fulfilled.

Revelation 3 v7-22

Philadelphia had very real opposition to face. Laodicea on the other hand, was a smug congregation, imagining they were self sufficient, and in reality quite poor in spirituality. They were the luke-warm congregation.

Proverbs 29 v23

Pride brings its problems.

December 13th

Obadiah 1v1-21

For various reasons, scholars date Obadiah's book to after the fall of Jerusalem in 586 BC and probably in the first half of the exilic period. The reason given for placing it in the first half of the exile is that it foretold the fall of Edom which eventually came in 533 BC. Location: Jerusalem itself. More details in (e.g.) the ESV Study Bible footnotes and similar Study Bibles in other translations.

Obadiah has a lot to say about Edom – the descendants of Essau. This is the southern end of what is now modern day Jordan. Instead of helping the people of Jerusalem, the Edomites exploited the situation with the Babylonians in every way, even to the point of selling refugees into slavery, and hunting down those being sought by the Babylonians. Edom had it coming – there was still time for Essau's descendants to repent – but their judgment came some years later.

Revelation 4v1-11

The fantastic scene in heaven above

Proverbs 29v24-25

Fearing the wrong person!

December 14th

Jonah 1v1-4v11

Jonah, the unwilling prophet.

The people of Nineveh (the capital of the Assyrian Empire) were very much the hated enemies of Jonah's people, so rather than evangelise them, Jonah decided to put himself out of God's reach, or so he thought. Instead of heading east, Jonah headed west, to the Mediterranean coast (modern Joppa or Jaffa on the outskirts of what is now Tel Aviv) and took a ship heading far west, to present day Spain (Good News translation) or an area approximately in that direction.

There is a lot of irony in the story – e.g. the pagans praying while the man who worships the one true God is sleeping.

By the time the whale vomits Jonah up, he obeys God. (Other examples of people swallowed by a whale do exist from the 1800s – at least one man was recovered live, quite mad, with his skin badly bleached by the acid in the stomach of the whale.) It gives us some idea of what Jonah must have looked like when he arrived in Nineveh. It was certainly effective!

Jonah's story ends on a particularly bad note. Because the people turned to God, Jonah is deprived of seeing his arch enemies, the Ninevites, burning in God's judgment. In fact he is more upset over a plant that God allows to wither, depriving Jonah of shelter while he sat on watching, hoping that God would not forgive the Ninevites.

In fact, it would appear that Jonah, who can't abide the people, doesn't even care about the cattle – see the last verse!

It was a hard lesson that more than Jonah had to learn – that there are people out there that we might not like, but our God of compassion and grace wants to bring them back to Himself.

Revelation 5v1-14

Only the Lamb – the Saviour – is worthy.

Proverbs 29v26-27

V26 – great expectations placed in the wrong people.

V27 – certain partnerships cannot be.

December 15th

Micah 1v1-4v13

Micah was working, roughly speaking, in much the same times as Hosea and Isaiah. In fact Jeremiah 26v18 mentions his influence on King Hezekiah – Micah prophesied God's judgement on both parts of the land, but he would have witnessed (most likely) God's deliverance of Jerusalem from the Assyrians during Hezekiah's reign. God's judgment did come upon Jerusalem later, through the Babylonians, as indeed Micah prophesied.

Micah also prophesied their rescue from Babylon.

Revelation 6v1-17

The seals are opened and God's judgment comes in terrible events. Prominent men would rather be hidden under the rocks than face the Lamb as He comes in judgment.

Proverbs 30 v1-4

Solomon was not the only one who made up Proverbs!

There are echoes of the Book of Job here.

December 16th

Micah 5v1-7v20

Micah prophesied the birth of the Saviour – see chapter 5 v 2.

The closing verses of the book are very much about God's forgiveness and compassion.

Revelation 7 v1-17

A much abused passage, by those who take the number very literally and make assumptions as to who exactly they are. There will be those from God's ancient people amongst the vast crowd in heaven, as well as those from every nation, tribe, people and language – Christians who have suffered terribly for Christ. Yet the point is that the Church is indestructible, and that God's people are safe with him. (Wilcock)

Proverbs 30v5-6 God's word is flawless. Trust in it, but don't amend it.

December 17th

Nahum 1v1-3v19

What Nahum has to say about the Ninevites helps us to put in perspective why Jonah had such a hatred of them, although it does not excuse Jonah at all. What Nahum said about the Ninevites was to bring comfort to his Jewish audience, whereas Jonah was required to deliver the message so that the people of Nineveh both heard the message and therefore had an opportunity to respond.

Scholars (see ESV Study Bible footnotes) date Nahum's book after the time of Jonah, when the repentance of the Ninevites had failed to last. The Assyrian/Ninevite empire was exceptionally cruel, rivalling some of the worst powers we have seen in more recent times (20th century Europe and Africa.)

Revelation 8v1-13

Sincere prayer is like incense to God.

Judgment continues. There were certainly ancient disasters which helped John to picture how that judgment would come – the eruption of Vesuvius, had already taken place,

Proverbs 30v7-9

A challenging prayer!

December 18th

Habakkuk 1v1-3v19

Habakkuk was a contemporary of Jeremiah, and although he saw the same corruption and disobedience of the Lord, his ministry is very much one in which he calls out to God to change all of these things. David Prior in his commentary in the Bible Speaks Today series believes that Habakkuk may have been one of the "official" prophets employed at the temple in Jerusalem. Hints to this come at the end where there are notes to the director of music. Given the very negative things we discovered about "official" prophets in Amos's day, it is good to realise, at least down in Jerusalem, that some were tuned into what God really had to say to His people.

One very challenging passage comes at the end – if the harvest is a complete failure, Habakkuk will still worship the Lord. As the introduction to Habakkuk puts it, in the ESV, "By the end of the book, Habakkuk is a changed person – he has learned to wait and trust in God, who works out all things for His glory."

Revelation 9v1-21

Despite the plagues sent by God, many refuse to repent.

Proverbs 30 v10

The "servant" may be powerless in this world to deal with wrong doings, but God the Judge takes him seriously.

December 19th

Zephaniah 1v1-3v20

Once again we have a prophet whose ministry coincided with King Josiah – a most godly king who did much to bring the people back from extreme paganism – but as I have said before, much of the reforms were imposed by Josiah, and only lasted while he was around. Zephaniah is preaching against a background in which many hearts remained unchanged after decades of uncontrolled paganism in the reigns that went before.

Revelation 10v1-11

The message of God's judgment will still be delivered. God's people have found God's Word sweet, but it is bitter to an unbelieving world.

Proverbs 30v11-14

Descriptions of arrogance and what it can lead to.

December 20th

Haggai 1v1-2v23

Haggai can be dated to within a few months – specifically late August to mid-December 520 BC (ESV study Bible.) The exiles are back from Babylon, but struggling to get God's Temple rebuilt. Haggai encourages the Persian appointed governor and the High Priest to complete the work.

Revelation 11v1-19

The temple in Jerusalem had already been destroyed by the Romans by the time this is written, so Wilcock cautions against assuming it is the actual Jerusalem temple here. God's people – the Church – are secure eternally, despite what is to happen.

How should we interpret the 2 witnesses? Some suggest this is the Church, which may actually vanish – for a time – from some parts of the earth. Others want to take them literally as two preachers resurrected. Terrible judgments continue, but some (v13) do acknowledge God in these end times.

Proverbs 30v15-16

Measureless ambition exposed as the craving leech it is. Comic, tragic, pathetic, repulsive are all adjectives used by commentaries (eg Kidner.)

December 21st

Zechariah 1v1-21

Zechariah begins his work as a prophet just after Haggai. Life was still hard for the exiles who had returned from Babylon and the people needed encouragement. However, Zechariah is a much longer book than some of the other prophets we have been reading recently, and there is a lot prophecy in this book looking well into the future – to the Messiah. It is not easy to read, and has many similarities to Revelation.

Regarding chapter 1, the Persians have brought a sense of stability and peace through the known world of their day. However, God's people are still trying to recover from all that has been done to them, and God will move in judgement against these other nations who are at rest and enjoying peace, but who were responsible for the horrible sufferings of God's people.

Revelation 12v1-17

There is a lot of argument over how to interpret these figures. The woman and the dragon are symbolic (Wilcock.) The child though is to be taken literally as Christ.

Here in Revelation we are told that there was a war in heaven, with fallen angels joining Satan as he was expelled.

The dragon, having failed to stop the Saviour, made war on the Church.

Proverbs 30v17

The chapter has had a lot to say on arrogance. Judgment is coming.

December 22nd

Zechariah 2v1-3v10

Humiliated Jerusalem will be restored. Those who are still in Babylon and playing cautious with any idea of going home to Jerusalem are told directly to go to Zion (Jerusalem.) It was a journey that some estimate at 900 miles.

Chapter 3: the long term damage to Jerusalem and its people was clearly immense. This Joshua was the High Priest, a godly man, and Zechariah sees Joshua, as representing the Lord's people, being given clean clothes and being restored. It is a vision of all the people being restored. "My servant, the (coming) Branch," is a reference to the coming Messiah.

Revelation 13v1-18

Christians from a Jewish background were already familiar with such language in the book of Daniel. They had already seen huge empires in the Old Testament and in the period between the Testaments. There are horrific stories of the desecration of the Temple and the torture of Jewish people from the period before the start of the New Testament. The use of false religion to give respectability and authority to despotic empires was well known then and now. They were also used to how the

Romans linked the state and worship in their own day, with ideas about the divinity of the Roman Emperors. So this chapter prophesied about what was ahead of the Church as various powers would arise and threaten God's people.

Proverbs 30 v18-20

We marvel along with verses 18 and 19 – and then are hit with the sickening description of v20. The sharpness of the contrast is very deliberate. As Kidner put it: "a person utterly at ease and in her element in sin."

December 23rd

Zechariah 4v1-5v11

Chapter 4: Zerubbabel was of the Davidic line, being the grandson of one of the kings of Jerusalem. He would never be king, but he was the governor of Jerusalem under Persian rule. He would know God's blessing as together with the High Priest they rebuilt the Temple.

We are told about the Lord being all seeing throughout the earth; the whole experience of exile had brought home to the people just how much bigger the world was than their little corner of the Middle East, and they had learnt that God was working on the grand scale of nations and empires, and not just in the affairs of the hills around Jerusalem.

The importance of olive trees may be lost on us, but they were an essential commodity, with the oil being used not only for cooking, but also for light. What we are shown is an inexhaustible supply of oil so that the lamps in the temple will never go out. Whether these trees also represent angels, prophets or the High Priest and Governor gets us into an area of debate. However, under God, things would not be as fragile as they might seem now. I suppose for us, imagine a present day situation in which you were never sure if we would have electricity today or not, and it gives you some idea of how people in those days relied on olive oil. It was a major commodity. A ready supply of oil – or not – was a sure sign of the stability (or not) of the land. We are seeing how fragile the returnees felt back in shattered Jerusalem, and we are hearing assurances from God to those needing encouragement to proceed with anything, never mind the rebuilding of the temple, which several of our prophets are calling Joshua and Zerubbabel to do.

Chapter 5. Sin is represented by the woman in the basket. Just as the storks migrated to the north every year, so all the sinful practices of the past would be purged from the people and carried off in the direction of Babylon. The winged women who carry this away are interesting, for if indeed they are angels, it is the only place in the Bible where we have female angels!

Revelation 14v1-20

The scene moves; the Lamb stands on Mount Zion surrounded by His redeemed. God's reaping begins.

Proverbs 30v21-23

Examples of reversals that are wrong.

December 24th

Zechariah 6 v1 – 7v14

God is in control of the whole earth as His chariots go out to patrol it all.

The crown for the high priest , and the promise of the Branch. Somehow, the Messiah is to be both king and priest.

Chapter 7. In exile, the need to repent had been brought home, very deeply, to the exiles. Should they continue all the rituals of fasting and mourning which had been their practice for the 70 years of exile in Babylon?

Zechariah stresses the need to live as they should, obeying God's laws, rather than just mourning past disobedience.

Clearly, "repentance" or the outer show of it, had been built into Jewish ritual during the 70 years of exile; now obedience was the answer as to how they should live.

Revelation 15v1-8

The plagues complete God's wrath on a sinful world.

Proverbs 30v24-28

The animal kingdom gives some fantastic examples of organisation and co-operation.

December 25th

Zechariah 8v1-23

Zechariah develops his answer as to what the exiles, so used to having fasts as a sign of repentance during the 70 years of exile, should now do, since they were back in the Promised Land. v19 - the fasts would become glad and happy festivals – but as before, Zechariah underlines obedience as the answer to the question from the people of Bethel.

Revelation 16v1-21

People under judgment curse God but still will not repent.

Proverbs 30v29-31

The writer is simply marvelling – as he did in yesterday's selection, as to how God has made things

---

December 26th

Zechariah 9v1-17

We have judgement proclaimed against those who exploited Israel and Judah – and then we have this wonderful prophecy, fulfilled by Jesus, as He rode into Jerusalem (v9.)

Revelation 17v1-18

People worldwide have been seduced into worshipping a false power. This "whore" has intoxicated rulers and peoples alike. This is extreme, corrupting evil.

Proverbs 30v32

There are consequences!

December 27th

Zechariah 10v1-11v17

There is judgement on those who have led the people falsely, but the Lord will care for His people. Scattered people will be brought back to the Promised Land.

There are arguments over how to interpret chapter 11. There are false shepherds, and the one deeply caring shepherd, whom the flock reject.

Cautiously, we see links between the rejected Shepherd, the thirty pieces of silver ("thrown into the house of the Lord to the potter") and what actually happened in the story of Judas at the start of Matthew 27. Matthew brings together both the promises of Jeremiah and of Zechariah (possibly from memory) and refers to them jointly.

Revelation 18 v1-24

Babylon falls; the most evil power which the world has seen, comes to a dramatic end. She is sadly missed by all those who grew rich on her evils.

Proverbs 30v33

Stirring up things has consequences.

December 28th

Zechariah 12 v1-13 v9

Prophecy concerning how nations that turn against Jerusalem will be punished.

Then we have a very clear prophecy of God Himself as the pierced one – a clear reference to Calvary.

In chapter 13 a fountain is opened to cleanse the people from their sins; idolatry is removed from the land. False prophets are punished. We also have reference to the good Shepherd being struck and the sheep scattered.

Revelation 19v1-21

The vast crowd in heaven break into worship. Now is the time for the great banquet in heaven that Jesus promised during His earthly ministry; meanwhile there is another banquet as birds gather to gorge themselves on the fallen armies on the earth below.

Proverbs 31v1-7

More proverbs, this time the source is King Lemuel, or more specifically, sayings taught by his mother. He was not a Jewish king, if Lemuel was his real name. (It means "belonging to God" and Kidner in his commentary did not rule out that it could be someone writing under this name.) Kidner comments: "These verses take away the glamour from loose living."

December 29th

Zechariah 14v1-21

Jerusalem is attacked and its people suffer – and then suddenly the coming of the day of the Lord – what a picture of Christ's return. We are also told of other nations who become members of God's people. The book ends with the prophecy of how there shall be no more traders in the House of the Lord.

Revelation 20v1-15

Judgment begins. How we should interpret things such as the figure of 1,000 years is another matter, and Satan could distract us into a multitude of cul de sacs that prevent us from living and witnessing for Christ, and instead lead to sharp and embittered arguments that have wrecked other denominations that have been obsessed with Pre-, Post-, and even Amillenianist theories, which are all to do with how everything else fits in around this number. There is also a problem as to whether we should even attempt to understand everything in a chronological way. Many assume that the thousand years is symbolic rather than literal.

Proverbs 31v8-9

A principle that is very dear to God's heart.

December 30th

Malachi 1v1-2v17

Malachi can be a proper name, or it can simply mean "messenger." The writer is seen as a contemporary of Ezra and Nehemiah, decades after the very first of the exiles had returned to Jerusalem. It was in 538 BC that Cyrus had allowed the Jews to return, but it was not until around 445 BC that Nehemiah got permission to rebuild the walls. The intervening years have been a hard struggle – Malachi's ministry is almost 100 years after the original decree allowing the Jews to go home (ESV introduction to Malachi) People are disillusioned, Judah is a small city state (ESV introduction suggests something like 20 by 30 miles in size – all a far cry from the empire of King David!)

The people's disillusion is shown by the worthless offerings they bring to the temple. The people have no respect for God's covenant and their attitudes to marriage are much the same. There are strong words on the subject of marriage, unfaithfulness, and the unfaithful husband who decides to get rid of the wife of his youth.

Revelation 21v1-27

Everything has been beautifully recreated. New Jerusalem is symbolic for the Church as Christ's bride.

Proverbs 31v10-24

A good wife is described.

December 31st

Malachi 3v1-4v6

The One who prepares the way is coming, and the Lord is coming. Judgement is coming, and we have the prophecy that Elijah will return (New Testament makes clear that this is a reference to John the Baptist.)

Revelation 22v1-21

Packed with symbolism, we have this beautiful picture of our home with Christ above.

Make sure you will be there – through faith and trust in the Saviour!

Proverbs 31v25-31

More on the godly wife! Certainly an interesting way to end our 365 days of studying God's Word!

And so the year ends!

If you have endured to the end, there will still be much to learn from the Scriptures, but you have begun to get an overall picture of how God's Word fits together. Think through how you are going to follow up this time of study, perhaps reading more slowly with the help of some good commentaries. Avoid extreme books that are going to take you off into elaborate theories and speculations. The attraction of "secret knowledge" was one of the things that took many Christians off the rails in Paul's time and developed into a very real problem in the next century, known as Gnosticism. It still has its counterparts, with all the arrogance of "superior" knowledge.

Better knowledge will lead to a more effective Christian life and witness – not petty party spirit.